CRACKERJACK BANDS
AND
HOMETOWN BOOSTERS

CRACKERJACK BANDS AND HOMETOWN BOOSTERS

The Story of a
Minnesota Music Man

Joy Riggs

NODIN PRESS

ISBN: 978-1-947237-22-3

Library of Congress Control Number: 2019943049

Design: John Toren

9 8 7 6 5 4 3 2 1

Photo Credits
Cover: Band photo courtesy of the Polk County Historical Society;
    G. Oliver photo from the Riggs family files
Riggs family files: 15, 33, 54, 95, 142-143, 165, 167, 271, 281, 287, 292,
    295
Polk County Historical Society: 20, 156,
Stearns History Museum: 46, 105, 129, 185, 191, 229, 235, 262, 273, 279
Minnesota Historical Society: 80, 213
Beltrami County Historical Society: 116, 121, 125

Nodin Press
5114 Cedar Lake Road
Minneapolis, MN 55416

www.nodinpress.com

Printed in USA

For my favorite music man:
my dad, William Johnson Riggs

Contents

CRACKERJACK BANDS
AND
HOMETOWN BOOSTERS

G. Oliver Riggs

1

ORIGINS

It all began during a family birthday party in October 2006 for my youngest child, Elias. He had turned six, and we gathered in the living room of our 1920s bungalow-style home in Northfield, Minnesota, to celebrate with ice cream and homemade angel food cake. I finished my cake and was half listening to my dad, and half keeping an eye on the boisterous activities of my three kids and their cousins, when Dad's turn of phrase jolted me to attention.

"My dad was a music man for a time. He organized bands for Holton, the instrument company," Dad said. He sat across the room from me, with his back to the fireplace. He was talking to my husband's middle sister, Beth.

Dad's calm baritone voice continued. "Then he got a job directing the high school band in Farmington ... this would have been in the nineteen thirties. That's where he met my mother. She played in the flute section. And his dad—my grandfather—was a music man, too."

Beth's ears perked up at the mention of Farmington, a town fifteen miles to the north; it's where she taught high school English.

From the way Dad's words hung in the air, I sensed he was not done with his story. I suspected from nearly four decades of experience, and the thoughtful look in his blue eyes, that he was just getting started. Dad grew up in St. Cloud, Minnesota, and his circuitous style of storytelling requires patience from the listener. I'm not sure if it's a Swedish Lutheran trait, a geographical influence, or simply a "Dad" thing, but he'll refer to people or places he assumes you're familiar with—like the supper club in Forada—and ten minutes later, he'll make a joke that assumes you retained knowledge you may not have possessed in the first place.

If you've never heard of Forada, that's probably because it's a village in central Minnesota about eight miles from my hometown of Alexandria. Forada has one hundred and eighty-five residents, a supper club, and a few bars. Don't worry—retaining that information is not important to this story. There is always a point to Dad's stories, though, and if you aren't a committed listener, you'll miss the joke.

At that moment in the living room, I was not a committed listener.

My brain was stuck on the phrase he uttered twice in reference to two ancestors in my family tree. A music man. A music man. It reverberated in my head, knocking loose a kaleidoscope of memories: me in third grade, attending a community production of Meredith Willson's *The Music Man* that co-starred my mom's bridge club friend Bonnie as Marian (I had, I recalled, felt desperately jealous I was not on stage as Amarillys since I, too, could play the piano); me in sixth grade, taking French horn lessons from my dad's friend Bud Christiansen, who sang snippets of a World War I song to me: "Oh joy, oh boy, where do we go from here?"; me in high school, sweat pooling behind my ears under my pointy silver helmet and drenching the T-shirt under my woolen uniform as our marching band captured the grand prize at the Minneapolis Aquatennial Parade; me in college, when I and other members of the Drake University Marching Band embraced the unfortunate acronym ("D. U. M. B. Drake University Marching Band!") and performed during halftime at a Kansas City Chiefs game; me at my wedding, when Steve and I hired a brass quintet to play the processional, since my dad was unavailable—he was too busy walking me down the aisle.

Actually, my first memory of my dad, when I was about four,

involved music, too: I remember him standing in front of the kitchen sink on a frigid winter evening, cleaning his trumpet with water so hot that it steamed up the windows.

But none of these memories drew forth images of my paternal great-grandfather, G. Oliver Riggs. I sheepishly considered the fact that I knew little about him. He had been a bandleader, and he gave his cornet to my dad; a black and white photo showed him instructing my four-year-old dad on that very instrument. G. Oliver died a few years after that photo was taken.

I knew more about my dad's dad, although I had no memories of time spent with him, either. My grandfather Ronald taught political science and died of a heart attack two months before my first birthday. His name often came up when Dad told stories about growing up in St. Cloud. Ronald had once directed bands, too, but the details of his career remained fuzzy in my head. As for my paternal great-grandmother, I knew almost nothing, except that she played the piano and had an unusual first name: Islea (pronounced *eye-lee*).

I looked at Dad, who was no longer the tow-headed kid of that old picture or the dark-haired young father of my early memory, but a silver-haired, sixty-seven-year-old grandfather. He had progressed with his story. He was telling Beth about his latest musical adventure: playing in the St. Cloud Municipal Band that G. Oliver directed for nearly twenty years. The band still gave concerts at Barden Park in Dad's old neighborhood.

"It had been on my bucket list to play in the band, so I asked some of the players I knew how I could do that. They said, 'Come on a Monday, and you can play on a Thursday,'" Dad said. "I'd only intended to play one concert, but . . . "

He paused for effect. "I've been in the band for several months now."

This was the punch line. Beth laughed. Dad laughed, too.

As I joined in the laughter, an insatiable journalistic curiosity bubbled to the surface of my thoughts. I wanted to learn more about the lives of my musical ancestors. I wanted to whip out a notebook and pen, and pepper my dad with questions: What did it mean to be a music man, back in the day? Was it like the portrayal in Meredith

Willson's famous musical? What had G. Oliver been like, as a band director? What did the G. stand for, anyway?

But I had to attend to other details first, like refilling coffee cups and clearing plates. So it wasn't until an hour later, as my parents prepared to leave, that I revived the topic.

"Dad, I'd really like to learn more about G. Oliver. Do you have any files at home about him and his career?"

Unlike my mom, who preferred to travel light through life, collecting friends instead of possessions, my dad was a pack rat, a sentimental collector of memories. The double garage of their townhouse held boxes of his papers and mementoes, much of it related to his forty-year career as a high school social studies teacher. So it didn't surprise me when he cracked a smile and replied: "Sure I do. My dad saved a lot of things from those years. It was always his intention to do something with it all, but he never got around to it."

Having joined the St. Cloud band, Dad was now helping it update the history section of its website with highlights from G. Oliver's career. The band still mentioned G. Oliver in its concert programs, and it still had a few members who had played for him. Dad also planned to make a scrapbook about the G. Oliver years for the band's 120th anniversary concert in the spring.

"Well, I'd be happy to help you with that, if you want any help," I said.

The timing was perfect. A decade earlier, when Steve started his family practice residency in St. Paul and I became pregnant with Louisa, I had taken a break from journalism to be a mostly stay-at-home mom. Now that Elias was in kindergarten, Sebastian was in third grade, and Louisa was in fifth, I wanted to rebuild my career. I was eager to sharpen my writing, researching, and interviewing skills on a good story. This seemed like a promising one, conveniently dangling from the lower branches of my family tree.

TWO DAYS LATER, I found a story from 2003 about the St. Cloud Municipal Band's uncertain financial future. The online *St. Cloud Times* article explained that the city had funded the band for years; the band received $40,000 a year to pay for a conductor, music, and stipends for band members. But this funding source was in doubt because the legislature and governor planned to drastically cut local government aid. Recreation programs—in St. Cloud's case, the band—were likely targets.

The cuts had affected cities statewide, and additional cuts were made after 2003. The St. Cloud band was still performing, however, so the city must have found a way to support it.

The article contained other facts: the band had existed in various incarnations since the late 1800s; it was composed of about forty members; its summer concerts attracted hundreds of people; and it played for civic events like the Fourth of July.

Halfway through the article, I spotted the (slightly incorrect) name I hoped to find:

"In 1923, under the direction of C. Oliver Riggs, the St. Cloud Boys Band was founded at the city's expense. At the height of its membership the boys band had almost 200 members and claimed to be the world's largest band."[1]

Wow. World's largest. Hard to verify—it sounded like an exaggeration to me—but impressive, nonetheless. The article didn't cite a source for this claim, and the incorrect initial in my great-grandfather's name didn't inspire confidence in the veracity of other facts in the article. I would need to dig deeper to determine what could be confirmed and what had become part of local legend.

When I pulled up the band's website on my laptop, a color photo of my great-grandfather appeared, accompanied by a timeline of his life and career. G. Oliver lived from 1870 to 1946. Underneath his photo was a quote: "I tell my boys that the only way to win success is by hard work and preparation."

The photo looked familiar. I had probably seen it at my parents' house, years ago. G. Oliver's band uniform jacket was navy blue or black, with gold buttons and gold braid around the sleeve cuffs. His silver hair was parted slightly off center and combed away from his high forehead.

He must have been about the same age my dad was now. The oval shape of his face reminded me of my dad's face. They had the same thick eyebrows, high cheekbones, and solid jaw. G. Oliver's firm, thin lips turned up at the edges, but he wasn't smiling. He looked like he was preparing to play the cornet he held in his left hand.

Below the photo, the timeline revealed G. Oliver was born on November 26, 1870, near Wapello, Iowa. This surprised me. I went to college in Des Moines, I worked for four years at a newspaper in the state's capital city, I married a native Iowan, and all that time I never knew my great-grandfather was born in Iowa.

My eyes continued down the timeline. G. Oliver had:

- attended the Oberlin (Ohio) Conservatory of Music;
- directed a band in Esbon, Kansas;
- taught music and directed a band at the Iowa Wesleyan Conservatory of Music;
- studied violin and cornet in Chicago; and
- led bands in Aledo, Illinois; Crookston, Minnesota; Grand Forks, North Dakota; Tacoma, Washington; Havre, Montana; and Bemidji, Minnesota.

At the bottom, it mentioned another curious item: his death of a heart attack at the Red Lake Indian Reservation school in northern Minnesota, where he ended his career.

The geographic mobility in my great-grandfather's life astonished me. He had traveled extensively, to towns with mysterious names, and to more than half a dozen states. Even though I knew he had been "a music man," which implied time on the road as a salesman, I had pictured him living only in St. Cloud, stuck like a pin in a map.

I sat at the dining room table and stared at the two-page timeline, which I had printed out from the website. The pieces of paper I held in my hands contained the bare bones of a life, condensed into two dozen bullet points. The real story waited in the spaces between those lines of text. I couldn't wait to fill them in.

A MONTH LATER, MY parents returned to Northfield for a band concert; Louisa had followed in the footsteps of both her parents by taking up the French horn. Dad delivered on his promise and dropped off some files and a scrapbook containing crumbly newspaper clippings and faded photos. A few days later, I uncovered a tantalizing tidbit in a *St. Cloud Times* article from 1977.

The reporter had interviewed several men who played under G. Oliver and still belonged to the adult municipal band. When asked to characterize their former director, the men called him "a tyrant, terrific, a carbon copy of his own hero, John Philip Sousa, with whose band he once played ... "[2]

Wait—my great-grandfather played with Sousa's band? He knew Sousa? This seemed like a big deal. Sousa was perhaps the most well-known bandleader in the world, dead or alive. If my great-grandfather played for Sousa, it indicated G. Oliver was not a run-of-the-mill musician, but a person worthy of more attention and respect.

Minutes later, I found a similar claim in an old *Escape to the Minnesota Good Times* article. It said G. Oliver "was an ardent admirer of John Philip Sousa, in whose band he once played, and emulated him to the extent that he never spoke during concerts and was strictly businesslike during rehearsals. Legend has it that Sousa once broke from his established norm and actually told a joke during one of his band's practice sessions. There is no evidence to indicate that Mr. Riggs ever permitted himself such a lapse."[3]

Sousa's name conjured up fond childhood memories of concerts on the courthouse lawn, fireworks, and deviled eggs on the Fourth of July. It also dredged up a grudge I held against Sousa, even though I'd never met him; he died in 1936, way before my time.

The grudge stemmed from the day my high school band director handed out the music for "The Washington Post" march. A cold, hard truth emerged as I scanned the notes: the French horn part was terrible. It mostly consisted of playing on the off beats, the pah of the *oom*-pah, *oom*-pah. It could not have been more boring. Convinced that Sousa hated French horns, I dismissed him from my mind when we were done with the piece. I didn't care if he was a famous bandleader and composer: He was dead to me.

However, this new information caused me to change my tune. Perhaps there was more to know about Sousa the man, who had been a real person and not just a cultural icon. Could it be true that G. Oliver played with Sousa? The writer of the first article misspelled Sousa's last name, which raised my doubts about his commitment to accuracy. The second article said G. Oliver lived into his eighties, which was false; he died at age seventy-five.

I wouldn't believe the Sousa claim until I found proof.

2

You Tell Me Your Dream,
I'll Tell You Mine

Islea Graham waited at the top of the stairs for her cue. The next day, she would turn twenty-four, and within the week, she would move to a northern Minnesota town she had never visited. She was taking a leap of faith, motivated by love.

Except for the months she studied piano in Chicago, she had lived with her parents and her younger sister in this Aledo, Illinois, home all her life. Among the eighty guests awaiting her appearance downstairs were members of her large extended family. She would no longer see them on a regular basis: her maternal grandfather, her half siblings, aunts and uncles, nieces and nephews, and a passel of cousins.

In her new town, she would perform and teach under a new name. No one there knew her, except for the man at her side, a man who had courted her for five years.

The strains of Mendelssohn's "Wedding March" filtered up from the parlor. Islea took the arm of her betrothed. They descended the staircase and walked down an aisle of pink and white satin ribbons to the bow window at the south end of the parlor, which was banked with palms and ferns and framed with bouquets of pink roses.

The Presbyterian minister's words, and the pledges the bride and groom made that December evening in 1898, are lost to time. But a newspaper clipping Islea later pasted into a scrapbook preserved details of the event.[1]

Islea wore a dress of white embroidered *mousseline de soie*—a crisp, gauzelike silk muslin—over white silk and carried a bouquet of Bride's roses and maiden hair ferns. Curly brown hair framed her heart-shaped face, which featured wide-set eyes and a friendly smile.

The groom's apparel was not noted in the newspaper, but by custom of the day would likely have been full evening dress—a black swallow-tailed suit coat, black trousers, and a white necktie. He wore his wavy brown hair slicked back and parted on the side, and his strong jaw and penetrating gaze projected a seriousness of purpose that made him appear older than his age of twenty-eight, and taller than his height of five feet nine inches.

Following the ceremony, a former piano instructor of Islea's played a classical piano solo, and three of Islea's female relatives performed vocal solos. Mr. and Mrs. G. Oliver Riggs received the guests' congratulations, and their gifts of silver, cut glass, and china. The celebration concluded with a bounteous supper in the dining room, where the guests had to take turns eating, since everyone could not be served at once.

The next day, the newlyweds attended a reception hosted by G. Oliver's parents, Jasper and Rebecca, at their home in the nearby village of Joy.

G. Oliver was not from Aledo, although his parents had grown up in the area. His father, Jasper, joined up with the 45th Illinois Infantry at the start of the Civil War and fought the Rebels at Fort Donelson, Shiloh, and Vicksburg, before joining Sherman's March to the Sea. Like many veterans, Jasper moved around in the postwar years, taking his young family to Missouri, Iowa, Nebraska, and Kansas before returning to northwestern Illinois in 1890.

As a schoolboy, G. Oliver went by the name Oliver. He hated his given name, George, and rarely used it. Both his parents were musical—Jasper played the violin and Rebecca played the accordion—and young Oliver became proficient in the violin and cornet. His younger sister, Daisy, played the piano, and the family provided the music for local dances during the lean economic times of the 1880s, supplementing Jasper's income from running a hardware store.

"I don't remember when I couldn't play some instrument. I started on the mouth organ and later played anything else I could get my hands on," G. Oliver later said.[2]

When he was thirteen, Oliver heard about the celebrated music conservatory in Oberlin, Ohio. He spent three months herding cattle to earn money for tuition, and he enrolled at the school in the fall of 1885. Years later, his son Percy wrote:

The picture of this fourteen-year-old boy, with his violin and cornet, and just enough money to get to Oberlin, starting on this long train trip all alone, gives you an example of this drive to succeed that was to stay with him all his life. His amazement at the number of teams and wagons in Chicago. Sitting up all night in the hotel room in this same city, because he was afraid to turn out the unfamiliar gas light. His bed in the furnace room of a theater in Oberlin, which he earned by taking care of the janitorial work. Working as a waiter in a boarding house for his meals. Practicing never less than eight hours a day. It is possible to understand why this man could never regard less than four or five hours practice per day as being a satisfactory effort on the part of a student.[3]

DURING A BREAK FROM SCHOOL when he was sixteen, G. Oliver organized and directed his first band. By that time his family lived in Ezbon, Kansas. The newly established village did not have many amenities, but it had a blacksmith and wagon shop, a livery barn, and its own nine-member cornet band, which included G. Oliver on E-flat cornet and his father on drums.

It was not unusual for a town as small as Ezbon to have a band. Town bands began appearing in the eastern United States in the 1820s. One of the earliest and most influential was the Independent Band of New York, founded in 1825. Members included Thomas Dodworth and his son Allen. The band dissolved in the early 1830s and reformed under the direction of the younger Dodworth; by 1836 it was known as the Dodworth Band.[4] Today a modern recreation of this band, the Dodworth Saxhorn Band of Ann Arbor, Michigan, travels the country performing nineteenth century music on antique horns.

In what used to be called the Northwest Territory and is now called the Midwest, bands began forming in the 1850s. Minnesota's earliest known bands included the Fort Snelling Military Band, which formed in the 1850s, when Minnesota was still a territory; the Great Western Band of St. Paul, formed in 1860, and the Mankato Saxhorn Band, established in 1862.[5]

Influenced by the European military tradition and the colonial bands of the eighteenth century, early town bands usually consisted of both woodwind and brass instruments. But once European instrument makers developed brass instruments like the keyed bugle and the ophicleide—a precursor to the tuba—musicians were able to play a greater range of notes. As a result, the number of all-brass or mostly brass ensembles in the United States expanded between the 1830s and the 1850s. This growth accelerated during the Civil War, when musicians joined regimental bands on both sides of the battlefield.

When the Civil War ended, musicians returned home and fueled the growth of community bands, which were influenced by the military bands' styles of music, uniforms, and instrumentation. By 1889, an estimated ten thousand bands were active throughout the country, and by 1908 this number had increased to eighteen thousand.[6]

Most towns in the 1880s and 1890s, regardless of their size, had at least one band. Some supported multiple ensembles. These bands performed in parks, theaters, and opera houses, providing regular entertainment before radio and talking pictures became popular. Bands also served an important civic function. They appeared at picnics, political rallies, and building dedications, playing a versatile repertoire of marches, classical works, and popular tunes.

Most band members were amateurs—laborers and shopkeepers, men from all walks of life with varying levels of talent, united by their enjoyment of making music. Because they evolved from military tradition, most bands were composed solely of men, although some novelty bands were made up of female musicians or children. Most musically inclined women sang, played piano—like Islea—or played orchestra instruments.

Successful bands were usually led by an individual who was not only a talented musician, but also an entrepreneur, able to raise money for uniforms and instruments, publicize and sell tickets to concerts, and convince donors their financial investment was worthwhile.

G. Oliver Riggs was that type of man: Talented. Entrepreneurial. Driven.

ISLEA'S NEW HUSBAND HAD his work cut out for him in Crookston, a railroad and lumber mill town a hundred miles south of the Canadian border. G. Oliver accepted a job there in October of 1898. It paid $100 a month. He had no job security and no guarantee of success—only a belief in his ability and a vision of the band he could develop.

His immediate concern was competition. The town already had one band, and with a population of five thousand people, Crookston likely could not support two bands. Also, the new band lacked adequate practice space.

"At my first rehearsal in Sam Wallace's old frame building … I had eleven players, a large kerosene lamp, one good window light in front, and a million dead flies," G. Oliver later said.[7]

Within two months, he solved both problems. The bands consolidated under G. Oliver's leadership, and the other director—who, unlike G. Oliver, had no formal music training—joined the new band as a cornet player. The city agreed to let the band rehearse in the new city hall and fire station, a two-story brick building topped by a bell tower. G. Oliver believed that an orderly, welcoming place to gather would attract musicians who would take the work seriously.

The combined band consisted of twenty-one members: one drum major, one E-flat clarinet player, one B-flat clarinet, six cornets, two baritones, four alto horns, two slide trombones, one tenor horn, one tuba, one bass drum, and one snare drum. Olaf D. Dahl, a candy salesman who recruited G. Oliver to Crookston, served as the band's manager.

Its financial organization worked this way: citizens and businessmen pledged a certain dollar amount annually to the band; in return, in the summer, the band would present open air concerts every Saturday evening, and in the winter, the band would perform monthly concerts in the three-story Grand Opera House, a brick structure built in 1891. The opera house seated five hundred people and hosted speakers and theatrical shows throughout the year; three years earlier, Mark Twain had delivered a lecture from its stage. The band's concert repertoire, modeled after that of professional bands like John Philip Sousa's, included solos by local and visiting artists. Subscribers received complimentary concert tickets for themselves and their families.

G. Oliver in 1899.

"It is the intention of Mr. Riggs and the band to give the people splendid entertainments from the first, and as the band improves the concerts will be advanced in merit and popularity, and in a short time the band entertainments will be among the best entertainment given in Crookston," an article in the *Crookston People's Press* explained.[8]

The Crookston Band's first indoor concert was held two weeks before the wedding of G. Oliver and Islea, and its quality exceeded audience expectations. So it was with great interest that residents flocked to the Grand Opera House in January 1899 to see the new Mrs. Riggs perform at the second concert of the Crookston Band and Riggs orchestra.

Local newspapers promoted the concert on their front pages.

Mrs. Riggs has spent the last two years studying under Emil Liebling, one of Chicago's talented teachers. She comes to

Crookston an accomplished musician and will be warmly welcomed by the musical circles of the city," the Polk County Journal *predicted. "She will play two piano solos and assist in a violin and piano duet, the professor himself making the violin speak. This will be a musical treat that Crookston people will most liberally patronize.*[9]

The newspapers at the turn of the last century were prone to boosterism and exaggeration, but Islea was indeed already an accomplished musician.

ISLEA WAS BORN ON December 23, 1874, in Aledo. Her father, William, had five children from a previous marriage; after his first wife died, he married Flora Bassett, daughter of Isaac Newton Bassett, a prominent local attorney and Republican Party activist. William worked as a bank cashier, and he and Flora had two daughters together, Islea and Ethel.

Flora may have named her elder daughter Islea as a tribute to her own mother, Scienda Isle Moore Bassett, who died when Flora was nine. That loss may also have influenced Flora's desire to maintain a close, supportive relationship with her daughters.

Islea pursued music from an early age. By the time she graduated from Aledo High School in May 1892, she had studied and taught piano for several years, and aimed to become a professional pianist. In her commencement address, titled "Sweeping Cobwebs Out of the Sky," she encouraged her classmates to likewise pursue a calling that suited them.

Having found out what you have to do—whether to lead an army or sweep a crossing—do it with all your might, because it is your duty, your enjoyment. Remember that life's battles cannot be fought by proxy, be your own helper, be earnest, be diligent, and if success is not soon, you will have done the next-best thing—you will have deserved it.[10]

What Islea wanted to do, at age seventeen, was improve her piano technique. She went to Chicago and lived with relatives while studying at the Chicago Conservatory of Music under the

esteemed Emil Liebling, a pupil of Franz Liszt. She also took courses in voice and pipe organ.

It was an exciting time to be in Chicago—preparations were
underway for the 1893 World's Columbian Exposition, also known
as the World's Fair. Islea's grandfather Isaac attended the dedication
ceremonies on October 21, 1892, with other dignitaries. The Fair
opened to the public on May 1, 1893, and ran through October
30 of that year.

Islea studied off and on with Liebling for two years, divid-
ing her time between Aledo (not far from Davenport, Iowa) and
Chicago. During that time, she attended the Fair with her parents
and her sister, and she attended concerts of the Theodore Thomas
Orchestra at the new Chicago Auditorium, a four thousand-seat
venue designed by Louis Sullivan and Dankmar Adler and known
worldwide for its innovative architecture and perfect acoustics.

G. Oliver also studied in Chicago during the heady days of
the Fair. In the summer of 1893, during a break from his work at
Iowa Wesleyan University's music conservatory, he studied violin
under the Austrian-born Luigi von Kunitz, who later directed the
Toronto Symphony.

G. Oliver and Islea had known of each other for years, through
family connections, but they didn't perform together until the
summer of 1894, when they both lived at home with their parents.
G. Oliver was directing the Aledo Cornet Band, and he and Islea
provided the accompaniment for a play staged at a hall a few miles
down the road in Joy. The two performances of *Tony, the Convict:
A Comedy in Five Acts* by Charles Townsend raised more than $160
for the village's new sidewalks fund.[11] But perhaps more impor-
tantly, the experience inspired G. Oliver and Islea to continue their
duet, both on and off stage.

The crowd that filled the Crookston Grand Opera House on
January 18, 1889, was not treated to selections from *Tony, the
Convict*. Instead, the concert kicked off with the "The Hamilto-
nian" march, followed by ten selections that alternately featured
the band, a G. Oliver-led orchestra, and a six-member guitar and
mandolin ensemble. G. Oliver and Islea performed a violin-piano
duet of Italian operatic melodies, and they each performed two

solos. The concert concluded with a lively, comic band number, J. O. Casey's "Squegee Polka," which incorporated percussive sounds like the triangle, sleigh bells, and "a grand chorus of squee-gees," a newfangled window-cleaning tool patented in 1891.

Afterward, the *Polk County Journal* praised G. Oliver's cornet solo as "one of the most skillfully rendered pieces of the evening,"[12] and the *Crookston People's Press* reported that Islea's "execution upon the piano surpassed the expectation of all. Every number on the program was heartily encored."[13]

Following the success of her debut, Islea and G. Oliver filled their days and evenings with music: rehearsing it, performing it, teaching it. Meanwhile, the town was abuzz with excitement about news that John Philip Sousa's world-famous band would perform in Crookston that spring.

As THE MARCH CONCERT neared, the Crookston papers printed numerous articles about Sousa's band, which was on its fourth grand "ocean to ocean" tour. One day the front page featured a line drawing of Sousa, with oval pince-nez glasses perched on his nose and a well-trimmed beard and mustache covering the lower half of his face; on another day, readers learned about Arthur Pryor, the band's celebrated trombonist.

By the end of the 1890s, Sousa had become a household name and an international celebrity. A prolific composer, he directed the US Marine Band for twelve years, molding it into a world-renowned military ensemble. He resigned from the Marine Band in 1892 and formed his own band of top-notch instrumentalists. The Sousa Band went on its first US tour later that year. It per-formed in Chicago at the dedication of the World's Fair buildings and during the Fair itself.

Sousa and his fifty-member band arrived in Crookston at noon on March 28, 1899. Most merchants and banks closed for the af-ternoon, and students and teachers received a half-day holiday. The Grand Opera House was "literally packed from the foyer to the stage"[14] when the concert began at two o'clock. It opened with the overture to "Paragraph II" by Franz von Suppé, then moved into the trombone solo "Thoughts of Love," written and performed by

Pryor. Soprano Maud Reese Davies and violinist Dorothy Hoyle performed solos, and the band played two selections from Sousa's operetta, *The Charlatan*. The concert concluded with Sousa's popular march, "Stars and Stripes Forever."

The *Crookston People's Press* said it was "the greatest musical event ever enjoyed by a Crookston audience."

"To say that 'Sousa and His Band' are simply magnificent does not express it—new words will have to be invented," a front-page article proclaimed. "The concert was a treat to the people of the entire region, and they left the house fully satisfied that they had seen the greatest musical organization on earth."[15]

It would be difficult for any amateur band to measure up after such a concert. But if the comparison intimidated G. Oliver, he showed no sign of it; at the Crookston Band's next concert, three weeks later, he opened with Sousa's march from *The Charlatan*.

G. Oliver may have viewed the Sousa event as an opportunity to raise community interest in his own band. Through the summer and into the fall, the Crookston Band continued to improve musically, and it attracted attention beyond the city's borders. In July, it performed at the Winnipeg Industrial Exposition in Canada, and in October, clad in spiffy new uniforms, members played for President William McKinley in Fargo, North Dakota, where McKinley greeted soldiers who had returned from the Spanish-American War.

Crookston residents puffed with pride upon hearing accolades about their band from out-of-towners.

"'Have you heard that Crookston band play?' was the question everywhere, and the answer was, 'Yes. It's the best that ever came to Fargo.' The prominence that Prof. Riggs' musicians gave Crookston yesterday among the North Dakotans was worthy of all it has cost this city to maintain the band up to date," the *Crookston Daily Times* reported.[16]

The first national recognition of G. Oliver's rapid success came in February 1900, when an article about the Crookston Band appeared in *The Dominant*, a monthly music magazine published in New York. A professional photo of the band and G. Oliver accompanied the text.

The Crookston Band, 1899

The article noted that the band received $1,800 a year from the city and local businessmen, and it said the combination of G. Oliver's talents and the receptive audience in Crookston made the band "the leading musical organization between Minneapolis and the Pacific slope."

"It is a pleasure to note the prosperity enjoyed by the Crookston band, and to be able to congratulate them on their having a leader who unites the dual capacity of business and music. These are qualities rarely united but they are invaluable when found," the article stated.[17]

The band's increasing fame caused some residents to wonder: would their ambitious young director remain committed to Crookston, or might he and his wife chase the dream of something bigger and better in another city?

3

ALIVE AND WELL

In May 2007, after several months of digging into my great-grandparents' musical past, I pulled the kids out of school, Steve took the day off from work, and we drove to St. Cloud for the municipal band's 120th anniversary concert. Who could deny the educational value of such a historic event? We stopped first at an Arts and Crafts-style house near my dad's old high school, which G. Oliver and Islea bought in 1923. From the outside, it reminded me of our house.

"I'm going to get out and take a few pictures," I said.

"You should go knock on the door and see if anyone's home," Steve suggested. "The car in the driveway has a Kerry-Edwards bumper sticker on it. They might be friendly."

He and the kids watched from the car as I walked up the steps and knocked on the front door. The screened-in porch contained assorted kids' toys, another sign we might have something in common with the occupants. If I was lucky, they would invite me inside to take a look around. Then, they would mention they had found an old photo under a floorboard that showed John Philip Sousa and another band director with thick eyebrows. Would I like to see it?

That's what would happen if this were a movie. As it turned out, no one was home, so I rejoined my family and we drove nine blocks east to Barden Park. Originally known as Central Park, it borders St. Cloud State University, where my grandfather Ronald once directed the college band and taught political science.

My dad, his brother, Bob, and his sister, Dana, practically grew up in that park. I hadn't visited it for years, but I recognized its distinctive feature: an octagonal granite bandstand. Constructed from blocks of locally quarried granite, it looked like a rook from a giant's chess set. The modern St. Cloud municipal band didn't play inside the bandstand because it wasn't large enough to accommodate all the performers and equipment.

If you stood next to the bandstand facing east, you could see the university alumni house. When my dad was growing up, it was the home of their neighbors, Dr. Claude Lewis—older brother of author Sinclair Lewis—and his wife, Wilhelmina. Behind the Lewis house had been the Riggs house; now, the space was part of a university parking lot. The house had been moved to another neighborhood, a victim of the university's expansion in the 1970s.

When my brother, Pete, and I were younger, Dad occasionally drove by the site of his former house and pointed it out. I had only one vague memory of being inside, when I was about four. My grandma had invited us to an indoor picnic, where the red and white striped bucket of chicken on the dining room table intrigued me; I had never eaten chicken from a bucket.

Thirty-five years later, I wanted to show my own kids the former location of this house. We crossed Fourth Avenue at Eighth Street and continued down the sidewalk, past the side of the alumni house and its garage, until we reached a set of steps that led to the parking lot.

"So, kids, this is where Poppa Riggs grew up."

I gestured toward the empty space where I imagined the house had stood.

Sebastian grinned and shook his head. "Poor Poppa, he grew up in a parking lot," he said.

"It must not have been very comfortable," Louisa said.

"Yes, it must have been rough," I agreed. "It's a good thing he was an Eagle Scout."

Louisa and Sebastian enjoyed the joke, but I couldn't tell if Elias knew we were kidding. I explained that the university moved the house later, once Poppa was an adult.

My visits to St. Cloud as a child and as a teenager rarely took me to the old part of downtown. When the university displaced my grandmother, she moved to a townhouse in nearby Waite Park, and we usually visited her there; it was an hour's car ride from our house in Alexandria. After she died in 1980, I only visited St. Cloud to shop at the Dayton's department store in the mall or to play basketball against one of the city's high school teams.

This time, I looked at the older buildings with more appreciative eyes. As we approached the stately red brick and granite Stearns County Courthouse, I almost gasped. I had no memory of walking past it as a child. It was built in 1921 and has six granite entrance columns, the same columns that grace the background of the photo I had purchased online three months earlier of the 1925 St. Cloud boys' band. The building is topped by a yellow terra cotta tile dome and four small clocks, each one facing a different direction.

The kids willingly posed for pictures outside the courthouse, and we rewarded them with some down time near the Mississippi River before we met my mom at a Thai restaurant (Dad didn't join us because he never liked to eat before a concert). By the time we entered the lobby of the Paramount Theatre a few hours later, a crowd had gathered.

We found Dad in the midst of the activity, mingling with people he knew and chatting up those he didn't.

"Hey, you're here!" Dad said. "How was dinner?"

We hugged him, and he helped us find seats on the main floor before ducking out to warm up with the other band members. I settled into my seat and gazed at the majestic chandeliers and the ornate side balconies. My great-grandfather had not been a religious man, but his devotion to music was unquestioned. If he ever felt the presence of a higher power, this seemed like a place where he would have had that experience, in this cathedral to the arts.

The concert opened with a slideshow of band photos from previous decades. Each time G. Oliver appeared, I whispered to the kids, "Look, G. Oliver!" After the slideshow, sixty band members filed onto the stage, and Elias climbed into my lap for a better view.

It felt momentous to see Dad among the musicians, knowing that his grandparents, father, and uncle had all performed in that space. If I squinted, I could almost picture G. Oliver taking the director's place, his arm taut as he raised the baton to lead the boys in his efficient, driven way.

I closed my eyes and breathed deeply. Elias' warm body nestled into mine. The harmonies and melodies filled my ears and reverberated until time and place dissolved.

After the concert, we lingered long enough to take a photo of Dad and me under the brightly lit marquee, smiling triumphantly.

ONE MONTH LATER, DAD AND I took a father-daughter research trip to Iowa and Illinois. My mom stayed in Northfield to help Steve with the kids. In addition to his daytime role as a family practice doctor, Steve was rehearsing his role as a villainous dentist in a community theater production of *Little Shop of Horrors*.

Dad and I hadn't taken a road trip together since 1988, when he drove me to Natchez, Mississippi, for a summer newspaper internship after my sophomore year of college. This trip would be a different kind of adventure. As Dad drove south out of Northfield, I popped in a CD that Steve had burned for me. It contained songs listed in G. Oliver-directed programs from the late 1890s and early 1900s.

Dad's eyes widened as the first few notes played. It was Sousa's march from *The Charlatan*. He grinned and glanced at me.

"You've thought of everything," he said.

Our first stop, at Iowa Wesleyan College in Mount Pleasant, yielded mixed results. G. Oliver had composed a march for the school's cadet band in the early 1890s, but no one there had heard of it. However, the library archivist found a photo of the band's two dozen uniformed musicians walking down a sidewalk in single file, carrying instruments. She also found a few articles about G. Oliver in the college newspaper.

Our second stop was the State Historical Society of Iowa in Iowa City, which housed the files of G. Oliver's mentor, friend, and fellow bandleader George Landers. The men met when G. Oliver was a student at Oberlin, and Landers helped him get a job directing the town band in Albia, Iowa. G. Oliver also played occasionally in an Iowa regimental band that Landers directed.

G. Oliver wasn't with Landers when the band fought in the Philippines during the Spanish-American War. However, because of a yellowed newspaper article I'd found in a scrapbook, I suspected my great-grandfather played in the band in 1906 when it traveled to the South to dedicate Civil War battlefield memorials, and I was hoping the archives would yield proof.

I had contacted the library in advance, and when we arrived, an employee placed the requested files on a long wooden table. They consisted of five sturdy boxes containing sixty-nine folders. Dad and I split them up, and twenty minutes before the library closed, as I sifted through one of the last folders in the last box, I found a piece of paper labeled "Band South." In old-fashioned cursive, it listed the names of twenty-three musicians, with check marks indicating whether they had paid. My eyes zeroed in on number nine: "G.O. Riggs," solo cornet. He had paid their band membership fee.

I squealed with excitement.

"Look what I found!"

Dad's face beamed. He knew what this meant. G. Oliver had indeed traveled with the band to Shiloh and Vicksburg, where his own father had fought. If we found nothing else of importance during the trip, I would be happy.

The next day, we crossed the Mississippi River and stopped long enough in Joy, Illinois, for Dad to take my picture next to the "Joy: Population 400" sign. Upon arriving in Aledo, we went to the historical museum where we found a few relevant obituaries. The highlight of the day was checking in at The Slammer Bed and Breakfast—the former county jail. It was built in 1909 and had been renovated by the former sheriff, Dick Maynard, and his wife, Jennie.

Jennie said we could have any room we wanted, since we were the only guests. We chose the top floor suite, with a view of the old opera house. That evening, I bathed in the porcelain tub and reveled in the break from parenting responsibilities; I could do what I wanted, when I wanted. I even had a driver/research assistant.

The next morning, we drove to Viola, a town eight miles east of Aledo, to visit two of Dad's second cousins. They were granddaughters of G. Oliver's sister and were about the same age as Dad. The directions Lorenda provided were exact, and ten minutes later we pulled up in front of a two-story bungalow farmhouse. The lawn was neatly mowed, and the barn looked well kept. I could easily be in rural Minnesota.

I'd had a warm telephone conversation with Lorenda's sister Nancy a few weeks earlier, but we were meeting the two women as strangers. What if they didn't like us?

Lorenda greeted us and led us into the living room, where Nancy waited. The home's built-ins and architecture reminded me of my own house.

Dad and I responded to questions about our trip, and we all talked about the weather—the oppressive humidity, the need for rain. Nancy was as bubbly in person as she had been on the telephone. She was extremely thin, but she had more energy than I expected; she was going through chemotherapy for ovarian cancer. I hoped the visit wouldn't overtire her.

Lorenda's husband, Jesse, didn't say much, but I liked him immediately. He seemed like the type of person who would plow your driveway without being asked and refuse payment for it.

We sat at the kitchen table, where Lorenda, more reserved than her sister, had gathered a collection of old family photos.

Dad had brought along a satchel of photos, and as we compared the two collections, we discovered we had some of the same images, including a portrait of Jasper taken at age fifty-five. He wore a suit, vest and a bow tie, and his bushy eyebrows matched his impressive mustache, which protruded over his lower lip. His hair was wavy and swept back from his forehead.

Next, Lorenda pulled out a black and white, fifteen-inch by eight-inch photo of a boys' band.

"We're not sure why we have this one; do you know what this is?" she asked.

Nearly two hundred boys stood to the side of a building. They were arranged in eight rows. Half wore light-colored uniforms, and the other half wore darker uniforms. G. Oliver and Percy stood in the back.

My dad's eyes met mine. I tried to contain my excitement.

"That's the St. Cloud band. But we haven't seen this one before," Dad said. "G. Oliver was the director of the band in St. Cloud for twenty years. He must have sent this to Daisy."

We asked Lorenda if we could have the photo and send her a copy. I didn't want to appear pushy, but I figured it meant more to us than it meant to her. Eager to offer something in return, Dad presented them with a bundle of letters their mother had written to his mother, and two postcards Daisy sent their father in 1919, when she visited G. Oliver in Minnesota.

One of the last photos Dad produced was a studio portrait of G. Oliver, seated, and Islea, standing behind him, her dark hair swept up in a pompadour. Lorenda produced a matching photo, with writing on the back: "G. Oliver and Daisy."

G. Oliver and *Daisy*? Not Islea? I stared at the swoops and curls of the letters, wondering if I had lost my ability to read cursive.

Lorenda also had a solo photo of Daisy, taken a few years earlier. It was clearly the same woman in both photos.

Dad's brain accepted this surprising information more quickly than mine.

"Here we were thinking this was Islea, and it's really Daisy," he said, shaking his head.

Nancy exclaimed, "He married someone who looked like his sister!"

She laughed merrily and we all joined in, unsure what to make of that psychological revelation. We moved into the dining room, where Lorenda had prepared a spread of ham and turkey sandwiches, potato chips, and fresh-cut watermelon, with sugar cookies for dessert.

As we ate and conversed, my mind drifted back to the photo of G. Oliver and Daisy. I had jumped to the wrong conclusion about the woman in the photo, and this made me question other things I had uncovered. (One of the first lessons I learned in journalism school was: *never assume*—which went hand-in-hand with: *Accuracy, accuracy, accuracy!*)

Before we said goodbye, I took a photo of my dad, his cousins, and Jesse standing on the front porch. Then Dad and I drove to the cemetery in Aledo to connect with relatives who wouldn't be able to answer our questions.

The temperature climbed past ninety, and the sun beat down on the backs of our necks as we wandered forty acres of lawn, searching for our ancestors. The cemetery office didn't provide a map, so we finally sought help from men working on the grounds, and they pointed us to the area where we found gravestones for Islea's parents.

We continued our graveyard tour at the nearby town of New Boston—incidentally, the first town Abraham Lincoln surveyed. It was also where Jasper was born and raised. The cemetery was bigger than I'd expected for a town of six hundred living people. Dad found a marker for Jasper, who was buried in Missouri; the grave of Rebecca; and the grave of their first child, Loie, who died at age four. Her gravestone was so covered by orange moss it was barely legible. Had she died of a disease? Did G. Oliver have any memories of his older sister? I left the cemetery with more questions than answers.

WE RETURNED TO Aledo in time for a band concert in Central Park. Jennie had loaned us two canvas camp chairs, and Dad set them up on a patch of lawn facing the band shell. Positioned across the street from the grand old courthouse and its clock tower, the band shell was only two summers old, but it looked like it belonged.

When G. Oliver directed the Aledo Cornet Band in this park, the courthouse was new, and merchants contributed money so the band could buy uniforms. That tradition of civic pride was apparently alive and well. Modern-day residents and businesses raised $250,000 to erect the new outdoor performance venue, where it accommodated everything from Christian rock to jazz to country. This evening, the spotlight shone on the Mercer County Community Band, directed by high school teacher Rusty Ruggles.

Before the band of thirty high school students and adults—including Rusty's mom on clarinet—took the stage, Rusty walked over to us and introduced himself. I had emailed him before the trip to let him know we'd be in the audience, and he'd clearly spotted us as the only people he didn't recognize. He appeared to be in his early thirties and exuded energy. He said he hoped the storm headed our way would hold off long enough for the band to complete its program.

As the musicians tuned their instruments and Rusty checked his cell phone, Dad and I grinned at each other. I could tell he was enjoying himself.

"Think it's going to rain on us?" I asked.

He glanced upward and pronounced his assessment, based on decades of cloud watching: "We're going to be cutting it close."

The concert opened with "The Star Spangled Banner," and then Rusty announced: "Tonight's all about playing fun stuff."

As the first few bars of "Theme from Scooby Doo" floated in the air, I scanned the faces of the other concertgoers, all strangers to me. Some were elderly, some were likely the parents of the younger players, and some appeared close in age to my kids. Although G. Oliver and Islea had moved from this town more than a century ago to pursue greater musical opportunities, the setting felt familiar. It was as though I were a child again, seated on a blanket in front of the courthouse in Alexandria, watching my dad play the trumpet with a different community band.

The sky grew darker, and the wind picked up. I continued to relive my childhood as the Aledo band played an arrangement of themes from old TV comedy shows including *Happy Days*, *The Brady Bunch*, *Bewitched*, and *The Addams Family*. Midway through the concert, Rusty grasped the microphone and faced the audience. He thanked the sponsors and introduced Dad and me.

"This is Bill Riggs, and his daughter, Joy, from Minnesota. Bill's grandfather—grandfather, right?" He looked at my dad for affirmation, and Dad nodded. "His grandfather directed the Aledo band in 1895."

We rose from our chairs and waved. The other concertgoers might think we were wacky, but I was pleased. I knew Dad appreciated the recognition, and the chance to connect in a new way to a long-dead grandparent he wished he'd known better.

The papa, the papa. Tradition! Questions flitted in and out of my mind while I listened to the next medley, from *Fiddler on the Roof.* What would G. Oliver think of this genealogical expedition to his old stomping grounds? How many of his concerts were foiled by rain? And—a question that begged to be asked—how would he have handled that arrangement of the Scooby Doo theme?

Storm clouds rumbled overhead as the band played its final number: the march from *El Capitan,* the operetta Sousa composed in 1895, the same year G. Oliver directed the Aledo band in the park where we were sitting.

If he were to appear before us, in a crazy sci-fi time travel scenario, it might please him to discover that Sousa compositions were still performed here, and it might amuse him to know that outdoor concerts were still at the mercy of the weather, despite a modern director's ability to receive storm updates from a telephone in his pocket.

But he might be most delighted by this truth: although community bands are not as numerous as they were 100 years ago, they're still alive and well—in Aledo, in St. Cloud, and in towns big and small across the country. Despite all the other entertainment options available to them on this June evening in 2007, more than 100 people chose to gather in a park to hear friends and relatives present a live band concert, and for forty-five minutes, we were united in that experience.

The wind carried away the final notes of the march, and Dad and I applauded enthusiastically. Then we folded our chairs and dashed to the car, minutes ahead of the downpour.

4

Song of Iowa

When G. Oliver and Islea moved to Crookston, they considered it a temporary diversion. They had struggled to make names for themselves in Chicago—a city bursting with musicians—following the economic Panic of 1893, and they correctly anticipated that the Minnesota town would provide them with steady work. Although the Crookston band had quickly become a financial and artistic success, G. Oliver longed to eventually return to the big city and become a famous concert artist.

In the meantime, he embraced his love of the northern Minnesota landscape. In the spring of 1901, he purchased one hundred and sixty acres of forested land northeast of Bemidji, near the village of Big Falls. G. Oliver's family had moved a number of times in his first sixteen years of life, and it's possible the security of owning land appealed to him. It also seemed like a wise financial move, given the anticipated growth of the area. He enlisted the help of half a dozen men to clear a portion of the land so crops could be grown on it.

A photograph G. Oliver took of a waterfall on the Big Fork River near Big Falls ran on the front page of the *Bemidji Pioneer* on November 7, 1901, two months after the Crookston Band performed at the Minnesota State Fair. The photo caption noted it

31

was the first time the newspaper had published a photo of the falls. "[It] has a drop of 40 feet in less than 130 yards. At this point the river is perhaps 250 feet wide …This is the best photograph we have seen of the falls, but it does not do it justice."[1]

The *Crookston Journal* reprinted the photo and said, "Much interest attaches to this portion of the state, as it is fast settling up and in the rapid development of Northern Itasca county this will become the leading point for manufacturing and milling purposes."[2]

In the spring of 1903, G. Oliver's adventures near the Big Fork River made the news again. The *Crookston Journal* reported on March 6 that a bear had chased the bandleader on a recent trip:

In order to make his escape the gentleman discarded everything he carried but his valuable violin. He finally "shinned" up a tree so small the bear couldn't hug it for climbing, and there they were. Bruin, when erect on his back feet could almost reach the music man's legs, but not quite, and finally decided to wait for his fruit until it fell from the limb … Mr. Riggs having heard of the efficacy of music in charming the savage beast, drew his bow and played an air from de Beriot which so pleased and affected Bruin that he went away to bring the balance of his family to the concert, and incidentally when it closed to let the cubs taste of a Crookston musician. When he returned Mr. Riggs was miles away up the trail.[3]

Accompanying the tall tale was a cartoon drawing of G. Oliver in a suit and a bow tie, sitting in a tree, playing the violin while a bear gazes up at him.

Islea stayed as busy as her husband, although her adventures did not involve bears. She performed in band concerts and orchestra performances directed by G. Oliver, she taught piano lessons, she played the organ at the First Congregational Church, and she participated in a women's music and culture club she co-founded.

Islea and G. Oliver also took on new responsibilities as the parents of future bandmasters Ronald Graham, born in 1901, and Percy Harrison, born in 1904. To accommodate their growing family, they moved into a modern, two-story wood frame home in

Four generations: Islea's mother, Flora Bassett Graham; baby Ronald; Islea; and Islea's maternal grandfather, Isaac Newton Bassett.

a neighborhood southeast of downtown, where many other young families lived.

The house was designed by architect Bert D. Keck, whom G. Oliver and Islea knew from Aledo. Keck had attended their wedding, and he played in the Aledo Cornet Band under G. Oliver's direction. Keck moved to Crookston in 1902 with his wife, Elsie, and the city's growing population meant he had steady work.

Islea also enjoyed, for a time, the occasional company of her sister, Ethel, who moved to Bemidji in 1904 with her husband, Ed Bigelow. Ed had taken a job as head bookkeeper at the lumber mill in Bemidji, eighty-seven miles east of Crookston. But the sisters' physical closeness was disrupted by scandal in the summer of 1905, when Ed was charged with embezzlement. The couple moved back to Aledo with their son, and although a judge dismissed the charges a few months later, the family did not return to Minnesota.

Fortunately for G. Oliver, his career enjoyed only positive publicity that year. He and his band were featured in two national music publications, the *Metronome* and the *Musical Enterprise*. The *Metronome* article described G. Oliver as "a competent business man, a thorough band master, a clever violinist and cornetist and a qualified musician," and said the organization "developed from nothing to one of the best bands in the State, and is, without dispute, the very best amateur band in the Northwestern States."[4]

Although they were amateurs, the Crookston band members knew they had to keep improving musically to meet the audience's growing expectations; the excited local residents who packed the Opera House to hear Sousa's band in 1899 and again in 1901 had demonstrated an appreciation for high-quality music performances. To build on that enthusiasm, and to motivate residents to purchase season tickets, G. Oliver varied the monthly concerts by adding new music and inviting out-of-town artists to perform.

GIVEN G. OLIVER'S REHEARSAL and concert schedule and the family's home life, fall of 1906 was not the most convenient time for him to leave town. But shortly before the first concert of the winter season, G. Oliver received an enticing invitation from his friend George Landers, the director of an Iowa regimental band.

Landers was ten years older than G. Oliver, and the two men had been friends since the late 1880s. Now Landers's band—renamed the Iowa 55th Regimental Band of Centerville—had been hired to accompany the Iowa governor and a host of officials and war veterans on a tour of the South. They would dedicate new memorials to Iowa soldiers at Vicksburg, Andersonville, Chattanooga, and Shiloh. It would be a two-week trip, mostly by train. Landers needed an accomplished solo cornetist to fill out the roster.

G. Oliver accepted. His father, Jasper, was nineteen when he enlisted in the Union Army. He was now sixty-three, and his war wounds had contributed to his worsening health. He suffered hearing loss in one ear from exploding shells, and a lead Minié ball was lodged in his left knee. This trip was G. Oliver's chance to see places where his father had fought, forty years after they became the final resting place for thousands of Union and Confederate men.

G. Oliver took a train to Chicago on November 11 to meet up with the one hundred and fifty Iowans. The next morning, The Governor's Special headed south on the Illinois Central Railroad. The special train consisted of nine Pullman luxury sleeping cars, a baggage car, and a dining car—G. Oliver later described it as "palatial."[5]

The band consisted of six men on clarinet; four on cornet, including G. Oliver; three alto horns; three tubas; two trombones; one baritone horn; one piccolo; a snare drum; and a bass drum. Some men were band regulars, and others were experienced musicians from across Iowa, brought in for the occasion. They wore dark pants with a stripe down the side, jackets crisscrossed with heavy braid, and military style caps. Their instruments were manufactured by the Holton company; a photo of the musicians later appeared in a Holton advertisement.

Notable Iowans on the trip included Governor Albert Cummins and his wife, Ida; General Grenville Mellen Dodge, a war hero and railroad builder; and Major Samuel Hawkins Marshall Byers, who had been a prisoner of war at five different camps, including Andersonville. Byers wrote the poem, "Sherman's March to the Sea," which was smuggled out of prison, set to music, and became a Union rallying cry.

Also on the train was Cedar Rapids journalist Ernest Sherman (no relation to the general). His newspaper articles about the trip were republished a year later as the book *Dedicating in Dixie*.

President Lincoln had recognized the strategic importance of Vicksburg early in the war; the city was perched on a three hundred-foot bluff above the Mississippi River. Lincoln was reputed to have said, "See what a lot of land these fellows hold, of which Vicksburg is the key. The war can never be brought to a close until that key is in our pocket."[6]

General Ulysses S. Grant's armies converged on the city in May of 1863, and after attempts to take it failed, the Union troops trapped the Confederate army there, along with the town's civilians, who took shelter in caves in the bluffs. The ensuing siege lasted until July 4, 1863, when Confederate General John Pemberton surrendered.

The Vicksburg National Military Park was established in 1899 to commemorate the battle and protect the ground where it was fought. It was the last of four battlefield parks established by the US Congress between 1890 and 1899; the others were Chickamauga and Chattanooga (1890), Shiloh (1894), and Gettysburg (1895). Congress wanted to preserve the sites for historical and professional study and to memorialize the armies on both sides of the war.

The Iowan veterans were unsure how they would be received by their former enemies. Conditions in the South had deteriorated for African Americans after the enactment of state and local "Jim Crow" segregation laws, and the current Mississippi governor, James Vardaman, was a white supremacist who did not hide his dislike of Yankees.

BOOMING CANNONS MARKED the delegation's arrival in Vicksburg on the morning of November 13. Governor Vardaman did not appear at the depot; he sent a staff member to drive Mr. and Mrs. Cummins to their hotel. Other members of the party took carriages from the station to the battlefield park. The Iowans drove past the national cemetery, a 116-acre burial site for seventeen thousand Union soldiers and sailors overlooking the river. It was the largest interment of Civil War dead in the country.

They also stopped at the newly dedicated Illinois Monument, one of the park's most impressive features. Made of Georgian white marble, it was designed by Chicago architect William Le Baron Jenney, a veteran of the Vicksburg campaign who later in life designed the first skyscraper. It cost the state of Illinois $194,432.92, equivalent today to nearly five million dollars.[7]

When the *Crookston Times* interviewed G. Oliver upon his return, he did not mention this part of the tour. If he ventured inside the memorial that day, it is likely he found the names of his father and two of his uncles. Sixty bronze tablets lining the monument's interior walls list all 36,325 Illinois soldiers who fought at Vicksburg.

That evening, Vicksburg citizens hosted a reception for the Iowans at the National Park Pavilion, which was brilliantly lit and decorated in red, white, and blue. Vardaman bypassed the reception and instead attended a Daughters of the Confederacy event in Gulfport. Other prominent residents also discovered they had previous engagements. Those who did attend showed warm hospitality toward the visitors.

The *Vicksburg Daily Herald* reported that the men and women from the two different states spent the evening becoming better acquainted. "The band played excellent music, and the friendly and fraternal feeling which prevailed made the occasion a most enjoyable one."[8]

Sherman described the scene this way: "The ladies were beautifully attired, there was gold braid in plenty worn by the Staff to relieve the somberness of the men's evening dress, the 55th regimental band gave an exquisite concert program, and the punch bowl, after the receiving line had done its duty, was the center of attention. That punch bowl, presided over by two of Vicksburg's society leaders, assisted by a bevy of Vicksburg's most charming young women, was a revelation to many of the Iowa party. They do not use water in their punch at Vicksburg."[9]

The next day, the weather was so agreeable no one wore overcoats. Two thousand people streamed to the park for the dedication of the Iowa Memorial. It was located on the opposite side of the park from the Illinois Memorial, along the Union line overlooking the old Confederate earthwork where many Iowa soldiers died in a bloody assault on May 22, 1863—including nearly nine out of every ten soldiers from the 22nd Iowa Regiment. Made of Vermont white granite, the semi-elliptical structure was to feature six bronze relief panels that depicted scenes from the Vicksburg campaign; however, these were not completed at the time. Sculptors Henry Hudson Kitson and Theo Alice Ruggles Kitson, a married couple from Massachusetts, also designed an equestrian statue for the monument.

The program opened with a prayer, and a speech by Henry Harrison Rood, secretary of the monument commission. One hundred Vicksburg schoolchildren sang, "America," and four young women from Iowa unveiled the monument. After the band played "Nearer My God to Thee" and "Dixie," the speeches continued for three more hours.

In his address, Governor Cummins struck a conciliatory tone. He said,

> *This monument is not reared to commemorate an event, not reared in the memory of a cause, not reared as evidence of a victory. It is reared to commemorate the work of the individual*

soldiers, and upon the same ground on which it stands as an everlasting tribute to the courage and heroism of Iowa soldiers, there will stand a monument built to do like honor to the like courage and heroism of the soldiers of the Confederate army. In the judgment day of history, Grant and Lee, Sherman, Johnston, Sheridan, Jackson, and all the other noble spirits of the war will stand as valiant commanders and followers who tried to do their duty as God gave them light to see it.[10]

When Cummins finished, Vardaman took the podium, and some Iowans in the crowd braced themselves for trouble. Known for his white suits and long black hair that hung down to his shoulders, Vardaman had caused an uproar the previous week. During the dedication of the Illinois Monument, he refuted Illinois Governor Charles Deneen's assertion that "all men are created equal."

"I used to think one Confederate was worth a dozen Yankees. Sometimes I think so yet," Vardaman said that day, in front of hundreds of Illinois veterans. He added, "all Caucasians, Anglo-Saxons especially, should have a hand in the government."[11]

Vardaman's speech before the Iowans repeated an assertion he had made the previous week: the real difference in the American people, he said, was not between the North and South but between those "who inhabit the great cities and the people who dwell in the country."[12] However, his speech overall was more conciliatory than incendiary.

Finally, the former prisoner of war, Byers, recited a piece he had written for the occasion. The forty-stanza poem "Vicksburg" ended with these lines:

Build to our own the marble bust
Where the great river laves
Yon hill that holds their honored dust —
Their twenty thousand graves.
The years go on, the living still
If Blue coat or if Gray,
May ask the mounds on yonder hill,
Where are they all today?

The Iowa delegation left Vicksburg that evening for Andersonville, Georgia, site of the infamous military prison where more than forty-five thousand Union soldiers were confined during the war. It was there that G. Oliver encountered what he later said was the "most impressive scene that he had ever witnessed in his life."[13]

Ernest Sherman, the journalist accompanying the band, later wrote of the cemetery at Andersonville that "the dead were buried without coffins, side by side, in trenches four feet deep, and there they lie today, nearly thirteen thousand of them, peacefully sleeping in one of the most beautiful God's Acres in all America." He added: "It is a somewhat singular fact that in spite of the heartlessness of the Andersonville management, the hospital records were kept in a fairly complete and correct manner, so that the burial place of 12,461 of the dead could be identified, while but 451 are listed among the unknown ... The Iowa Memorial has been erected in this cemetery."[14]

The Vicksburg dedication had pomp and glory, but Andersonville was a funeral. A gentle rain greeted the Iowans when they got off the train, adding a tone of cathartic sadness to an already solemn occasion. The Iowa visitors were met by a platoon of US soldiers based at Fort McPherson, Georgia. No former Confederate soldiers were included in this event, unlike other ceremonies on the trip.

The unveiling ceremony began at half past ten. The regimental band led the procession into the cemetery playing a dirge. The musicians put their best efforts into the music, and G. Oliver described it as "the finest music he had ever heard."[15]

Governor Cummins gave a moving speech that many listeners assessed as his best of the tour. He noted that the American flag "flies for all her citizens, without respect to condition in life, whether they be high or low, rich or poor, white or black,"[16] and he concluded with words from the "Battle Hymn of the Republic."

"As he came to the final [words], many a man who had not wept for years was wiping his eyes, and covertly looking at his neighbors, was feeling better because he saw them doing the same," Sherman wrote.[17]

Mrs. Cummins unveiled the Iowa monument at Andersonville: a weeping, kneeling granite woman set atop a marble pedestal. It was dedicated to the one hundred and seventy-eight Iowa soldiers who died in that cruel place.

If things had gone differently for Jasper during the war, he might have been buried at Andersonville. That thought may have crossed G. Oliver's mind as he toured the grounds. That afternoon, G. Oliver played a solo during a concert of sacred music at Providence Spring in the prison stockade. A freshwater spring had appeared there in August of 1864—an occurrence some parched and emaciated prisoners believed was an act of God. People were invited to wander the grounds after the concert, and as dusk approached, they boarded the train.

AFTER STOPS IN Atlanta and Chattanooga, the delegation traveled by steamboat to the 3,600-acre Shiloh National Military Park in southern Tennessee. It commemorated the two-day battle in April 1862 that produced more than twenty-three thousand Union and Confederate casualties.

The Shiloh dedication was also a two-day affair. The delegation spent the first day visiting the eleven Iowa regimental monuments spread throughout the park, identical except for their inscriptions. A brief ceremony was held at each, complete with a speech, a prayer, and a different song by the band. The procession took G. Oliver over ground his father had covered; a memorial to Jasper's 45th Illinois regiment was near those of Iowa's 11th and 13th regiments.

Jesse A. Miller, son of Lt. Colonel Alexander Miller of the Sixth Iowa Regiment, spoke at the dedication of that regiment's monument. His words may have resonated with G. Oliver:

> *I, as one who was born after the war, as one who knows nothing of the war except as I have heard and read, feel that I am a better man and will live a better life for having visited these battlefields. I believe that the people of all the states of this Union would be better citizens if they would visit the battlefield and see what we have seen and hear what we have heard. I hope that as the days go by and as the years roll on ... these memorials will*

ever tend to raise the citizenship of this country and make the people of this nation a better and higher type of civilization than any that has gone before.[18]

The towering Iowa State Memorial was formally dedicated the next day. Located near the Shiloh National Cemetery, high above the river bluff, it featured a thirty-six-foot-high shaft topped by a bronze eagle, and a twelve-and-a-half-foot bronze statue of a woman inscribing the words of another Byers poem into marble.

G. OLIVER CELEBRATED his thirty-sixth birthday during the return trip north, and within three weeks of arriving in Crookston, he received another enticing offer. Grand Forks businessmen wanted to know: would he consider taking over the direction of their city band, for a higher salary and generous expense budget?

The offer came as a surprise. He and Islea had many friends in Crookston and felt valued by the community. However, the trip South had reinvigorated his soloist aspirations. Grand Forks might offer greater opportunities for this aspect of his career.

G. Oliver had to weigh his options and make up his mind quickly.

5

LENNIE

"He was a real *martinet*. Did you know that? Oh, he'd give those kids hell."

I couldn't see Leonard Jung's face as he relayed this information over the telephone, but I heard him chuckle.

Martinet. It's not a word I had ever used in conversation. I inferred its meaning as Lennie rattled off memories supporting his characterization of my paternal great-grandfather: G. Oliver once mercilessly chewed out a traffic cop during a parade because he didn't adequately clear the way for the band to pass. G. Oliver would not tolerate absences from rehearsal; even a family vacation was not an approved excuse. G. Oliver would poke boys in the stomach with his baton if they hadn't practiced, calling them "boneheads."

"He never said that to me because he liked me—because of my older brothers," Lennie confided, referring to Richard and Herbert, who played trumpet and drums, respectively, in the St. Cloud boys' band. "He'd put me on the spot all the time—he'd say, 'Leonard, you show them.'"

As Lennie talked and I typed frantically on my laptop, trying to keep up with his recollections, a surge of adrenalin raced through my body. It thrilled me to speak with someone who had known G. Oliver. The eighty-seven-year-old US Navy Band veteran had recently moved from his D.C. home of sixty years to a place in Maryland, and I wasn't sure how long he would want to

42

talk, so I tried to work in as many questions as possible. Ten minutes into the conversation, his voice grew fainter, and he suggested I call him back in a few weeks, when he would be unpacked and more organized.

My fingers still trembled from excitement when I set down the phone. I grabbed a dictionary from the nearby bookshelf and leafed through its pages until I found martinet: a rigid military disciplinarian, or "one who demands absolute adherence to forms and rules," after a French army officer named Jean Martinet who died in 1672.

That fit other descriptions of G. Oliver I had gleaned from newspaper clippings. A 1977 *St. Cloud Daily Times* article described him as "stark, gaunt, precise, terrifying and eminently respected." It noted that his baton "served more purposes than mere direction." Band members recalled that their former director ruled by fear and would rap their knuckles and the backs of their necks when they didn't meet his performance standards.[1]

When I first read this description, I wondered if it was an exaggeration. I instinctively felt defensive of an ancestor I had only begun to know through photographs and news accounts. I wanted to believe there was more to him than this image of a crusty, old-school director who terrified his charges. I wanted to like him. I also wasn't sure I could completely trust the source. The newspaper article, published more than thirty years after G. Oliver's death, contained other inaccuracies. Ferreting out the truth proved to be an ongoing challenge, especially given the dearth of primary sources and the unreliability of memory.

As I gathered more material, I began to find confirmation of my initial instincts. Although there was no disputing G. Oliver's reputation as an imposing and demanding director, individual boys responded differently to his approach. What made talking with Lennie so rewarding was that I could hear warmth and admiration in his voice as he described his former bandmaster.

SIX MONTHS LATER, my dad and I headed toward Lennie's home in Bowie, Maryland. It was a sunny, forty-degree day in January—a pleasant change from below-zero temperatures in Minnesota. While Dad drove the rental car, I tried to relax by listening to the calm voices of the public radio reporters. It didn't work. I had trouble concentrating on anything except the man I was about to meet and the interview I was about to conduct. I had built it up in my mind as an occasion of personal importance, and I didn't want to screw it up.

My initial phone conversation with Lennie convinced me that I had to interview him in person, and I invited my dad to join me. Given Lennie's age and the uncertainties of life, it seemed imperative not to wait too long. I planned a three-day trip that gave us enough time to interview Lennie, locate articles about G. Oliver at the Library of Congress, and meet with friends in D.C. before flying home.

I normally conducted interviews with a notebook and a pen, but for this occasion I'd brought along a laptop computer, microphone, video camera, and tripod.

If Dad was nervous, he didn't show it. He carried a black nylon briefcase stuffed with assorted band photographs and concert programs to kindle the conversation.

Lennie greeted us at the door with the smile of an old friend. Behind his gold-framed glasses, his blue eyes were clear and bright. Slim and energetic, he looked spry and younger than his age. He wore a red chamois shirt and crisp blue trousers, and he carried himself with the air of someone accustomed to military efficiency and discipline.

He ushered us into his immaculately kept townhouse, decorated with a collection of Russian nested dolls in all sizes and colors. They belonged to his wife, he informed us. His terrier raced up and down the hallway, her collar tags jingling with excitement.

I set up my recording equipment in the living room as Lennie and Dad exchanged pleasantries. Dad knew Lennie's niece, Karen, and she had given us her uncle's contact information. She had assured my dad we'd have no problem getting Lennie to talk. Keeping him on track—that, she joked, would be challenging.

Lennie repeated some of what he told me over the phone and added new details. He was born in St. Cloud in 1919, the youngest of five children. His father and both grandfathers played in the Perham Cornet Band; his oldest brother, Francis, played violin and clarinet; his sister Mildred taught piano; and his brothers Herb and Richard played for G. Oliver. Although

Lennie was more interested in hunting and sports, his mother cajoled him into joining the beginners band in about 1931, when he was twelve.

"I started against my will. It turned out I took to it; it was right up my alley. So I stayed with it," he said.

This was an understatement. He had been an active musician for seven decades and had only recently given up playing the tuba.

Lennie also told stories I'd never heard before, one of which focused on a rivalry between G. Oliver and Erwin Hertz, the director of the Tech High School Band. Hertz was still directing at Tech in the 1950s when my dad played in the band.

"Here's what happened," Lennie said, leaning forward on the floral-patterned couch. "Some of these kids, by the time they got to high school, they were pretty damn good players. They had been trained by G. Oliver, but Hertz was getting the credit for it. G. Oliver would say, 'Damn it, here I develop these kids and he gets all the credit. Damn it, *I* want the credit'—that's the way he was."

Lennie was clearly enjoying himself.

"There was a concert of high school bands somewhere—not in St. Cloud, somewhere else. I guess they were being graded for a contest. The St. Cloud Boys' Band wasn't in it, but Hertz had the St. Cloud high school band there. G. Oliver knew one of the other band leaders involved, and he said, 'You beat him, you beat that damn Hertz, and I'll buy you a new suit of clothes.'"

Lennie laughed heartily and leaned back on the couch. Dad and I laughed, too. Lennie's amusement was infectious.

"He told me that himself; he just didn't like Hertz," Lennie said, "You knew where you stood with him. There was no holding back. And he was sincere."

Lennie was quiet for a moment, and my dad took the opportunity to interject a comment.

"Hertz ended up being my band director. And a lot of what I've been doing with her," Dad said, looking in my direction, "is going back through my own life. Some things are making a lot more sense now. I mean, I'm kind of putting things together."

I wasn't sure if Lennie caught my dad's meaning, or if the words had even reached his slightly hard-of-hearing ears. I understood, though. My dad grew up in St. Cloud as the grandson of

G. Oliver and the son of Ronald, the band director turned college professor. People must have formed opinions of my dad because of his last name, or had expectations of him that he couldn't possibly have understood as a young man.

I wondered if Dad was experiencing what I'd experienced since we started the project: my adult brain was slowly piecing together fleeting details and bits of information that my younger self had stored in a miscellaneous file, and a new version of my past was emerging.

I was also beginning to see my dad's life from a different perspective. And it was clear to me that although he and Lennie were almost twenty years apart in age, they were like two peas in a pod. They grew up in houses a few blocks apart, they graduated from the same high school, they both attended St. Cloud State, and they understood music in a way I never would.

Unlike Lennie, who pursued music as a career, my dad went into teaching. He took a job at the high school in Alexandria in 1960, about the time Lennie retired from the Navy Band. Dad taught social studies for more than thirty years, and he worked part-time in the education department at the University of Minne-

Leonard "Lennie" Jung, a former boys' band member who had a career in the US Navy Band.

sota–Morris for many years. Music remained his passion, however, and he played trumpet in numerous bands, including the Alexandria Big Band.

Lennie knew about big bands. After college, he played all over Minnesota and its surrounding states in Don Strickland's Twin Cities-based dance band. He then followed in his brother Herb's footsteps and enrolled in the Navy School of Music in Washington, D.C.

Lennie showed us a photo of Herb from 1930 and dug out a

letter G. Oliver wrote in January 1937 on City of St. Cloud stationery, recommending Herb for the Navy School of Music. I held the letter in my hands and read the words G. Oliver had composed:

[Herb] showed great interest and unusual talent from the first, and soon earned the right to be named the best drummer in the band. Since his boyhood days he has played tympani, snare drum, BB♭ sousaphone, string bass, and other instruments which we in the St. Cloud Municipal Concert Band use and has always been absolutely dependable, both musically and as a clean cut intelligent young gentleman, Herbert Jung is worthy of any confidence. He will make good at anything he attempts.

Herb's promising career was cut short in 1952. Lennie recalled in a shaky voice how his brother, who suffered from asthma, caught double pneumonia and died at age thirty.

"His nemesis was when he caught a cold, and he couldn't breathe," Lennie said. "I was on tour with the Navy Band, we were somewhere—I think Brookings, South Dakota—on tour when I got this long-distance phone call about how Herb had died."

Lennie had his own close call with death as a young man. After the attack on Pearl Harbor, Lennie was assigned to play in a twenty-one-piece band on the battleship the USS *Northampton*. During a night battle off the coast of Guadalcanal on November 30, 1942, two Japanese torpedoes struck the *Northampton*, and it sunk.

"If I hadn't been a good swimmer, I wouldn't be here right now," Lennie said.

His tuba wasn't so lucky. It went down with the ship and is presumably still at the bottom of the Pacific Ocean.

For his efforts in rescuing other sailors that night, Lennie received a commendation from Admiral William F. Halsey. He showed us the letter, which was framed and hanging on the wall in the side room off his living room.

While home on leave in 1943, Lennie visited G. Oliver. It was the last time he saw his former bandleader.

"Was G. Oliver proud of how some of you went on to continue in band work?" I asked.

"Well, if any of his players got any kind of good notice, he was proud of that, he was glad to see it, and of course he would want his name to be mentioned, too, 'a student of Mr. G. Oliver Riggs,' sure," Lennie said.

Lennie's friend Pullman "Tommy" Pederson was perhaps the most famous former pupil of G. Oliver's. He played in Hollywood and was a prolific composer; you can still buy his trombone instruction books. Lennie said he and Tommy were practically inseparable. Tommy's mother would often ask Lennie to invite her son to go outside and play, because all he wanted to do was practice the trombone.

"When he was 10 or 12 years old, he was playing all these big, dynamic Herbert L. Clarke trumpet solos on the trombone flawlessly. What a player," Lennie said.

Another boys' band friend of Lennie's, Chester Heinzel, joined the US Army Band, and—two decades after G. Oliver's death—led President Lyndon Johnson's inaugural parade as the band's assistant leader.

Dad then brought out some photos and programs. Lennie recognized many faces and threw out asides about former bandmates: Bill Goblish, a great tennis player; Paul Fleming, who became a dentist; Bobby Kollman, who joined the National Guard Band during the war.

When Lennie asked if we knew of Herbert Streitz, a friend of his brother Herb, Dad and I nodded; we had seen Streitz's name in several concert programs.

"As far as I know, he became the band leader in Waseca, Minnesota. I don't imagine he's alive anymore, but he was the solo cornetist for a long time in that band," Lennie said.

The conversation turned sober when Dad asked Lennie about a 1960 airplane crash involving US Navy Band members on tour in Brazil. I wasn't familiar with the incident—it occurred before I was born—but the pained look in Lennie's eyes indicated he remembered it like it happened yesterday.

A plane carrying the band collided with a Brazilian commercial plane over the bay in Rio de Janeiro. Sixty-one people died, including all nineteen musicians. Lennie was scheduled to go on that tour, but he'd begged off. The assistant bandleader, Harold Fultz, approved his request.

"He said, 'Lennie, don't worry about it. My god, you're on every single job. Every conductor we have, they want you on there, whether it's a dance job or a gig job or whatever it is, they want you. Don't worry.' He told me I didn't have to make that trip. That saved my life."

Lennie continued, haltingly. "All these bodies—one bystander saw stuff floating down—music and bodies and …" He paused for a few seconds to regain his composure. "And instruments and everything else coming falling down. Yeah."

"And Harold Fultz was on that plane?" Dad inquired in a soft voice.

"Yeah, he was on it, he was killed. And if it hadn't been for him, I'd have been on that damn plane, too."

We sat in silence for a few minutes, sobered by the thought and unsure how to proceed.

Dad had been waiting to spring a surprise on Lennie, and he must have decided it was time.

"So, you knew a trumpet player by the name of Attridge?" Dad said, posing it as a question but already expecting the answer.

"Oh, god, Paul Attridge, one of my good friends," Lennie responded with zeal. "He's from Minnesota—no, his wife's from Minnesota. Yes, he was one of my good friends. He had a great sense of humor."

"Do you know who one of my good friends was?" Dad asked.

"Who?"

"Paul Attridge."

"Is that right!" Lennie's face beamed with pleasure. "Yeah, well, did you know his wife, Sandy? Sandy's dad was a banker."

I listened as they swapped stories about Attridge, who played trumpet in the Navy Band from 1939 to 1962 and then retired to Alexandria, where he played in the Alexandria Big Band with my dad. He also taught elementary band and had my brother as a trumpet student. Attridge died in 1999 at age eighty-six.

My dad showed Lennie a picture of Attridge and promised to send another one he'd accidentally left at home.

"You'll love it because we're playing 'Bugler's Holiday,'" he said.

Lennie started humming a few bars of the tune, and then

switched topics as another memory surfaced. "You know who guest conducted us a couple of times, and I'll never forget? Henry Fillmore. This was on our 1946 tour."

I supposed he meant *the* Henry Fillmore—I had played his marches in band. Dad responded, in a collegial way: "I met Henry Fillmore in 1956, and he guest conducted us. Wasn't that a thrill?"

This was news to me also. I began to feel out of place, not having a famous conductor story of my own to share, and my neck started to tire from turning my head back and forth between them as they carried on their rapid-fire conversation. I found it endearing, but confusing.

"Oh, god, yeah. What a great guy," Lennie said, referring to Fillmore.

"And you've never played the Fillmore march better," Dad said.

"We'd get through and he'd say, 'Neatly done, boys, neatly done,'" Lennie said. "I like his marches, I always did. And I believe he would take a drink if you played your cards right."

My dad chuckled. "I don't know about that, I was still in high school. But I did meet him."

After Lennie retired from the Navy Band in 1964, he worked for the Navy for twenty years in a civil service job, creating music and sound effects for motion pictures. For many years, he played string bass in a jazz combo that performed in D.C. clubs, and he played his tuba in a community band composed of retired Navy, Air Force, and Army band members.

He and my dad could have talked about music all day, discovering other common experiences, but we had specific questions we hoped he could answer, such as whether G. Oliver had played for Sousa. Lennie had no information to share on that subject, unfortunately. He couldn't even recall G. Oliver *talking* about Sousa, although he said his dad once invited G. Oliver to the house to listen to a live Sousa concert on the radio.

Lennie also didn't remember meeting my grandfather or Percy. He did, however, relate a story about how Islea played the organ for silent movies at the Paramount Theatre.

"Sometimes she could be playing background music for a movie, and she was reading a magazine at the same time," he said, chuckling. "He told me that; that's what he told me."

Lennie's memories were vivid and detailed, but many aspects of his time in band remained beyond recall. That made sense to me. I couldn't recount many details about junior high band, but I could still picture tar melting in the streets on the July day my high school band marched in the Minneapolis Aquatennial Parade. And I could still see the look on our director's face when he announced that we placed first in the competition.

Toward the end of our four-hour conversation, after we had moved to the kitchen table for coffee and doughnuts, Lennie shared one more helpful piece of information. When I asked whether he knew that G. Oliver had composed two pieces in his early career, a cadet march and something called the "Reel Rag," Lennie replied, "Oh, yes, the 'Reel Rag.' G. Oliver got that out for the band to play one day."

Dad and I exchanged glances of delight; at last, confirmation that as recently as the 1930s—which isn't recent at all, come to think of it—the composition was in the St. Cloud Band's music library. Maybe it was still there. I added that to my mental checklist of follow-up items.

Lennie did not appear fatigued by our lengthy visit; if anything, he seemed energized. But we had already stayed longer than we'd planned. We said goodbye and promised to stay in touch.

Feeling exhilarated by the marathon interview, I settled into the passenger seat and exhaled deeply. Meeting someone G. Oliver had cared about was as close as I could get to being in his presence. For that, I was grateful.

As Dad maneuvered the car toward our hotel, one of Lennie's comments kept replaying in my head. If G. Oliver could have heard the tribute—his own verbal letter of recommendation from one of the Jung boys—I believe it would have put a smile on the old martinet's face.

"I tell you, in all my years of playing with different conductors, he was pretty hard to beat," Lennie had said. "He had something on the ball, he really did. To this day I highly respect him and his memory."

6

You Won't Do Any Business
If You Haven't Got a Band

The first time Grand Forks businessmen tried to lure G. Oliver away from Crookston, in December of 1906, he turned them down. For three more years, he continued to direct the Crookston city band, the Riggs theater and dance orchestra, and the Burnham Creek Band, composed of a dozen men from the outskirts of Polk County. Music was not taught in primary or secondary schools at that time, and in 1907, he formed a youth band and began to provide free lessons to boys aged twelve and older. As they matured, they were allowed to advance into the adult band.

Years later, his son Percy wrote, "He was one of the first men to work with young people in class lessons, and since there was no material available for this type of instruction at the time, he wrote the first workable courses of study. He did not think that they were very good methods, so did not try to have them published."[1]

The *Polk County Journal* ran a column about the venture and encouraged parents to insist that their sons practice an hour a day as a necessary part of their education.

"Do not be afraid of them becoming professionals because the chances are they will not have either talent or application to become anything but an average performer, but being an average performer to a business man is a great pleasure as an accomplishment," the column said. "There is nothing that will take a young man in to the best society in his hometown or in a strange town or city as quickly as the fact of him being a good performer on some musical instrument or possessing a good voice."[2]

The column continued: "Possibly a boy who is accomplished has more temptations than one who is not, but that is no argument against the boy spending his time learning something. Keep the boy busy and have him taught as much as possible and to know right from wrong and even though he may do a few things that are not just perfection, he will come out right in the long run and make an accomplished, useful man."[3]

Eager to advance as a performer himself, G. Oliver played occasionally in the Iowa regimental band, and in the spring of 1908, he spent three weeks in Chicago studying cornet with Alfred F. Weldon, one of the best brass teachers in the country. Weldon was a friend of Herbert Clarke, Sousa's famed cornetist, and several Weldon students went on to play for Sousa, including trombonist Arthur Pryor.

The bustle of big city life in Chicago must have provided an invigorating change from G. Oliver's routine in Crookston. More than a decade had passed since he studied violin in Chicago, and the city had grown by 400,000 residents—its population stood at roughly two million, making it the second-largest US city.

A few months after studying with Weldon, G. Oliver received an invitation to play at the North Dakota State Fair in a professional band directed by C. S. Putnam. G. Oliver had played with Putnam the previous year, although not as a soloist, and he jumped at the new opportunity.

Putnam taught arithmetic at the North Dakota Agricultural College, and he directed the college's ROTC cadet band. Like G. Oliver, Putnam was the son of a Civil War soldier; his father had led a Union regimental band and died during Sherman's March to the Sea, and his mother was a trained opera singer.[4]

Putnam asked G. Oliver to serve as the band's assistant director in addition to his soloist role. The North Dakota State Fair ran July 20–26 in Fargo, and the band performed each day.

"Overtures, marches, and popular airs were played and the crowds gave evidence of their appreciation by spontaneous and generous applause ...[G. Oliver] pleased thousands of visitors at the fairgrounds by playing a beautiful cornet solo, the Air 'Facilita' by Hartmann during the band concert," one newspaper reported.[5]

G. Oliver with sons Ronald, left, and Percy.

Amid all this activity, G. Oliver organized another amateur band closer to home—the thirty-member Bygland Band, comprised of men from a township outside of Crookston.

How Islea felt about these developments, and how she managed during his absences, was not mentioned in any news stories. Her teaching and performing schedule became more complicated with the arrival of daughter Rosalie, born June 24, 1908, and the illness of son Ronald, who spent several weeks in the hospital in July recovering from typhoid. It was around this time that G. Oliver began a regular practice of taking Ronald and Percy to band rehearsals, for their education—and also, perhaps, to gain favor with his wife.

IN NOVEMBER OF 1908, G. Oliver returned to Chicago for more instruction from Weldon, but he made sure to return home in time for his orchestra to play at the opening of Crookston's new Carnegie library, designed by his friend Bert Keck, and he spent the winter preparing for a spring concert featuring three of his four bands: the city band of Crookston, the Burnham Creek Band, and the Crookston Juvenile Band.

On March 16, 1909, the sixty-five musicians squeezed onto the stage of Crookston's Grand Opera House for the concert. They wore black tuxedos, white shirts, and long black ties. The size of the combined band tested the dimensions of the performance space: one man in the front row was perched precariously close to the edge of the stage.

The size of the audience also tested the auditorium's capacity. No seat was unoccupied for the concert, which featured two piano solos by Islea and a challenging cornet solo by G. Oliver—Herbert Clarke's "Valse Brilliante." The consolidated band performed eight pieces. G. Oliver thanked the audience and the bands for making the event a success. He also "called attention to the disadvantages under which the bands had been working and gave a well directed boost for a [new] opera house."[6]

The local papers uniformly praised the concert. The *Polk County Journal* described Islea's numbers, "Hungarian Dance" by Johannes Brahms and "Polka de le Reine" by Joachim Raff, as "a genuine treat" and said G. Oliver was "forced to respond with a second piece" after playing "one of the most difficult solos ever heard by a Crookston audience."[7]

A mere two weeks later, the residents of Crookston received startling news: G. Oliver had resigned as director. He had accepted an offer from businessmen in Grand Forks, a city nearly twice as large as Crookston. He announced the news on March 29. His new job, directing the thirty-piece Grand Forks Military Band, started April 1. The band was not affiliated with the military—its name reflected the style of music it played.

At a gathering of city and juvenile band members, G. Oliver said that while "he deeply regretted leaving Crookston, he had, after careful consideration decided that he would not be doing justice to himself unless he accepted the offer."[8]

The *Crookston Daily Times* said it would be difficult to find a successor who had the musical ability and business skills that G. Oliver possessed, a rare combination among band leaders. It also noted "during the past year the organization of the Juvenile band marked a new era in musical endeavor which had great possibilities in store for the city."[9]

An article in the *Crookston Chronicle* seemed to especially mourn the loss of Islea, noting she was a valued member of the Matron Club and the Current Events Club and was the longtime organist at the Congregational Church. It added: "A faithful mother, a true friend and a musician of rare ability, it will not be an easy task to fill her place ... She is a brilliant pianist who has pleased many a Crookston audience, being always received with the same enthusiasm."[10]

Putnam, the Fargo band director, sent a letter of congratulations to Grand Forks band member Fred Redick. "You ought to have a cracker-jack band soon, and the more the merrier. He ought to be able to do good work with you and I heartily wish you success," Putman wrote.[11]

The *Minneapolis Morning Tribune* even ran a story about G. Oliver's new position: "Music authorities place him as the most successful director of amateur bands in the United States, and one who is thoroughly competent to direct a professional band, should he decide to take up this line of work. He not only is a master at directing a band, but his ability in financing the band organization makes his services doubly valuable."[12]

G. Oliver began work almost immediately, while Islea and the children remained in Crookston for three more months. Islea seemed in no hurry to leave her friends and pupils.

A Grand Forks newspaper article indicated that the lack of an adequate opera house in Crookston had played a role in G. Oliver's decision to move. Whether or not this was true, the band facilities in Grand Forks were superior. G. Oliver had an office in the three-story Metropolitan Opera House, often described as "the finest opera house between Minneapolis and Seattle." Minneapolis architect Warren B. Dunnell had designed the Romanesque Revival building, which was built in 1890 at a cost of $91,000. Its nine-hundred-seat auditorium hosted operas, concerts, plays, and political speakers, and the Grand Forks band performed there in the winter. For the summer concerts, G. Oliver had a mobile bandstand constructed that seated up to fifty musicians and could be wheeled to different downtown locations each week.

In Grand Forks G. Oliver once again organized a youth band to feed his adult group. By mid-May, thirty-eight boys had joined. He told the *Grand Forks Evening Times* he wanted bright, energetic boys who behaved as "little gentlemen."

"[G. Oliver] does not permit smoking or profanity in the meetings or at any time while the boys are under his direction and told the boys at the meeting Wednesday night that if any of them were addicted to either habit they would have to quit the habit or the band," the newspaper noted.[13]

In July, G. Oliver's adult band had a four-day paid engagement at the North Dakota State Fair. Dressed in blue uniforms, the Grand Forks band performed at the grandstand from half past ten each morning through the later hours of the evening, with some breaks. Two other bands also performed, but the main attraction was an exhibition race between the "fastest horses in the land," Dan Patch and Minor Heir. It was the first time either horse had set hoof in North Dakota, and the race attracted nearly twenty-eight thousand spectators.

When Dan Patch appeared in the grandstand, the *Grand Forks Evening Times* reported, "The suppressed enthusiasm broke forth into a great cheer, a cheer that swept over the waiting thousands, drowned the music of the bands and rolled out across the fertile prairies. It was the greeting of a great crowd to a great horse."[14]

The man who owned both horses, Marion Savage, staged the race, but his plans went awry, and Minor Heir won by half a length, to the great disappointment of Dan Patch fans in the crowd.

Although G. Oliver wasn't as famous as Dan Patch, three national music magazines published stories about him that summer: *The Metronome*, the *American Musician and Art Journal,* and *The Dominant*. The *Metronome* called him "one of the leading cornet soloists in the West" and "one of the most successful directors of amateur bands in the United States."[15]

Islea and the children joined G. Oliver in Grand Forks in July, and the family moved into a house located south of downtown near the new city park. G. Oliver's band played for the park dedication in August, and several thousand people attended.

By fall of 1909, the population of Grand Forks was pushing past twelve thousand; two decades earlier, it had been five thousand. Railroads fueled much of the growth. Other major industries were flour milling—"Cream of Wheat" was invented in Grand Forks in 1893—and lumber milling. Grand Forks prided itself on its cultural offerings, and this must have helped ease the transition for Islea, who sought out opportunities to perform and teach. She joined the Thursday Musical Club, a group of talented society ladies who met regularly to discuss and perform music.

Hiring domestic help was a fairly common practice for middle-class families at the time, and the Riggs family made enough money in Grand Forks to hire a live-in servant named Lena Gorder. The daughter of Norwegian immigrants, she was single and five years younger than Islea. She helped with household chores and the care of the three children.

G. Oliver's job appeared to be going well, but dissatisfaction bubbled under the surface. His visits to Chicago may have fueled his ambition. It's also possible that turning thirty-nine made him reevaluate his career goals. For reasons he did not explain in the newspapers, he began to look outside the city for the next great opportunity.

IN JANUARY OF 1910, Americans went crazy for comets, in anticipation of the return of Halley's Comet. They planned comet-watching parties and wrote comet-related music, and hucksters peddled amulets and other products to those who feared the comet would destroy Earth. Perhaps no one was more attuned to the expected reappearance of Halley's Comet than author Mark Twain, who was born shortly after the comet's previous appearance in 1835.

In 1909, Twain said, "I came in with Halley's Comet in 1835. It is coming again next year, and I expect to go out with it. It will be the greatest disappointment of my life if I don't go out with Halley's comet. The almighty has said, no doubt: 'Now here are these two unaccountable freaks; they came in together, they must go out together.'"[16]

As it happened, Halley's was upstaged by the unexpected appearance of a second comet, later referred to as the Great Comet of 1910. Five times brighter than Venus, the awe-inspiring comet was first widely sighted in the Southern Hemisphere, but became visible in the sky above Tacoma, Washington, around the time G. Oliver arrived there on business.

He had come to assess the prospects for organizing a fifty-piece professional concert band in Tacoma, a city easily six and a half times larger than Grand Forks. Tacoma had once had an impressive band, but after its leader departed it collapsed, and musicians organized into a dozen smaller bands that competed for work.

While the *Tacoma Times*, the preferred paper of working-class residents, kept up a steady stream of front-page comet coverage, the more staid *Tacoma Daily News* covered the meeting between city leaders and G. Oliver.

"A first-class band, like a first-class baseball team, is an excellent advertisement in addition to its great entertainment value for the people who support it," the newspaper opined.[17] It's likely that G. Oliver knew he was walking into a delicate situation, but he may have underestimated how resistant some men would be to an "eastern" outsider leading them.

A February 10 article in the *Tacoma Daily News* said of the local musicians: "They have been at loggerheads among themselves for a long time, and it is the belief of many of them that the only hope of uniting them is to bring to this city an able leader who is a stranger to both sides. The music lovers of Tacoma desire a first-class organization, and they believe the only way they can get it, if the musicians do not unite, is to go away from home for it."[18]

After the meeting in Tacoma, G. Oliver returned to Grand Forks and rehearsed his band for its last concert under his direction—although members didn't yet know it. The February 27 concert at the Metropolitan Theater featured Islea on piano and guest soloist Jeremiah Schefstad on violin.

The *Grand Forks Herald* reported, "Musicians noted a vast improvement in the band even since the first public concert, which attests to Mr. Riggs' ability as a director. Both Prof. Shefstad and Mrs. Riggs added greatly to the program and their work was above criticism."[19]

Although the concert reflected well on G. Oliver, he was ready to move on. With the plans out west still unsettled, he announced he was moving to Tacoma on April 1. He told the *Grand Forks Herald* the Tacoma opportunity "is one that comes but once in a lifetime."[20]

The *Grand Forks Evening Times* reported, "Both Mr. and Mrs.

Riggs are delighted with Grand Forks as a home and their year's residency in the city has been one of pleasure. Both regret the change and both will cherish many memories of the year."[21]

G. Oliver returned to Tacoma alone, and Islea moved with the children to her mother's house in Aledo, where she enrolled the boys in school (Islea's father had died in 1907).

Eager to get the band organized, G. Oliver met with trustees of the Tacoma Commercial Club, who agreed to contribute $100. Under the plan developed by the band association, which included Commercial Club and Chamber of Commerce members, thirty-two musicians would be hired, and G. Oliver would organize a series of ten summer concerts and four winter concerts.

Businessman James H. Dege expressed enthusiasm about the prospect.

"There is no city in the west that I know of that needs a first class concert band any more than Tacoma needs one," Dege told the *Tacoma News*. "This is a music-loving city, and I believe the people will support such an organization. It will do much toward advertising the city, and more than that, it will be a source of pleasure to the people of Tacoma."[22]

G. Oliver hoped to swing public opinion his way. His first test was a concert on April 17.

People began strolling into the twenty-seven-acre Wright Park two hours early to find seats in front of the bandstand, an unusual structure built atop a giant tree stump. The *Tacoma Daily News* later estimated the total attendance at between six thousand and seven thousand people, noting: "Almost everybody in Tacoma went to the band concert yesterday instead of taking the usual trips to the islands, beaches and country places."[23]

The musicians had only rehearsed together four times before the concert. When they made their way onto the pavilion, the *Tacoma Tribune* reported, "a rousing cheer went up. Director Riggs smiled and bowed in response, making himself popular with Tacomans at the outset."[24]

The program opened with "The First Brigade I. N. G. March," written by Weldon, G. Oliver's teacher. People continued to stream into the park, and when space in front of the bandstand became packed, concertgoers gathered on terraces overlooking the park. The program continued with seven more numbers, and the band played four encores.

The next day, the *Tacoma Daily News* ran a letter to the editor supporting G. Oliver. Tacoma newcomer M. J. Sheridan, who had known G. Oliver in Chicago and Omaha, said the bandmaster proved his ability at the concert. He also attested to G. Oliver's ability as a businessman.

"If Seattle can pay an orchestra leader $6,000 or $7,000 a year," he wrote, "and pay 65 players besides, in addition to buying music and meeting the other expenses, surely Tacoma ought to readily raise $5,000. I am informed that Seattle's subscription for the orchestra is $30,000 a year. That ought to be enough to encourage Tacomans to act immediately. From what I have learned of this man Riggs he is going to make every other band on this Coast get up and dust, if Tacoma will give him the opportunity."[25]

Later that week, G. Oliver met with the band-organizing committee and said he needed a guarantee that it would raise $4,000 to fund the first year of operation. He appeared to be growing impatient. He intimated to a *Tacoma Ledger* reporter that "he would not waste much more time in Tacoma unless the money for the maintenance of the band is soon forthcoming."[26]

On the same day that G. Oliver held his conference, April 21, Mark Twain died in his sleep at his New England home. Within a week of Twain's death, Halley's Comet was close enough to be seen in the United States with the naked eye. Interest in its approach continued to build.

Meanwhile, G. Oliver held the businessmen to their $4,000 promise. In late April, he sent a letter to local newspapers, in which he reiterated his credentials, explained the proposal in detail, and assured citizens he would make the band a success.

He wrote, "This band plan that I hope to have this city adopt is very similar to the way in which many of the principal cities of the United States are keeping up with their concert bands and symphony orchestras of 75 and 100 artists, and the work I have outlined comes pretty near being two men's work—that of the musician and that of the business man.

"I have only a few days left now to decide whether I remain in Tacoma or go elsewhere ... I hope that the people of this city will see the necessity of immediate action."[27]

As a last-ditch effort, G. Oliver tried to connect the band to a military unit based in Tacoma. He mentioned this in a postcard he mailed to Ronald. The postcard featured a picture of the Washington State Armory, a brick structure with a five-story tower.

G. Oliver wrote to his son: "Dear Ronald, This big building is where I have the band practice now. We play to-day 14 musicians. Give concert tomorrow with 32. Your father, G. O. Riggs."[28]

G. Oliver's Coast Artillery Band performed its first—and last—outdoor concert on May 29 at South Park in South Tacoma. The band of thirty-two musicians performed eleven numbers. Later that evening, Halley's Comet made an unusually brilliant appearance over Tacoma.

"It was observed soon after twilight and was visible until it set after midnight," the *Tacoma Times* reported. "Many expressed the opinion that the comet was brighter and the tail more distinct than on May 23 when the eclipse of the moon brought it into relief."[29]

One week later, G. Oliver announced he was leaving Tacoma. His stay had been temporary after all, just like that of the comets. He said it was impossible to form a band of the size he had hoped, and he was not interested in scaling it back. Instead, he told the *Tacoma Daily News*, he would pursue similar opportunities in four or five eastern cities, including Chicago.

"Businessmen, upon whom the success of a band would depend, have been assessed for so many things that they are not ready to stand behind a big musical organization. They have been building the Stadium, a mighty worthy institution, the YMCA, another credit to any city, and they have been assessed for many other purposes."[30]

G. Oliver also cited the weather as a factor.

"When I came here I was under the impression that the summer evenings were hot. I find that to be untrue. Chilly evenings do not encourage open air concerts, and that militates against the success of the band," he said.[31]

What he did not cite in the interview was the chilly reception he had received from a significant percentage of the musicians. The supposed "chance of a lifetime" had fizzled, and G. Oliver was left with no job. Despite what he told the newspaper, he had no solid leads on a new one. He returned to his family in Illinois and began to work his connections.

When he spoke of Tacoma years later, it was only to mention that he directed a professional band in that city. He never elaborated on the fact that in Tacoma his effort to organize a band had fizzled for the first time.

That summer, Islea performed in Aledo with Jane Abercrombie, an up-and-coming Chicago opera star who had married the brother of Islea's childhood friend Lallie. The two women gave a joint recital on August 18 at the First Presbyterian Church. A newspaper article about the event called Abercrombie "the leading prima donna in English Grand Opera in this country," and it said of Islea: "Her work as a sterling artist is almost too well known to require comment. She has taken first rank both as instructor and soloist in the northern states where she has resided for the past few years, and where her reputation was such that her name on a program was enough to excite great interest among the musical circles and to insure a large and enthusiastic audience."[32]

In late summer, G. Oliver performed as a cornet soloist with Landers's band at the Iowa State Fair in Des Moines, and in October he wrote to Weldon to ask if his teacher could line him up with any gigs. Weldon responded that the prospects from late fall through January were not great for either band or orchestra work.

"In either case it is a case of hustle and become acquainted before you can get a start in Chicago," Weldon responded. "As far as playing is concerned, you are head, neck and heels better than 9/10ths of the cornetists in Chicago."[33]

In January G. Oliver returned to Iowa Wesleyan University, his former employer, to lead the conservatory's cornet department. He also started an adult band and a thirty-five-member boys' band in Mount Pleasant. G. Oliver's family joined him there, and as spring approached he went on tour with the Iowa Wesleyan Glee Club as a violin and cornet soloist. The group performed in nine Iowa cities including Ottumwa, where G. Oliver received a glowing review.

The *Ottumwa Courier* said: "There has never been a more artistic cornet solo played in Ottumwa than Mr. Riggs' rendition of Herbert L. Clark[e]'s 'Bride of the Waves.' Mr. Riggs' playing compared very favorably with that of [Bohumir] Kryl and other well known artists who have visited Ottumwa."[34]

When the school term ended, G. Oliver announced he would teach music in Burlington, Iowa, and would play solo cornet in the Fischer Band. He cited, among his qualifications, his organization of the "famous coast artillery band" in Tacoma and his five-octave range on the cornet.

But he abruptly abandoned those plans to take a directing job in Havre, Montana, a rough-and-tumble railroad town halfway between Fargo and Seattle. A former member of his Crookston city band, Bert Gourley—owner of a thriving Havre bakery—must have convinced G. Oliver the Montana job would be a better fit than Burlington. More money likely helped, too.

Director J. Henri Fischer told the *Burlington Hawkeye*, "Of course, nobody blames him. He is to get $1,800 per annum for looking after a band, and will have plenty of time for giving lessons and doing other work. He will no doubt do very well."[35]

G. Oliver headed west and wired for Islea once he rented a house. His family arrived the first of May and prepared for new adventures on the plains of Montana.

7

BIG G AND THE FAMILY

Throughout the winter of 2008, unanswered questions about G. Oliver's connection to Sousa gnawed at me: Why had St. Cloud band members told a reporter in the 1970s that G. Oliver once played with Sousa? Who or what was the original source for this information? If it was true, when had it happened and under what circumstances?

On April Fools' Day, Dad told me he had uncovered new information about this mystery. He wasn't joking. At a St. Cloud Municipal Band rehearsal the previous evening, trumpet player Tom Pattock revealed to my dad that the source of the story was a now-deceased municipal band member named Lloyd McNeal, who was stationed in California during World War II.

McNeal "entered the Coast Guard Band, where he met Herbert Clarke," Dad emailed to me. "Herbert asked him where he was from. Lloyd said St. Cloud, Minnesota. Clarke asked him if he knew his close personal friend G. Oliver Riggs. Then he said they had met while playing with Sousa. Tom said it was a military band."

Dad continued. "Lloyd has died recently of course. But I knew him and played some jobs with him ... This is not it—but we are closer."

The news excited me, but it also left me stymied. I wrote back: "Dad, you deserve extra bonus points for getting the Lloyd Mc-Neal story from Pattock. It gives us some more clues—and more detective work."

Email had become a regular form of communication between Dad and me. He wasn't opposed to talking on the phone, especially to hear good news, but after a few minutes he would hand the phone back to my mom. Now that we were a research team, however, we exchanged G. Oliver updates almost daily via email, along with news about the kids' activities or dinner guests my parents had entertained. I had always felt close to my dad, and the project was bringing us even closer.

Dad had a hunch that G. Oliver met Sousa in Chicago during the World's Fair. It seemed plausible, but I'd had no luck finding documentation. I did know Clarke had joined Sousa's band by the time it performed for the World's Fair dedication in October 1892 and returned to perform at the fair from May through June of 1893. Islea was in Chicago during much of this time, and G. Oliver was there, too, studying violin. I also knew Sousa's band performed in Crookston twice after G. Oliver moved there. But that still didn't explain the assertion that G. Oliver had once played in Sousa's band. The Riggs family scrapbooks contained no mention of Sousa, no scrap of a concert program, no photo of G. Oliver and Sousa. The search continued.

Another line of detective work I pursued related more to genealogy than bands, although it seemed like it could be important to the greater story. Following the success of meeting my dad's second cousins in Illinois—descendants of G. Oliver's sister, Daisy—I tracked down descendants of my grandfather's brother, Percy.

Percy and Ronald grew apart after they both married and had children. However, letters Percy wrote to Ronald late in life showed they made efforts to strengthen their relationship before Percy died in 1959, following heart surgery in Minneapolis.

Percy's wife, Patricia, and my grandmother Eleanor kept in contact after Ronald died in 1968, but their relationship became strained in the 1970s, after they were in a multi-car pileup on the Houston freeway; Patricia was driving, and Eleanor broke her leg.

Following my grandmother's death in 1980, the families of Ronald and Percy communicated mainly through Christmas cards.

Dad gave me outdated addresses for his first cousins and their children, and through Facebook and Google, I located some of my second cousins, who seemed friendly but knew even less than I did about G. Oliver and Islea. I also learned that Patricia and her daughter Mary Jane had both died (in 1990 and 1993, respectively).

THAT SPRING, DAD AND I collaborated on creating a G. Oliver exhibit for the Stearns History Museum in St. Cloud. Dad and his siblings decided the museum was an appropriate repository for G. Oliver's band items, including his baton, his band hat, a folder of his cornet solo music, and several band photos. Permanently housing the items at the museum meant they would be preserved for future generations. We were elated when the museum agreed to host a special day in June to highlight the exhibit.

On the afternoon of G. Oliver Riggs Day, also known as June 29, Steve, the kids, and I arrived at the museum half an hour before the exhibit opened to the public. My parents arrived at about the same time—I spotted my dad right away, wearing his bright yellow St. Cloud Municipal Band polo. I was excited but nervous. What if no one showed up? We would look foolish for thinking anyone would be interested in a long-dead band director. And we'd also have a lot of cookies to eat.

Planning for G. Oliver Riggs Day was like preparing for a graduation party, except we didn't have to clean our house. For the entertainment of anticipated guests, I created a twelve-minute movie of G. Oliver's life and career—a slideshow of photos, concert programs and newspaper clippings, with accompanying descriptions, set to band music. We set up the movie in the main gathering room and kept it running on a loop. I also found a spot to display "Big G," a three-foot-tall cardboard cutout I'd had made from an 1899 photo of G. Oliver in a tuxedo.

Among the first visitors to appear were Louisa's friend Alexa and her family. Alexa's mom, Kelly Lynn, was Louisa's Girl Scout troop leader, and she was always up for an adventure, but I was touched nevertheless that they'd driven two hours from Northfield to St. Cloud for the event. I also was thrilled to see our longtime friends Laurie and Bryan and their kids, Sam and Katy, who lived in the St. Paul suburb of Eagan. Laurie and I bonded over a mutual love of books during our first week of college, and she had been a stalwart supporter of the G. Oliver project from the beginning.

Steve gave our video camera to Louisa and suggested she interview guests about the exhibit. Laurie became her first "victim."

"Hello, I'm with the history museum crew," Louisa said, embracing her new role as a documentary filmmaker. "We're wondering what you think of the exhibit so far."

Laurie gamely played along. "I think the G. Oliver exhibit is great and very interesting, especially for me, as someone who used to play in bands," she said.

I chimed in. "Laurie was a member of the Drake University Marching Band."

"That's true—the D. U. M. B.," Laurie added. "Kudos to Joy for putting the exhibit together."

An hour later, my mom introduced me to her new friend, Francis Schellinger. Mom was a retired French teacher, and she had a knack for befriending interesting people at social gatherings. The man seated next to her seemed to fit this profile. Francis had white hair, a matching close-cropped beard, and a kind smile. He had played the sousaphone in the St. Cloud Boys' beginner band, and although he was not a star player, he said he learned valuable life lessons from G. Oliver.

After he told me his story, I found Louisa and asked her to capture his comments on video. Francis was still sitting next to my mom when Louisa approached, wearing a nametag that identified her as a great-great granddaughter of G. Oliver Riggs.

"So, I hear you knew G. Oliver," she said to Francis.

"I knew him very well. He was my band director," he said.

He didn't seem to mind being grilled by a ten-year-old girl with pigtails and a video camera.

"Was he strict?" Louisa asked.

It was a leading question; she'd heard me talk about G. Oliver's martinet ways.

"We didn't use the word strict then—he was a disciplinarian."

Francis pronounced the word slowly, emphasizing each syllable. "He wanted you to practice at home so when you got to band practice you didn't ..."

"You didn't stink?" Louisa said, supplying the adjective. "Did he ever call you a bonehead? I heard he said that to some people."

He smiled ruefully. "No, but I know he didn't have too much of an opinion of my ability to play the sousaphone ... I struggled with it." Francis said. "But they needed the bodies there. As long as I could carry that horn, I was in. I used to ride to band practice on my bicycle with the horn on my shoulder—I'm talking about the wrap-around sousaphones."

He pointed to my mom and asked Louisa, "Is that your grandma?" Louisa nodded.

"I was telling her that I learned things from him like, after you brush your teeth, you stood there and went like that," he closed his mouth and demonstrated, puffing his cheeks in and out like he was swishing water in his mouth, "so that your breath doesn't stink."

Mom laughed. "He taught you more than just band," she said.

The "Big G" cardboard cutout was popular with my Riggs relatives. We took a photo of him with all twenty family members in attendance, representing three generations (four if you count cardboard representations). Later, when Louisa interviewed my aunt Dana and my cousins Jessica and Kristina, Kristina said the group photo was her favorite part of the day.

"Maybe in another one hundred and twenty years they'll have another group photo," Jessica said.

We ended the afternoon with a Riggs family picnic at Hester Park, where we used to go to hear the community band play on the Fourth of July. My grandma would bring deviled eggs, and we'd stay for the fireworks. One year, Kristina's older twin brothers—Brent and Scott—had taught Kristina how to mimic the Fonz from the TV show *Happy Days*. She'd stick her thumbs up and say, "Ayyy!" on command.

I must have been about Louisa's age then, and Kristina must have been about the age of her younger daughter, Piper. As I sat at a picnic table now, watching family members interact, I couldn't predict what my kids and their second cousins would remember from G. Oliver Riggs Day. I could only hope their memories would include a glimmer of the laughter and warmth of family connectedness that made it feel so special to me.

THE FOLLOWING WEEKEND, we visited my parents in Alexandria. After breakfast on Sunday, Steve and the kids disappeared into the basement, and Mom stayed in the kitchen to load the dishwasher. Her love of a tidy kitchen was not a trait I had inherited. Dad and I moved into the adjacent living room, where sections of the newspaper rested on the coffee table, already read and refolded. The two thousand pieces of his latest jigsaw puzzle lay on a nearby card table, awaiting his patient attention.

But I needed his attention first. Ever since we started working on the G. Oliver project, I had wanted to record an interview with Dad. I couldn't trust my forty-year-old brain to recall all the details of his stories, even if I'd heard some of them several times. I had finally interviewed him in May, and now I wanted him to listen to a podcast I'd created of the interview. If he approved, I planned to put it on the website I'd created about G. Oliver's life and career.

Dad and I sat side by side on the leather couch. I balanced my laptop on my knees and clicked on the audio player. We listened as my recorded voice asked questions and Dad gave the same thoughtful answers about his memories of his grandparents and of his dad. Near the end, I had asked Dad if there was anything else he wanted to say about the G. Oliver project, and he explained that we had already gone way beyond his original expectations.

His podcast voice continued: "You're the reason that we have this awesome research project on our hands, and I'm very appreciative of that. You were even able to do some genealogy work that's been very important. So one of the things I want to say is thank you. I want to tell you that it's been a great journey ..."

I stared at the computer screen, listening intently. It took me a minute to notice something was wrong. Dad's broad shoulders were heaving up and down, his head was bent toward his belly, and tears streamed down his face.

Had something I said upset him? I had never seen my dad cry like that, not even during those scary hours a decade earlier when my mom underwent surgery for ovarian cancer. The only time I remembered seeing him cry was when I was in sixth grade, and he received a phone call giving him the news that his mother had died.

Dad always knew what to say to make me feel better. He was the calm, soothing presence in an emergency situation. He was an Eagle Scout, for goodness sake. I tried to put my arm around his shoulders, but it felt awkward with the computer in my lap. I wasn't sure if he wanted comforting, or if that would make it worse.

Mom must have heard the unfamiliar noise. She appeared in front of us, a dishtowel in her hands, an expression of alarm on her face. They looked at each other. Dad's sobs subsided and he caught his breath. He looked into my eyes, his cheeks still wet with tears.

"It isn't the first time you've made me cry tears of happiness, but it might be the first you've known about it," Dad said.

He smiled. I exhaled a sigh of relief. Mom did, too.

"I thought you were having the big one," she said.

She could joke now that she knew he was OK.

It had not occurred to me that my dad might be having a heart attack. I harbored that fear in the back of my mind, though—Ronald, G. Oliver, and Jasper all died of heart attacks.

On the drive home that afternoon, my thoughts kept returning to that moment in the living room with my dad. Even if I stopped the research the next day, if I never interviewed another person or found another tantalizing fact buried in an old newspaper article, I had given my dad a gift that I didn't know he wanted or needed. I had given him the chance to look at his life, and his family, from a different perspective, to fill in some puzzle pieces he didn't realize were missing.

8

M-O-N-T-A-N-A

If G. Oliver and Islea found it challenging to introduce high-minded culture to Crookston at the turn of the century, that challenge paled in comparison to the obstacles they faced in Havre. In 1911, the north central Montana town was not as notorious as lawless places like Deadwood, South Dakota, and Tombstone, Arizona, but it was not for lack of effort.

Havre was located on the Milk River, at the junction of the Montana Central and Great Northern Railways. The city was two hundred miles northeast of the state capital of Helena and forty miles south of the Canadian border. Before the arrival of Euro-Americans, the area served as a trade thoroughfare and as seasonal hunting grounds for several Indian tribes. The city of nearly four thousand residents now served as home to a diverse cast of characters: miners and railroad men, robbers and gamblers, saloonkeepers and prostitutes, cowboys and soldiers.

Diversity was not limited to occupation; the town was a melting pot that occasionally boiled over with ethnic and racial tensions, as immigrants from China and Japan mingled with those from Italy, Greece, Sweden, and Bulgaria. The town also had a significant African American population because of its proximity to Fort Assinniboine. Members of the all-black 10th Cavalry, known as "Buffalo Soldiers," had been stationed at the fort since the 1890s. In 1911, the federal government announced it wanted to turn the fort into a home for displaced Cree and Chippewa bands. Many white residents bitterly opposed this; they wanted the land opened to homesteaders.

Havre was named after the French city of Le Havre because several early citizens were of French descent. Coal mining had been its original industry, but agriculture was surpassing it. Great Northern Railroad Company founder James J. Hill encouraged immigrants to move to the area, promoting its untapped potential for a new type of farming known as "dry land farming."[1]

When the Riggs family arrived, Havre had three banks, three newspapers, eleven restaurants, a department store, four pool halls, and a dozen saloons. Bawdy vaudeville shows were staged at the Montana European Hotel and Grill, the fancy name for a shady business also known as the Honky-Tonk; it housed a brothel, saloon, and gambling hall. Its owner operated a slightly classier joint next door, the Parlour House—also a front for a brothel.[2] At least one opium den operated in the maze of steam tunnels that connected the basements of downtown buildings.

To counter the dens of sin and corruption, residents established four churches: one Catholic, one Presbyterian, one Methodist, and one African Methodist Episcopal. The town had one high school and three primary schools. It had two music stores, an opera house, and one hundred and fourteen electric streetlights.[3] Businessmen who formed the Havre Chamber of Commerce in 1909 aimed to boost Havre's population to fifteen thousand by 1916.[4] They believed a successful brass band would help promote the city as a place of culture and civility.

Two of those businessmen organized the original Havre band in the early 1900s: G. Oliver's friend Bert Gourley, and Bill Wiltner, owner of the Havre Meat Market. Relatively new residents themselves, they understood the challenges G. Oliver would face in adjusting to the politics and rhythms of life in the western town.

G. Oliver wasted no time organizing his new band of nineteen musicians. They performed their first concert at the end of May on a portable bandstand illuminated by electric lights and positioned at a downtown intersection. A week later, the band performed a new program at a different intersection. The June 8 program included "Moonlight on the Nile," the first copyrighted work by twenty-year-old Karl King of Ohio. King and G. Oliver would cross paths several years later, after King moved to Fort Dodge, Iowa.

G. Oliver also organized a band of thirty-three boys, ages ten to eighteen. The Junior Band of Havre included nine-year-old Ronald on clarinet and seven-year-old Percy on bass drum.

"This work of Riggs is just splendid, and is more commendable as there is not a word in the band's contract that in anyway binds him to this extra exertion," the *Havre Plaindealer* enthused in an article about the junior band. "It is in reality a labor of love, and the evidence of a sincere desire on his part to build up the musical interests of Havre in every possible way."[5]

G. Oliver's ambitious schedule was soon disrupted by sad news: his sixty-eight-year-old father, Jasper, died while napping in a hammock outside his home in Hunnewell, Missouri, where he and Rebecca had moved after his retirement from the hardware business. G. Oliver took the train to Missouri for the funeral and spent several days with family.

Jasper's obituary described him as "a good solider, true husband, devoted father and faithful friend," and it concluded: "He had always been a lover of everything good, enjoyed music very much and played the violin well. ... He did good in the world at the right time and did it because it made him happy to do it."[6]

G. Oliver had tried to follow his father's example, except when it came to Jasper's main vice: cigarettes. G. Oliver was virulently anti-tobacco long before people understood its toxic effects on the body. He steered young men away from the habit all his life.

When he returned to Havre, G. Oliver may have discussed his grief with Islea. From the outside, though, it appeared he coped with the loss by taking on more work. He organized a new adult band in Chinook, twenty-two miles to the east, and announced plans to start a juvenile band there, too. The eight hundred residents in that entertainment-starved railroad town were thrilled. Only six of the seventeen men in the adult band had any prior musical training.

74

G. Oliver and Islea also opened a studio in Havre, where G. Oliver gave cornet, violin, and harmony lessons, and Islea taught piano. She started a musical club for women, played the organ at the Presbyterian church, and performed with the Riggs Concert and Dance Orchestra. Throughout the winter, the adult band and the orchestra performed at the McIntyre Opera House, and in April, the city renewed G. Oliver's contract for another year, praising his "indefatigable work." The *Havre Promoter* also urged businessmen to renew their financial support of the band.

"From a business standpoint the value of an up-to-date band to a community as an advertising medium can hardly be estimated," it stated. "Under the present arrangement Bandmaster Riggs will be in position to perfect the work he has begun with the junior band, and with the addition of its members to the regular organization, Havre will have a band of which any city could be justly proud. Let the good work go on."[7]

Another newspaper, the *Plaindealer*, praised G. Oliver's ability to turn a chaotic band situation into a success in one year.

"The public will realize a splendid return on the money expended in retaining him for this city," the editorial said. "Good music is an educational feature that no city can afford to neglect, and so long as Prof. Riggs remains in Havre, the aesthetic tastes of the public of this city along musical lines will be nourished."[8]

When he wasn't directing his own ensembles, G. Oliver kept up his soloist skills. In the summer of 1912, he, his friend Bert Gourley, and three other Havre band members joined a thirty-five-member band in Kalispell, a town on the other side of the newly opened Glacier National Park. Director Marion B. Riffo worked in both Kalispell and Havre as an architect. The Kalispell Elks Club organized the band specifically to perform at the state convention in Kalispell, and at the national convention in Portland, Oregon.

Outfitted in white uniforms trimmed in purple, the Kalispell band spent the first evening of the state convention on a steamboat, performing for an excursion on Flathead Lake, the largest body of fresh water west of the Mississippi River. The next day, the band participated in the grand parade, which featured a drum and fife corps from Great Falls and a corps of young women dressed in

Grecian costumes. The convention concluded with an evening ball attended by more than a thousand couples.[9]

From Kalispell, G. Oliver and his bandmates went to Portland for the six-day Elks Grand Lodge Reunion. It was the 48th annual convention of the fraternal club officially known as the Benevolent and Protective Order of the Elk (BPOE). Portland went all out to welcome thirty-eight thousand visitors from all forty-eight states, plus the Philippines and the territories of Alaska, Hawaii, and Puerto Rico. Guests enjoyed a nearly non-stop schedule of entertainment.

One highly publicized event was a barbecue at the Oaks Amusement Park, "the Coney Island of the Northwest," where within the first hour the "Elk herd" consumed three tons of Chinook salmon, 3,300 pounds of clams, 6,300 loaves of bread, two tons of potatoes, 500 bunches each of onions and radishes, 100 of celery, 428 rolls of butter, 148 boxes of crackers, 100 pounds of coffee, and 300 cases of soft drinks.[10]

The barbecue served as the site of the preliminary round of a contest between the Kalispell band, Theodore "Dad" Warner's band from Seattle, and the Fifth Regiment National Guard Band from San Francisco. Warner's band was favored to win, and it did not disappoint; it received a score of 100. The Kalispell band placed second with 72 points, and the San Francisco band trailed with 60 points.

One judge explained that in comparison to the San Francisco band, the Warner and Kalispell bands were "so extremely superior from all points of view in concert work" that the judges expected them to take first and second place in the finals.[11]

The bands were scheduled to perform twice the following day. However, after the San Francisco musicians' union filed a protest against the San Francisco band, the national musicians union issued an edict asking union members to boycott the parade and other official Elks events. To show their solidarity, the Kalispell and Warner bands escorted their local clubs in the parade but did not play their instruments, and they were thus disqualified from further competition.

G. Oliver must have felt disappointed, but he may also have

felt the players, as members of the union, had no other choice. Thirty bands and more than twelve thousand people did participate in the parade, and the National Guard Band from San Francisco placed first, followed by a band from Moscow, Idaho. Third prize went to the boisterous Pendleton (Oregon) Cowboy Band, whose members played musical instruments on horseback.

The Tacoma Elks won a prize for the largest parade delegation. Since the city still did not have its own band, another town's band performed with the Tacomans. G. Oliver may have taken satisfaction in knowing no other director had yet succeeded in the effort that stymied him.

The final band concert was canceled due to the union dispute.

Although the Kalispell band did not receive any prize money, G. Oliver must have considered its second place finish in the preliminary contest to be a moral and technical victory. He later listed "cornet soloist Montana State All-Elks Band; second prize national Elk music contest, Portland Oregon, 1912" among his accomplishments.[12]

WITHIN TWO MONTHS, G. Oliver had joined another band. Led by Bill Houle, a professional cornetist from Chicago, the Helena-based band resembled the boisterous cowboy band from Pendleton. It performed with a handsome singer named Bill Pruitt, known as the "Cowboy Caruso" because of his operatic baritone voice. G. Oliver and the other eleven musicians wore cowboy costumes complete with chaps, bandanas, and hats, and they played while on horseback.

The Montana Cowboy Band performed daily at the 1912 Montana State Fair in Helena with a group of Blackfeet Indians from Glacier National Park. Other events included aeroplane flights by aviator T. T. Maroney; and appearances by Fannie Sperry, female world champion broncho buster, and Weasel Head, a member of the Blackfeet tribe billed as the one-armed world champion broncho buster.[13]

On the fair's last day, Louis W. Hill led a parade of tribal members around the racetrack. Hill had succeeded his father as Great Northern Railway chairman, and he was a driving force in the development of Glacier National Park, but he had a complicated relationship with the Blackfeet tribe because the park had been established on sacred Blackfeet land. The tribe had been displaced, and it now lived on a reservation east of the park, near where Hill had erected the $75,000 Glacier Park Hotel. He often hired members of the tribe to promote the park, and he "genuinely liked the Blackfeet." The feeling appeared to be mutual. A month before the fair, the tribe adopted him and gave him the name "Crazy Grey Horse."[14]

Seeing the cowboy band and the Indians at the fair gave Hill an idea; he and fair secretary James Shoemaker decided to send the costumed ensemble to perform in Minneapolis and Chicago to promote Montana and Glacier National Park.

The image of G. Oliver as a cowboy contradicted his reputation as a straight-laced man of culture. It was not as ridiculous as it seemed, however, since he grew up riding horses on the plains of Kansas and Nebraska and had cattle-herding experience.

He seemed to enjoy his new persona. In November, he wrote to a friend in Crookston to report that his cowboy band was appearing in Minneapolis. The *Crookston Times* printed the letter and noted the incongruous concept of G. Oliver passing for a cowboy: "Mr. Riggs stated that the members of the band were all artists but himself, and that they were sending him because he was 'tough,' which is very ludicrous to those who know Mr. Riggs."[15]

The *Grand Forks Herald* informed its readers that a tall tale about the cowboy band—which included former city residents "Ollie" Riggs and "Windy" Warner—was circulating in the *Minneapolis Tribune*: "The boys have never before been out of Montana on a tour. Riding the ranges within a hundred miles of Great Falls and Helena, they have headquarters at the Riverside ranch near Helena, and call it home and get together there when not punching cows."[16]

The twelve-day Northwestern Products show at the Minneapolis armory highlighted the products of Minnesota, North Dakota, South Dakota, Montana, Idaho, Washington, and Oregon. The cowboy band spent the first week entertaining thousands of attendees by shooting pistols, performing western tunes, serenading

Louis Hill at a dinner, and parading through downtown.

Escapades ramped up in the second week, when the Black-feet Indians arrived. Led by Fred Big Top and Two Guns White Calf, the delegation dressed "in full regalia: feather head pieces, gay blankets, beaded buckskin suits and war paint." Following a reception for the Blackfeet at the Great Northern Railway booth, the band and the Indians held a race in front of the armory "with what Mr. Hill called 'Montana runabouts.'…The Indians were mounted on one traction engine and the cowboys on another. The huge machines, with full steam up, raced along side by side for some distance to the accompaniment of whoops from the Indians and a fusillade of revolver shots from the cowboys. The Indians won the race, which, while not remarkable for speed, was remarkable as a spectacle."[17]

For the Montanans, the height of spectacle came on November 21, "Montana Day," which attracted nearly eight thousand visitors—the highest daily attendance of the expo. The band and the Indians led Montana Governor Edwin L. Norris and a group of prominent Montanans in a parade, followed by a lavish banquet. People left the event whistling the refrain from the state's official song, "Montana," one of the band's oft-played tunes:[18]

> *Montana, Montana, glory of the west;*
> *of all the states from coast to coast you're easily the best.*
> *Montana, Montana, where skies are always blue;*
> *M-O-N-T-A-N-A Montana, I love you.*

AFTER THE EVENTS IN Minneapolis, the costumed group boarded a train to Chicago. G. Oliver had traveled regularly to Chicago for twenty years, usually to take music lessons, socialize with other musicians, and purchase the latest in band music. Traversing familiar streets in cowboy boots, posing as a "rube" from Montana, was a new, and possibly liberating, experience.

Hyped as "the greatest exhibition that has been held in Chicago since the World's Fair,"[19] the fifteen-day New Land Show took place at the Chicago Coliseum. The building had been the site of high political drama in June when it hosted the Republican Par-

The Montana Cowboy Band and the Blackfeet Indians at a football game in Chicago.

ty convention. Former President Theodore Roosevelt challenged President William Taft for the nomination, and more than six hundred police officers were called in to calm the crowd. Roosevelt later formed the Bull Moose party and returned to the Coliseum in August, where he was elected the new party's presidential nominee.

The politics of the land show were not as dramatic, although states did compete for attention as they displayed their products: golden oranges from Florida, red apples from Washington, and fresh pecans and peanuts from Georgia. Geraldine Dunne, the eleven-year-old daughter of the Illinois governor-elect, opened the show by cutting the white silken ribbon stretched across the entrance. As she did so, G. Oliver and the other musicians fired a volley of celebratory blanks, and Pruitt uttered a "western ranch call."[20]

Ten thousand people filed into the Coliseum on the first day. Outside, the temperature ranged from the mid-30s in the morning to the low 40s in the afternoon. Inside, twenty queen bees from Russia and Austria made themselves cozy in the apiary, joined by one hundred stingless bees from Italy.[21] Deer nibbled vegetation near a stream that wound through a fenced enclosure.[22]

The cowboy band performed in the Glacier National Park booth that morning, startling the hundreds of pheasants, ducks,

geese, and swans in the nearby aviary, while the Blackfeet performed dances and songs. In the afternoon, the ensemble marched
around Marshall Field before the start of the Chicago Maroon-
Minnesota Gopher football game. Chicago won, 7-0.[23]

The band and the Indians also paid a surprise visit to Andreas
Dippel, general manager of the Chicago Opera Company. Dip-
pel was preparing for the season opening performance of Puccini's
Manon Lescaut at the world-renowned Chicago Auditorium.

The cowboy band played in the theater lobby for the opera
stars, chorus members, and other employees, and Pruitt's voice
made a big impression on Dippel. He made Pruitt an offer: he
would pay to send him to Europe for training, if he returned to
Chicago to sing with the opera.

"[Pruitt] said that he would like to go back home to talk the
matter out with his mother before he made up his mind to accept,
for he was earning a good living as it was, having lots of fun, and
besides that, he had his mother to support," the *Chicago Evening
Post* reported.[24]

The cowboy band received accolades in the *Chicago Sunday
Tribune* for its harmonies and precision: "Although the boys waddle when they walk, as do all men who ride hard to cattle for years,
they do not waddle when they play. 'Heinie' Houle is a leader who
brings response from his men and quick results by the merest motion of his head or the slightest wave of his hand. No baton is
needed, and no Sousa-like bends and bows or bodily curves are
brought into play to get the boys together."[25]

Photos were taken of the band and the Indians at the football
game, at the opera, at the office of motion picture producer William Selig, and at a luncheon of reporters and editors, sponsored by
the Chicago Press Club. Louis Hill did not attend the land show,
but Shoemaker, the Montana state fair secretary, and other participants kept him informed of their activities.

In a letter to Hill dated November 28, Fred Big Top wrote: "Like
the people here in Chicago, and same way the people here like us
very much, and we went to Press Club with the cow boys for lunch,
and we had good time, and good dinner. Very sorry you not there.
Lot of speeches by newspaper people, all speak very well of you."[26]

When G. Oliver returned to Havre on December 2, he told the *Havre Promoter* that the cowboy band "made a decided hit and was a great advertisement for Montana."[27]

Ten days later, Pruitt performed with the Havre band. Six hundred people packed the Orpheum Theater in Havre for an evening concert. The *Havre Plaindealer* said Pruitt "had a voice of remarkable flexibility and purity and sweetness. He took the high notes with the greatest ease and apparently without effort and it was in these notes that he was sweetest. Of course his voice is as yet without any cultivation whatever, and it is not improbable that after his training, that is to begin in Berlin, Germany, in the spring, Pruitt will develop into one of the great opera singers of the age."[28]

Dippel offered to pay for two years of Pruitt's opera training in Germany, and to cover the expenses of Pruitt's mother. In return, Pruitt would sing for the Chicago Grand Opera for one year, receiving $250 a night; if he became a star, he would get $1,000 a night.[29]

As of mid-December, Pruitt had not decided whether to accept.

EVENTS IN THE SECOND HALF of 1912 took G. Oliver away from home for long stretches of time. Whether Islea was wholly supportive of this is unclear, but according to a Crookston newspaper item from early in 1913, neither she nor G. Oliver were fond of Havre. The boys were now eleven and nine, and Rosalie was four.

"Friends in the city have heard from Mrs. G. O. Riggs ... Mr. and Mrs. Riggs are not satisfied with Havre, itself, but like Montana as a state to live in. Mrs. Riggs has a large class in music which she enjoys very much. Ronald is solo clarinet in both bands and Percy is bass drummer in the junior band, but will soon start playing the cornet. Mrs. Riggs hopes to visit Crookston in the near future, which is the earnest desire of her many friends here."[30]

G. Oliver put away his cowboy boots and returned to directing his city band and orchestra. In the summer of 1913, the Havre band performed at the state Eagles convention in Great Falls, and in the fall, it played in Havre for the closing day of the Hill County Fair and its special guest, James J. Hill. A week later, G. Oliver and four other Havre men performed at the 1913 Montana State Fair with the Great Falls-based Black Eagle Band. In the sky above the fairgrounds, twenty-two-year-old Katherine Stinson, the world's youngest female aviator and the fourth American woman to earn an aviator license, wowed the crowds with her aerial feats.

G. Oliver's hard work reaped rewards in December of 1913, when a prominent New York-based magazine, the *American Musician and Art Journal*, featured him on its cover. The accompanying article said G. Oliver started in Havre with eight men and no equipment and within two years had developed a forty-two-piece band many Montanans considered the "largest, best-equipped and finest amateur band in the Northwestern States."[31]

The interview was conducted in the Chicago office of G. Oliver's cornet teacher, Alfred F. Weldon, who said G. Oliver was "one of the most satisfactory students he ever taught and that he was an artist of rare ability on the cornet." The article devoted several paragraphs to G. Oliver's thoughts on how to successfully fund municipal bands, and why he felt smaller cities tended to have stronger bands than cities with more than twenty-five thousand people.

The reason for this is that it is not so difficult to get musicians and business men together on a business proposition in the smaller cities. The time is not far off when business men and musicians in the cities of the size I have mentioned will come to realize that they should come closer together and do something to help their bands.

A plan copied somewhat after the way the Havre Band is maintained will succeed in most any city, large or small. Our plan is similar to the way in which symphony orchestras are kept up in most large cities. The growth of the symphony orchestras in the United States during the first fifteen years is more than wonderful, and they will continue to grow, because most of them are founded on a high business principle and are doing a grand work.

Band organizations are just as useful as symphony orchestras and should be encouraged and financed just the same. The orchestra and band are both necessary to the country in order

*to develop a higher musical environment and make the United
States a greater musical center. By the proper understanding between business men and musicians every city should have at least
one fine band and I look for a wonderful change along this line
in the near future.*[32]

By the time the article reached Havre, Islea was nearing the
end of her pregnancy. G. Oliver Jr. debuted on January 15, 1914.
One newspaper announced: "Mr. Riggs has purchased a hat two
sizes larger than the one worn before the advent of the bouncing
baby boy."[33]

The birth of their fourth child may have influenced G. Oliver's
next career decision. In February, he accepted an offer to return as
manager and director of the Crookston city band. Havre residents
did not try to retain him; perhaps they knew his mind was set.

By the first of May 1914, the Riggs family settled into their
old house in Crookston, which they had never sold. Maybe this
time they would stay.

9

Borrowed Time

In July 2008, after the success of G. Oliver Riggs Day, *St. Cloud Times* reporter Adam Hammer left me a phone message. Given his last name, I figured he'd be a hard-hitting investigative reporter—but no, he covered the entertainment beat. He wanted to talk about the G. Oliver exhibit at the Stearns History Museum.

I hesitated before calling him back. Answering off-the-cuff questions was not my strength. I preferred to compose my thoughts on paper—that was why I went into journalism, not comedy improv. Also, I knew reporters approached interviews in different ways. Some excelled at sifting through a conversation to grasp the greater point, while others focused more on getting good quotes. I didn't know what to expect from Adam Hammer—if that was indeed his real name.

But the main reason I hesitated was that I didn't want to be the focus of the article. I wanted it to be about the goal Dad and I were pursuing, to tell the story of G. Oliver's St. Cloud band and the men who played in it. I didn't want Dad to feel like I was taking over our team project. Although he wasn't the type of person to seek the spotlight, he deserved recognition for his role in the developing story. He was the musician, after all, and the one who had known G. Oliver, if only briefly. I was not the interesting part of the tale; I was merely the conduit.

Of course, when it came to sound bites, my dad was possibly less able to speak concisely than I. Don't get me wrong—he had coached high school speech and debate teams and was comfortable in front of crowds. But he was a slow talker. Would Adam Hammer be patient enough to sift through my dad's Ole and Lena jokes and obscure references like "Phoenix" and "Northfield"—his Secret Service-type code names for my brother's family, and my family—to grasp the point of the exhibit?

But when I mentioned the interview to my dad, he encouraged me to do it. We agreed that it would help us reach new people who might have long-forgotten band items stashed in their attics or stories about G. Oliver to tell. As Dad said, referring to the man my mom befriended at G. Oliver Riggs Day, "There are more guys like Francis out there."

I jotted down a few key points and called Adam. He seemed friendly and professional. I told him how the project started and where the research had led, and I emphasized that Dad and I hoped to gather more stories and memorabilia.

The article appeared on St. Cloud doorsteps two days later, but I didn't know it at the time. That was the day Steve, the kids, and I headed north to attend a family gathering near Finlayson. Unfortunately we were involved in a major fender-bender on the way up and abandoned the excursion.

Steve and I spent the rest of the day at home, considering how much worse the accident could have been. Although I didn't say it out loud, I thought: I can't die yet. Who would finish my research?

Before I went to bed, I read an email message from Dad. He had picked up the St. Cloud paper on the way to the family gathering, and he delivered the best news I had heard all day.

He wrote: "Remarkable! You have G. Oliver on the front page. The story accomplishes exactly what you want and includes excellent personal quotes. I have two copies, and it is one of my favorites!"

He also reassured me that I had not stolen his thunder by doing the interview.

"We are a team. We know that is the case," he wrote. "I think the great-granddaughter focus is great. You deserve all the praise."

I found the article online, and read it with clenched teeth. Seeing my words in quotes was like hearing a recording of my voice—odd and uncomfortable. The reporter's emphasis wasn't quite right, but by the time I finished the article, I was pleased. He had covered the important points and concluded by explaining that I planned to continue my research in Crookston and Bemidji. When I saw the print copy a week later, I was even happier with it.

On the front page, a small version of the G. Oliver portrait peered out from the top right corner with the teaser headline: "St. Cloud's Own Music Man; G. Oliver Riggs Had An Illustrious Career." The article ran on the front page of the Life section with a headline proclaiming, "Music Man: Minnesota Legacy of G. Oliver Riggs is Revived by His Great-Granddaughter." The whole thing made me smile.

IN THE AFTERMATH of the car accident, I bought a Mazda5 "mini" minivan, and later that summer I drove it to St. Cloud. A few people had contacted us after the article ran, including Ray Galarneault, whose two older brothers had played in the boys' band. I arranged back-to-back interviews with Ray and with Francis Schellinger while my kids were in Alexandria visiting my parents.

I met Ray in the coffee shop of a Barnes & Noble. He wore a white polo shirt and appeared to be in his mid-70s. He had thinning white hair, gold-rimmed glasses, and a forthright manner. As we sat across from each other at a small café table, he told me that his brothers Tom and Dick played for G. Oliver in the late 1930s and early 1940s. Tom, the oldest of five siblings, played the French horn in the band and later played in the St. John's University orchestra. Dick, who was five years younger, played the clarinet in the boys' band for two years, mainly to please his mother.

The Galarneault family attended all the band's events, including summer concerts.

"We would finish eating our evening meal, wash the dishes, and away we went. They'd usually start at 7 and play for about an hour or an hour and a half. I don't remember exactly but it was about that, and they'd always close with one of those strong marching band numbers—John Philip Sousa, and so on, 'Stars and Stripes Forever.' Even as young kids, we would go there."

Ray also remembered the uniforms. The old ones were blue, but the uniforms of the late 1930s and early 1940s were more colorful: maroon coats, gray pants with maroon piping, and military-style hats with a visor and gold braid.

This was news to me. I couldn't glean this type of information from looking at black and white photos, and it made me grateful for his perspective. It added color, in more than one way, to the picture forming in my mind of what it would have been like to hear and see the band.

Even though he hadn't played in the band, Ray had clear memories of G. Oliver.

"He made everybody toe the line, and he was businesslike. He'd march perfectly himself, and the guys didn't get out of line with him. He was a disciplinarian," Ray said.

"Did your brothers enjoy playing for him? Were they scared of him?" I asked.

He shook his head. "No. My oldest brother, who played the most, he wasn't afraid of him. It was more that he respected him, you know? And compliance starts mostly with respect. Dick also toed the line, I remember that clearly, but he just wasn't blessed with the enamored love of music that Tom was ... Tom, he got his start in music from G. Oliver Riggs. There's no two ways about that."

Ray said he never understood why G. Oliver left St. Cloud in 1944. Ray was in high school at the time. I explained the story as I understood it, that G. Oliver was forced to retire.

"He was pretty old by that time," I said.

"Sure, he would have been old," Ray said. "But also he didn't allow for any monkeying around, and that may have rubbed some of the parents the wrong way, because he required people to be on time and to practice."

That remark reminded me of a story Lennie told me about a boy who was kicked out of the band, to his parents' dismay, for lack of practicing. I was not surprised that Ray knew Lennie.

"Lennie Jung—he lived west of the college itself, right near Barden Park. Lennie was a musician. He was, I think, in the service, too," Ray said. "The Jungs were musical. Music kind of ran in families back in those days."

Ray's parents were not musical, but they encouraged it in their children. His father, Thomas, worked at a bank, and his mother, Wilhelmina, worked as the office manager for the St. Cloud Milling Company. For many years—until Ray began playing baseball and basketball—attending their older children's concerts was their main social activity.

When I pulled into the driveway of Francis' home, outside the town of Avon, I spotted him tending the flower gardens. He welcomed me warmly and invited me inside. He was as easygoing and intellectually curious as he'd been on G. Oliver Riggs Day. We sat down in the living room, and I posed my first question: When was he born?

"Nineteen twenty-two. I'm in my 86th year, and I'm not impressed at all by it," he said.

He smiled, and I laughed.

"Were you born in St. Cloud?"

"Yes. I moved out here in 1974. My first wife had passed on in '66, and I remarried in '68. I had four children—one was in kindergarten at that time—and my second wife would settle for nothing less than four children also, so we had four more."

I asked about his children, and then moved on to the topic of the band. Why did he join, and how old was he? Those questions launched him into a lengthy response that began with his parents.

Francis' father, Leo, played the French horn in pre-G. Oliver versions of the St. Cloud band. He and his brother owned a construction business their father started in St. Cloud in 1889. Francis took it over in 1953. Francis's mother, Anna, came from a farm family and was determined to get an education. She graduated from the College of St. Benedict, went on to Valparaiso University, and became a nurse.

"She was for her time very well educated. We learned how to pronounce words, and we were told rather than put something on the table you place it there, and you said sufficient, you didn't say enough. There is a nice way of saying just about anything," he said. "The biggest one was 'Yes, I'm done.' 'No, Francis, something that gets put in the oven is done. When you've completed your work you're finished.'"

I laughed at his imitation of his mother's words; he had clearly heard them many times as a boy.

His mother exposed him to Metropolitan Opera radio broadcasts and encouraged him to play the violin. He and his younger brothers Lawrence, Louis, and Paul all joined the boys' band.

He showed me a black and white picture of himself with Lawrence and Louis, taken outside their home. All three boys wore band uniforms and stood straight with their arms at their sides.

Francis examined the writing on the back.

"It says here '38, probably? No, well, that could be. I graduated from high school in '40, and I look like I could be a freshman in high school here. Lawrence hadn't had his growth spurt yet, I guess, Louis looks like he's caught up to him."

The boys marched in many parades, but Francis only recalled going out of town once.

"What I remember about it was that drunken celebrants threw coins at the players out of a third or fourth floor of the hotel. It was a little bonus," he said.

"Did you catch them in your sousaphone?" I asked.

He smiled. "I might have done that and not remembered," he said.

"I bet G. Oliver wouldn't let you get out of line to pick them up," I said.

"No, we were gathered below. We were on the sidewalk there, we had just disbanded and were getting ready to disburse, and these guys showered us with coins."

He paused. "It's the little things that you remember."

Francis said he was not a talented player, but he appreciated G. Oliver's lessons on topics like hygiene. When I asked what he learned from being in the band, he had a ready answer.

"The most important thing is, I believe, the lasting impression he left and the guidance we got from him. It didn't have anything to do with music at all, it had to do with growing up and being man enough to come to practice."

Francis offered one last thought before he escorted me to my car. It summed up his band experience so perfectly, I almost got goosebumps:

"I feel I owe G. Oliver Riggs something. He made my life better. I can mention him in the same breath I mention my mother. If it hadn't been for him, I might have found other ways to spend my time that were not as positive."

As I drove back to St. Cloud, I thought about how Francis took G. Oliver's lessons to heart. As an adult, Francis became a positive influence in the lives of many other people. It was an ongoing ripple effect.

I had spent so much time identifying the career highlights of G. Oliver and his talented former players, I hadn't considered the benefits gained by the less-gifted musicians. Talking to Francis reminded me of what I had gained through my own band experiences. I had been a decent player, and performing in an ensemble enriched my life. That's why Steve and I encouraged our own kids to participate in music. I didn't expect them to become professionals—that was highly unlikely, considering their practice habits. But I did want them to become good people.

As the visits with Ray and Francis replayed in my head, a new question surfaced: Who else was out there? If other former players with ordinary and extraordinary stories were still living, I needed to find them before it was too late.

10

WHERE DO WE GO FROM HERE?

On his first day back to work in Crookston in May of 1914, G. Oliver stopped by the *Crookston Daily Times* and told the editors: "Crookston looks mighty good to me. It is a real homecoming to us all. While I have enjoyed the work elsewhere, and have profited by the wilder experience, I, as well as Mrs. Riggs have always regarded Crookston as home and we are both glad to return and renew the old associations."[1]

The town had grown in his absence. Not in population—that held steady at about eight thousand—but in amenities and transportation options. New buildings graced the downtown, the streets were paved, and Crookston boasted six businesses that sold and serviced automobiles. Like the rest of the country, residents had embraced the "horseless carriage."

G. Oliver's friend Bert Keck played a key role in both developments. Keck was a leading member of the Crookston Automobile Club, which advocated for better roads, and he was busy designing buildings throughout northern Minnesota and eastern North Dakota. Notable Crookston projects included the three-spired Cathedral of Immaculate Conception, a Gothic Revival church that could seat one thousand people; and the three-story Central High School, designed to accommodate two hundred students.

Keck also designed an armory for the Crookston National Guard. Captain Peter Eide, leader of Company I, envisioned the armory as a multi-purpose venue that could host dances, shows, and other civic events; thus, the design included a concert hall with excellent acoustics.

Another national trend residents had embraced was the playground movement of the early 1900s. The city planned to install a slide and sand box that summer in Central Park, a fifteen-acre green space along the Red Lake River. This news may have excited the Riggs children.

Ronald was now a lanky twelve-year-old with straight, dark brown hair and hazel eyes. The often-serious expression on his oval face disguised his dry sense of humor. His clarinet skills had improved enough to earn him a place in the adult band that spring.

Nine-year-old Percy looked nothing like his older brother. Percy had his mother's wider face, wide-set eyes, and a mischievous grin. His blond baby hair had darkened to a light brown. G. Oliver worried that Percy's quick temper would get him into trouble; it's possible his charming smile got him out of it more than once.

Five-year-old Rosalie most resembled her father, without the penetrating gaze. She had warm, chocolate brown eyes, and her smile seemed as wide as the bows that held her wavy, dark brown hair away from her face. She loved helping with her baby brother, Oliver, and she loved dogs—including the family's collie, Prince.

Islea rejoined the women's current events club and resumed teaching piano and performing as much as she could with a baby at home. G. Oliver revived the Riggs Orchestra and plunged into band work, determined to make the Crookston Citizens' Band one of the state's top ensembles.

DURING THE RIGGS family's first two months in Crookston, a string of disturbing national news stories left many Americans feeling uneasy. First was the Tampico incident, a misunderstanding involving US sailors and Mexican land forces that nearly resulted in a war. Other noteworthy events included a miner's strike in Colorado and a mining disaster in West Virginia. Locally, a fire damaged the Grand Theatre, and two men were charged with arson.

Those events were eclipsed at the end of June by news that a Serbian nationalist had assassinated Archduke Franz Ferdinand of Austria.

For the next month, developments in Europe dominated the front pages of the local papers. Yet, daily life in Crookston was largely unaffected. Music and social activities likely provided a welcome respite from worries about global and national unrest. In mid-June, one thousand people attended the band's concert in Central Park, and on July 11, the *Crookston Daily Times* praised the growing national popularity of outdoor band concerts.

"In large towns like Crookston, band concert night is about the most typical festival occasion of our hurrying American life. Ball games and horse races and athletic meets have the note of competition and miss the festival spirit. The cattle show has much of that atmosphere, but is, at least theoretically, an industrial and business gathering. At the band concert, the Americans cast aside the stress of the game, and for once meet with pure enjoyment."[2]

In July, while the council of Austro-Hungarian ministers pondered how to respond to Serbia, the Crookston Band performed at the city's first Northwestern Fair, held at the new fairgrounds. While German forces mobilized on the French border, Crookston youth—including, perhaps, the Riggs children—took picnic lunches to Central Park, where they tried out the new slide.

Riggs family photos taken that summer include one of Percy riding a bicycle, one of a smiling Islea holding Oliver, and one of Rosalie sitting on the lawn with her arm around her baby brother, with Prince resting in the grass next to them.

Austria-Hungary declared war on Serbia on July 28. That set off a series of actions and reactions across Europe, as countries took turns declaring war on each other. The US government remained neutral. Meanwhile, Islea helped draft the bylaws for the Philharmonic Club. Made up of thirty-five men and women, it aimed to educate members about music and promote music within the city. Islea was elected chairman of its instrumental music department.[3]

Rosalie with baby G. Oliver Jr. and the family dog, Prince, in Crookston.

IN JANUARY 1915, Germany launched an aerial bombing campaign against Britain using zeppelins, and it deployed poison gas for the first time in the war. Fortunately for the Russians on the eastern front, frigid temperatures prevented the gas from vaporizing properly.

Crookston also experienced frigid temperatures. It hit a record low of 33 degrees below zero on January 27, but the cold spell didn't keep residents from socializing. G. Oliver's orchestra played three dances at the end of January, each one attended by more than a hundred people.

News about death and destruction overseas must have affected G. Oliver and Islea to some degree. However, it was nothing compared to their anguish after an unexpected death at their home: One-year-old G. Oliver Jr. fell ill with a gastrointestinal virus on January 31, and his condition worsened the next day. He suffered a series of convulsions during the night and took his last breaths a few hours before sunrise on February 2.

The front page headlines of that day's *Crookston Daily Times* announced that a German officer had dynamited a bridge in Canada, that Russians had claimed a victory over the Germans, and that F. Melius Christiansen's St. Olaf College Band would perform in Crookston on February 8. Readers who hadn't already heard the Riggs family's news may have learned it from two news items on page five announcing that the Crookston band's rehearsal was canceled because of the death, and that funeral arrangements were pending.

The Reverend Paul Albert of the First Congregational Church, where Islea was a member, led a service at the family home on February 4. Islea's mother, Flora, stayed with the family for a few weeks. Oliver was buried two miles from home at Oaklawn Cemetery.

In 1915, Crookston had fourteen doctors and surgeons, six dentists, two chiropractors, and one electrologist—a person skilled at removing moles and unwanted hair by using an electric current. There were no psychologists or grief counselors. So the Riggs family did what others in the early 20th Century did when they lost loved ones to illness or accidents, and still do today: they kept on with their lives as best they could.

When school let out that summer, Ronald and Percy spent a month with their paternal grandmother, Rebecca, and other relatives in Illinois. The boys played with their nine-year-old cousin Oliver (Daisy's son), they rode horses, and they had a formal picture taken with their mother's grandfather Isaac, who was turning ninety.

Rosalie stayed home with her parents, and G. Oliver busied himself with musical tasks. He scheduled twenty band concerts that summer, and the musicians performed one hundred and forty-three songs, including the war-inspired tune, "I Didn't Raise My Boy to Be a Soldier."

The twenty-seven-member band included Nels Thorson, county school superintendent; Marshall Byrne, high school orchestra director; and two students from the Northwest School of Agriculture.

When Ronald and Percy returned, G. Oliver wrote his mother a three-page letter:

> ...They had the best time when they visited you folks and they liked Oliver the best of the bunch of cousins. They both thought he was a fine little fellow.
>
> Their uncle Art made quite a hit with them also, in fact I

think everything you had from the sheep up made a hit with
them. They talk a whole lot about the visit. They think you folks
are the real thing, so I guess you must have showed them a fine
time. They will no doubt always remember the visit and you
folks in a most kindly manner.

G. Oliver mentioned that he had a band concert that afternoon and concluded:

We are about ready for dinner. Have had several messes of home
grown peas and beans, potatoes, radishes, lettuce and onions—
are using from the second crop of radishes. Well I guess I have
written all the news for this time—will write Daisy soon.

He signed the letter, *"Your son G. Oliver Riggs."*[4]

As the death toll climbed for young men overseas, G. Oliver
turned his attention to the boys of Crookston. In January 1916, he
organized a band for boys under age sixteen. More than one hundred boys signed up. He continued to direct the adult band, and
he took a job directing the student band at the agriculture school.

Six months after launching the juvenile band, G. Oliver arranged for its first public concert on July 10. Ronald and Percy
were among the seventy-five boys who participated. The *Crookston*
Daily Times described the ensemble as "the largest volunteer juvenile band in the United States."[5] The boys performed downtown
on an elevated platform, and the city block was closed to automobile traffic. One thousand people gathered to listen, and the
quality of the music by a band of children, some as young as ten,
astonished many residents.

The *Crookston Daily Times* said the boys played with the as-
surance of "old troopers." "Prof. Riggs had the members of the
organization under complete control and every wave of his wand
was answered by a correct response from the section to which it
was directed. 'Oh, isn't that just too lovely,' as one of the girls in
the crowd said, expresses the feeling of the audience better than
anything the reporter can think of just at the present time."[6]

Editors at the *Times* were so impressed, they secured an invitation for the boys to perform at the North Dakota State Fair in Grand Forks. The *Times* also helped raise $200 for uniforms. Islea's pastor was among the first to contribute; he gave $5. Rosenthal & Falk, a men's clothing store, donated $5 and ordered the Boy Scout-type uniforms from New York at actual cost.[7] They arrived in time for the July 27 trip to Grand Forks, where the band performed three concerts. Afterward, Fair officials treated the boys to dinner.

G. Oliver wrote a letter to the editor thanking those who had contributed to the uniform fund and supplied cars for the trip.

"Crookston has a wonderful lot of boys in the Juvenile band, the best I have ever worked with during my 30 years' experience, and I am sure anything done for them will come back to the city ten fold," he said.[8]

IN THE FALL of 1916, G. Oliver replaced the departing director of the high school orchestra. The group of three girls and sixteen boys included Ronald on clarinet and Percy on drums.

Americans went to the polls on November 7 to choose between incumbent president Woodrow Wilson—who campaigned on a slogan "He Kept Us Out of War"—and his Republican challenger, Supreme Court Justice Charles Evans Hughes. Wilson narrowly won the popular vote and the majority of electoral college votes. In Minnesota, the edge went to Hughes. Although G. Oliver did not publicize his views on the election, it's likely he voted for Hughes; as the son of a Union soldier, G. Oliver was a lifelong Republican.

In early January 1917, G. Oliver stepped away from directing the adult band to focus on the juvenile band. And at the end of the month, he stepped into his cowboy boots once more and reunited with Montana friends for a week of uncharacteristic frivolity.

Louis Hill had revived the popular St. Paul Outdoor Sports Carnival the previous year, and he was reprising his role as president of the Carnival Association. The 1917 festival ran January 27 through February 3, attracting participants from throughout Minnesota and six other states. When Hill invited the Havre Cowboy Band to participate, its members recruited G. Oliver.

Each day was packed with performances in different parts of the city. Perhaps the most memorable event for G. Oliver occurred on the fourth day. At half past eleven on January 30, the dozen members of the cowboy band—sporting chaps, cowboy hats, and striped woolen Mackinaw coats—assembled on the front steps of the Minnesota State Capitol. They were joined by a twenty-five-member fife and drum corps from Glendive and two hundred and fifty other visitors from Montana.

The crowd moved inside to the rotunda, which offered an inspiring upward view—an unsupported dome constructed of white Georgian marble. The architect, Cass Gilbert, had modeled it after St. Peter's Basilica in Rome. In the center of the floor, an inlaid star design reminded visitors that they were in the North Star state. But these visitors showed no reverence for marble or fondness for solemnity. They started singing at the top of their lungs, and the cowboys repeatedly shot their pistols into the air, firing blanks.

The noise was deafening. It bounced and echoed off the limestone walls and marble columns. In the glass cases against the rotunda walls, regimental battle flags from the Civil War and the Spanish-American War appeared to flutter under the bombardment of sound. The surrounding balcony filled with curious state officials, clerks, and other employees, while legislators in session upstairs wondered at the source of the commotion.

"Capitol attachés declared it the 'biggest noise'... ever heard in the State House," the *St. Paul Dispatch* later reported.[9]

The Montana contingent was joined by another fifty "buckaroos" and female carnival-goers from Pendleton, Oregon, and the massive group proceeded to Governor Joseph A. A. Burnquist's reception room, down the hall from the rotunda.

The sumptuous reception room featured chandeliers and a hand-carved mahogany table. Decorative Minnesota symbols overlaid with gold leaf adorned the walls and ceiling, and six oil paintings depicted scenes from Minnesota history. The visitors were unfazed by the ceremonious atmosphere. The band, with G. Oliver on solo cornet, played "Montana," the state's official song, and Burnquist "shook as many hands as he could reach,"[10] perhaps seeing in the disruption an opportunity to boost interstate relations.

Next, the rowdy group processed to the guarded, closed door to the Senate chambers. Inside, where men sat at wooden desks, a quote from Daniel Webster encircled the walls: "Let us develop the resources of the land, call forth its power, build up its institutions, promote all its great interests, and see whether we also, in our day and generation, may not perform something worthy to be remembered."

What happened next was certainly remembered by those who were present or who heard tell of it later. Senator Patrick McGarry, owner of a popular resort on Leech Lake, suggested that the Senate invite the entire group of merrymakers into the chambers. The motion carried. Moments later, costumed Westerners sang and cheered while G. Oliver and the other musicians performed.

"The Havre cowboys, becoming enthusiastic, emphasized their music with frequent pistol shots that reverberated against the ceiling and caused the senators to put their fingers in their ears," the *St. Paul Daily News* reported.[11]

Chief Long Pine, an Indian man from the Umatilla reservation in eastern Oregon, was introduced, and the room quieted. Through an interpreter, he explained that he had come a great distance to attend the carnival, and he invited people from St. Paul to visit his reservation.

"When he had finished, one of the Pendleton men said the chief would like to speak a few words in 'halting English.' Much to everyone's astonishment, the Indian gave an eloquent talk in perfect English, explaining that many Indians on the Umatilla reservation were well educated. He recited a poem, telling of the Spirit of the Great West. He was given an ovation," the *St. Paul Daily News* reported.[12]

Later that evening, the cowboy band held a position of honor behind the grand marshal of the torchlight parade. An estimated fifteen thousand marchers participated, and one hundred and fifty thousand people lined the streets to watch.[13] The frolicking and merriment continued until the last day, when sobering news curtailed the celebrations: the United States had severed diplomatic ties with Germany, and the country's entry into the war seemed inevitable.

G. Oliver returned to Crookston the next day. His cowboy days were over.

On April 6, Congress approved President Wilson's request and declared war on Germany. In May, Congress passed the Selective Service Act, and on June 25, the first American troops landed in France. In Polk County, where Crookston was located, 3,500 men between the ages of twenty-one and thirty-one registered for the draft in its first month.[14] G. Oliver, at forty-six, was too old, Percy and Ronald, at thirteen and sixteen, were both too young.

G. Oliver resumed directing the juvenile band that fall. After several girls requested instruction, he considered forming a girls' saxophone group. Rosalie may have played a role in the idea. G. Oliver proposed that the auxiliary unit of twelve to twenty girls would perform separately and also with the boys' band.[15]

The stores in Crookston had a sparse selection of Christmas toys that winter, particularly dolls. Because of the war, the popular bisque porcelain dolls made in Germany could not be purchased in the United States. Christmas trees, however, were in bountiful supply[16] in northern Minnesota, and the town bustled with music events and holiday preparations.

On the last day of school before winter break, Rosalie played a starring role in her class skit in the afternoon Christmas program. That evening, Ronald, Percy, and other high school orchestra members furnished music for a farce at the Grand Theatre, a benefit for the Red Cross.

The family spent the 22nd—G. Oliver and Islea's nineteenth wedding anniversary—decorating the Christmas tree and preparing gifts for each other. Rosalie also delivered presents to her friends. By evening, she complained of feeling ill.[17] The next day, Islea's forty-third birthday, Rosalie walked to the doctor's office. She had an ear infection, but it didn't appear serious.

Even if the doctor had known how Rosalie's illness would progress, he could not have prescribed what she needed—penicillin. It hadn't been discovered yet. The bacteria in Rosalie's middle ear spread to the mastoid bone behind her ear, causing swelling and pain. During the night, the abscess broke. The doctor was summoned.

There was nothing he could do. The infection became meningitis, an inflammation of the membranes surrounding her brain. At seven in the morning on Christmas Eve, Rosalie died.

The shock reverberated throughout the community. The *Crookston Daily Times* ran a short story about the death that day. Two days later, it published a longer story about Rosalie, whom it described as having "a splendid disposition and artistic temperament."[18]

The newspaper expressed sympathy to the bereaved parents, whom, it noted, suffered a similar experience two years earlier with the death of G. Oliver Jr.

The family held a funeral at their home on December 27. The Crookston Juvenile Band attended, without instruments. A public service was held a week later at the First Congregational Church. The newspaper announced that Pastor W. E. Dudley was to speak on Rosalie's "contribution," and the thoughts that occurred to him "as a result of Rosalie's passing from life to life."[19] His words were not recorded for posterity.

G. Oliver coped by diving into work. He rehearsed the juvenile band on January 2 and directed a concert at the Armory the next week. He dropped the idea of forming a girls' band.

As for Islea? She kept framed photos of her daughter in the house, and she continued to speak of Rosalie, but she never again celebrated Christmas.

THE FIRST SIX MONTHS of 1918 provided no relief from illness and death. An influenza virus spread across the world, killing millions of people. More Polk County men enlisted, trained, and went overseas as US forces took on a greater role in the war.

The Riggs boys spent the summer playing in the juvenile band and playing with a new collie, Laddie. In August, G. Oliver took Percy along on a trip to Kansas City and left Ronald in charge of the juvenile band. The war had reduced its ranks from a high of one hundred and thirty-five to fewer than sixty members.[20]

By fall, G. Oliver's enthusiasm for Crookston affairs had waned. He traveled to Bemidji at the end of October, and again in mid-November. Between those two visits, Germany signed an armistice with the Allies. Although peace had not yet been negotiated, the fighting was over.

G. Oliver returned to Bemidji in December and accepted an

offer to reorganize its adult band and form a juvenile band, starting January 1. He thanked Crookston residents for their support of the juvenile band and expressed confidence it would continue without him.[21]

He was already planning a larger, more accomplished band for the city on the lake.

11

Never Quite Satisfied

When a new St. Cloud boys' band photo surfaced in December of 2008, I considered it an early birthday present. Unlike photos staged in front of the courthouse, this glossy black and white photo was taken inside a former church where the band rehearsed in later years. The room had a high, arched ceiling, a bank of multi-paned stained glass windows along one wall, and a polished wood floor. Most of the ninety boys pictured sat in chairs; a handful of percussionists and two dozen younger boys stood in the back. It was a lot of adolescent testosterone for one room, even one with a tall ceiling.

The man who sent the photo to my dad could identify several boys pictured, including himself. Roman Schneider sat in the second row, first French horn player from the left. Three seats to his right sat his friend Tom Galarneault—brother of Ray, who had told me his family's story in August.

Roman became a dentist and moved to California in 1959. He kept up with news about St. Cloud, though, and when he heard about our project, he contacted my dad.

Dad had seen a grainy newspaper copy of the photo before, but this 10-inch by 8-inch photograph, taken in 1939, provided greater detail of the boys' faces.

"I always thought that picture was earlier," Dad wrote. "It's a great addition to the collection."

G. Oliver rehearses the St. Cloud Boys' Band in the band hall, 1939.

He and Roman talked briefly on the phone, but since they had trouble hearing each other, Dad gave me Roman's number and suggested I call him.

"Tell him the picture arrived and how appreciative we are to have it. He wants some pictures from that same era. I told him that was not our strength but we would get right on it."

My mom and dad were driving to Phoenix to celebrate Christmas with my brother and his family. Along the way, they planned to stop in Clarinda, Iowa, where G. Oliver's friend George Landers once lived; in Dorchester, Nebraska, where G. Oliver spent his boyhood; and in Esbon, Kansas, where G. Oliver formed his first band. I hoped, for my mom's sake, that at least one of those places had a coffee shop with good pie, since visiting rural historical societies was not high on her list of vacation priorities.

I called Roman a week later. His hearing had lost its sharpness, but his memory hadn't. He said he joined the band when he was eight or nine years old. He and his younger brother, Ardwin, who played clarinet and saxophone, were "in it for the duration."

"What was G. Oliver like as a band director?" I asked.

"Unfortunately, my self-image was shallow at that time; his strictness was very difficult for me," Roman said.

Talented boys with self-confidence had no problem with G.

Oliver, he said, and all the boys learned to perform difficult pieces. But Roman feared incurring G. Oliver's wrath.

"He demanded so much, and there was very little that was fun. Yes, he was successful, but he was successful as a demanding person. We could compete anywhere, and in that sense it was good. But the price we had to pay to get to that was pretty high," he said.

Roman played French horn in the St. John's University orchestra and through dental school at Marquette University in Milwaukee, where he served as drum major and student band director. During World War II, he served in the Army and played in a band of dental and medical students. He gave up performing when he started his dental practice.

As I listened, I pictured the fresh-faced boy in the band photo and wished I could hug him. Poor little guy. When Roman joined the boys' band, he was about the age Elias was now. Even though I had played no part in diminishing Roman's adolescent self-esteem, I felt like I should make amends.

"I'm sorry that my great-grandfather wasn't kinder to you," I said. "I appreciate your honesty."

Roman's perspective reinforced my developing picture of G. Oliver's methods. He had developed a reputation as a martinet for a reason. His techniques may have been effective, but they hadn't worked well for every child.

It also was possible that G. Oliver became more cantankerous with age. The boys who knew him at age sixty-nine perhaps had a different experience than those who knew him at forty-nine.

Three days later, I googled G. Oliver's name after the kids had gone to bed. It was something I did occasionally in search of promising research leads.

One of the top results was an obituary for Herbert Streitz, a name I recognized from concert programs and from talking to Lennie.

The fact that Herbert Streitz was dead didn't surprise me—he had been in the first St. Cloud boys' band—but his date of death did. "Herbert J. Streitz, 94, a longtime resident of Waseca, died Monday, August 25, 2008 at St. Mary's Hospital in Rochester, Minnesota."

I stared at the date and let the information sink in. Waseca was forty miles southwest of Northfield, and Rochester was an hour's drive south. Herb had practically been in my neighborhood all this time and had been very much alive—until four months ago.

I wanted to kick myself over the missed opportunity.

The obituary included a photo of Herb in his later years and a paragraph about the boys' band. It also mentioned G. Oliver by name—which was why it had appeared in my Google search:

"Herb began his band career in 1923 at the age of 10 with the St. Cloud Boys' Band. There were very few high school bands in those days. The city of St. Cloud hired a professional band director by the name of G. Oliver Riggs on a full-time basis to organize and direct boys' bands for any who qualified. The band became well known for its performances in Minnesota and Iowa. Travel in those days for the large 100 member band was by train, a fun deal and incentive for all boys who could make the 'First Band.' He played 1st chair solo cornet with the band for a period of 10 years ..."

Herb worked his way through St. Cloud State by playing in dance bands. He completed his advanced musical studies at Bemidji State and the VanderCook College of Music in Chicago, and received a master's degree from the MacPhail College of Music in Minneapolis. He taught school band and orchestra in Grand Rapids, Minnesota, before he was hired in 1940 as the first full-time band and orchestra director in Waseca. He taught there until he retired in 1969, except for the two years he played in the US Navy Band during World War II.

"Shortly after he returned from World War II, the band started a series of 22 consecutive years of winning 'A' or first ratings in any and all contests and events entered. In his spare time, he organized the first band for Sacred Heart and Morristown High Schools making it possible for them to hire a full-time band director of their own," the obituary explained.

Well, what do you know. He sounded like G. Oliver. He would have been the perfect source.

I sent a message to the funeral home director, asking for help contacting Herb's second wife, Polly. When I didn't hear anything after a couple of days, I put it out of my mind.

NEW BEGINNINGS IN EARLY 2009 gave me hope for the year ahead. My cousin Scott and his wife Robin became the parents of twin boys. I accepted a job as the new tween/teen columnist for *Minnesota Parent* magazine, which meant I would get paid to write a monthly column on parenting topics of my choosing (my first regular journalism gig since my part-time stint with the local newspaper when Elias was a toddler). And Barack Obama was inaugurated as the 44th president of the United States.

I pulled Louisa out of middle school, and together we watched the country's first African American president swear an oath on the Bible that Abraham Lincoln used in 1861. It seemed like a meaningful excuse for missing a few hours of seventh grade.

Knowing more about my ancestors' connections to history— like G. Oliver's band performing for President McKinley—enhanced my connection to this occasion. When the US Marine Band played Sousa's "The Washington Post" march, I wanted to join in, off-beats and all.

News announcers noted that the tradition of the US Marine Band performing at inaugurations started in 1801 with Thomas Jefferson. I hoped current band members, looking smart in their brimmed white caps, scarlet jackets, and crisp white pants, would take time to record their thoughts about the day. Their future great-grandchildren would surely thank them.

It didn't compare to playing for the president, but I experienced a thrill of my own that winter when I heard the sweet elderly voice of Polly Streitz, whose husband I had failed to reach a few months earlier, on our voice mail. I returned the call, and we decided to meet in the spring.

Polly met me at the front door of her townhouse on April 17. She had short, silver hair and wore small gold hoops in her ears, and she bubbled with excitement.

"Come in, come in! Oh, how I wish Herb was here to meet you," she said. "He talked so much about G. Oliver Riggs and that boys' band."

Fortified by cups of coffee and cookies, we sat at her dining room table for two hours discussing Herb's career and its parallels to G. Oliver's.

Polly said Herb had a reputation for being a strict teacher.

"The students all admired him for, what should I say... because he was a little on the tough side. They admired him for that, and through the years we've heard from different ones who have said what they learned from him. He was strict but he was also nice, you know, so I guess that's what you have to be to be a teacher."

"Yes," I agreed. "When you have so many different kids, and you need to work as a group."

Polly smiled. "I was never good at teaching. I wasn't strict enough! I was more like a friend than a teacher."

I smiled back. She seemed like the opposite of strict. She was fun. She must have complemented Herb's personality the same way I imagined Islea complemented G. Oliver's.

Herb developed high standards for himself as a boy. His perfectionist tendencies may have passed to him from his mother, who kept a spotless house and ironed everything. Herb's father played the violin, and Herb also took up that instrument. Herb earned money for his first cornet by delivering newspapers.

Polly said Herb and his best friend, Ray Hermanson, both traveled to Des Moines in 1931.

"For them at that age to travel by train that far away, I guess that was really a treat."

"Did he talk about that trip?" I asked.

"Yes. He talked to different people, for different reasons, about his life," she said. "I often said, you know, it's too bad we didn't have a recorder and record all those stories. I've heard them, but I'm not good at remembering all the details."

Polly said Herb did tell her he'd played in the pit band at the Paramount Theatre before talking movies displaced silent ones. I told her that the theater had been restored, and that the St. Cloud Municipal Band performed there twice a year.

"They had a big concert in May of 2007—it was the 120th anniversary concert of the band—and we went to hear my dad play," I said. "It was really something to be in that theater where the band had played for so many years and where G. Oliver had directed them."

"Did they memorialize G. Oliver then?"

"They did. They mention him in every concert program, which is neat," I said.

"They do the same thing for Herb," Polly said. "Last year, the year that he passed away, the band here, every concert they did was in his memory. I was thanking the band director for doing that, and he says, 'His memory should be kept alive.' He says as long as he's here, he plans to keep his memory alive."

Polly was in high school when Herb came to Waseca in 1940 with his first wife, Aileen. The school's concert band grew larger under Herb, and he started a marching band. When he left to play in the US Navy Band, his replacement didn't maintain the high standards Herb set. Herb returned after the war, and the band took off with even greater success.

It was almost eerie how this echoed G. Oliver's experience in St. Cloud—except G. Oliver left because of a dispute with the band committee, not because of a world war.

Herb and Aileen raised four children, and Aileen died of cancer in 1981. Polly and Herb started dating two years later; she was divorced and had four children of her own.

Polly and Herb both loved golf and married within a year of their first date. Herb was eager to marry so they could take golf vacations to California. That's how they spent much of their retirement, on the golf course. Herb golfed until he was in his early 90s.

Polly stood up. "I've got to show you something. You're probably going to think I'm crazy."

She went into another room and returned with a drawing; it was the design for the headstone of their cemetery plot. It featured Polly and Herb riding in a golf cart and incorporated a music note and a treble staff.

"Oh that's so fun!" I said.

"The artist used a picture of us and the golf cart and drew around the rest," she explained.

"I have never seen anything like that," I said.

This was a true statement. I didn't think she was crazy, though. Her enthusiasm was endearing. I could tell she missed Herb terribly.

Polly said she played violin in the school orchestra when Herb arrived in Waseca.

"He decided that the school was not big enough to have an orchestra and a band, and a lot of the people wanted to be in the band, so they cut the orchestra. That was the end of my career."

She gazed upward and pointed a finger at the ceiling as though addressing Herb in heaven.

"It's your fault I'm not a world-famous violinist," she joked.

Polly sang in the school and church choirs, and she wanted to join band, but her parents couldn't afford to buy her an instrument. No assistance existed then for financially strapped music students. It was one reason Polly strongly supported the Herb Streitz Memorial Band Fund, established in 2000. An anonymous donor gave $100,000 to create the fund. It honored Herb for inspiring young musicians to excel, and for starting the tradition of Waseca residents taking pride in their high school band.

Every year, she explained, students with financial need could apply for scholarships to pay for the rental or purchase of instruments and to cover band trip and band camp expenses.

Polly showed me a *Waseca County News* article about the fund. It included a quote from Herb in which he explained his response when an administrator asked why the band had to be so good.

"I was speechless," he said. "I answered, 'That's what they pay me for.' I was hired for a job and I was just doing it the best I could do it."

The article said Herb emphasized practicing until students perfected their songs, and "no matter how good the band was, he says he was 'never quite satisfied.'"

This could have been uttered by G. Oliver. It perfectly captured his attitude.

Polly said two of Herb's favorite former students visited him in July 2008, when they were in town for an all-school reunion. Herb had hoped to attend, but didn't feel up to it physically. I told Polly this was the same time period the G. Oliver exhibit was at the Stearns History Museum.

Polly shook her head and smiled. "I still get excited when I think about how you were so close in Northfield. He could have filled you in on all that stuff."

She gazed up at the ceiling again. "Herbie, come back for a little bit. We need you!"

I hugged Polly when I left and thanked her for sharing her memories of Herb. If I traced the careers of Herb's students, I expected I would find people like Lennie, Francis, Roman, and Herb himself. The ripple effect continued.

By establishing his own legacy in Waseca, Herb had, in a way, honored his former director. G. Oliver likely expected nothing less from a fellow perfectionist.

12

SITTING PRETTY IN A PRETTY LITTLE CITY

Islea had many reasons to remain in Crookston in January 1919, when G. Oliver left to start yet another job in yet another city. Ronald was one reason. He was class president, he was a forward on the basketball team, and he was set to graduate in May. He likely had no desire to move in the last few months of high school.

Another reason was uncertainty. The first time the family left Crookston, Grand Forks seemed like a promising opportunity, too. But after one year, G. Oliver left for a seemingly better job prospect in Tacoma, which fizzled. Better to let her husband get settled before upending her life and moving from her friends, her students, and the cemetery where Rosalie and G. Oliver Jr. were buried.

On the other hand, leaving an environment fraught with memories may have held appeal. In 1919, Bemidji residents touted their city as a place of escape, a place to seek relaxation amid the beauty of nature. It was situated on the southern shore of Lake Bemidji and surrounded by pine and hardwood forests. When the Ojibwe arrived in the area around 1750, they called the lake "Bemijigamaag,"[1] which meant to cut sideways through or diagonally—a reference to the path the Mississippi River took across the south end of the lake. French fur traders passed through the area in the early 1800s, and in 1883, the first permanent settler arrived. People called him "Chief Bemidji," but his Ojibwe name was Shaynowishkung.[2] White settlers arrived in 1888, and once the Great Northern Railroad extension was completed in 1898, the population boomed with the growth of the lumber industry.

By 1919, Bemidji had about seven thousand residents. It also had eleven parks, a golf club, and comfortable accommodations, including the posh Markham Hotel, located downtown, and the popular Birchmont Beach Summer Hotel on Lake Bemidji's northwest shore. Tourists came from as far away as Chicago to fish in the area's clear lakes and breathe the clean air.[3]

Bemidji residents and visitors also appreciated theater and music; since the late 1800s, the city had been served by various bands. It never had a youth band, though, and businessmen were eager to see what G. Oliver could do with the local supply of prospective musicians.

By mid-February, more than one hundred and fifty boys between the ages of ten and fifteen had signed up for the juvenile band. Most had little or no musical experience. G. Oliver assigned them instruments and began giving individual and small group lessons.

When he wasn't rehearsing the adult city band or teaching music to boys, G. Oliver formed two rural community adult bands. One was in Gonvick, population four hundred, located forty-five miles west of Bemidji. The other, the thirty-piece United Community Band, was composed of farmers from four townships in southern Beltrami County.

After Ronald's graduation, the family shipped their belongings to Bemidji and moved into a new house. As suggested by the address, 1213 Lake Boulevard, it had a view of Lake Bemidji, and it was located near the new teachers' school. Islea's mother, Flora, visited in July, and the following month, G. Oliver's mother, Rebecca, and sister, Daisy, stayed for a few weeks. During the visit, they all drove to the popular tourist area of Lake Itasca—the source of the Mississippi River—located thirty miles south and west of Bemidji.

Ronald was still tall and thin, but his face had matured, and he wore his hair parted and slicked back, in the popular style of the day. Percy's face had lost some of its boyishness, but he retained his impish smile. Islea had put on weight since the deaths of her younger children, and G. Oliver had succumbed to a common sign of middle age: he wore eyeglasses.

G. Oliver took a week off from work in September to drive Ronald to college in Minneapolis, where his son gained a spot in the University of Minnesota marching band. By October, G. Oliver had hoped to start rehearsing the Bemidji band boys as a large group. However, the $16,000 City Hall renovation—which included a new band rehearsal room and an office for G. Oliver— was delayed.[4] When the building finally reopened in November, the adult band celebrated with a venison and oyster dinner and reelected G. Oliver as bandmaster for another year."[5]

Although its concerts attracted respectable crowds, the adult band held steady at about twenty-two members. G. Oliver hoped 1920 would bring an increase in membership. One major reason for the lack of growth had to do with unions. At least a dozen men had not joined the band because they belonged to the local musicians' union, and they were disgruntled that G. Oliver was not a member. A letter they sent to the *Bemidji Daily Pioneer* did not name G. Oliver, but its meaning was clear:

> *Gentlemen: At the last meeting of this local, held January 11, 1920, the local resolved that it was deemed advisable to notify the daily press that the members of the Bemidji Musicians' Association, local No. 331, cannot play under the non-union director, but we want to cooperate with the City to the best of our ability. Thanking you, we remain, Respectfully, Bemidji Musicians' Association.*[6]

The newspaper ran a follow-up article about the situation on January 14.

"Attention has been called to the fact that the Bemidji band as a whole is not composed of members of the Bemidji Musicians' Association, and it is asserted that the association is composed of but few in this city, and the large majority of the regular band is bitter in comment over the action and refusal of the local union taking the position that they won't play with the other members under a 'non-union' director."[7]

The Bemidji adult city band in front of the courthouse, 1920.

G. Oliver had been a union member in the past; however, in 1920, during a time of increasing anxiety about the Bolshevik takeover of Russia, and concern about the growing influence of "Reds" within the United States—combined with growing labor unrest about working conditions and big business profits—being a union member had become somewhat of a political statement.

The newspaper did not reveal G. Oliver's reasons for not joining the local union. It was clear, though, that the division between union and non-union musicians detracted from his efforts. One week later, the city council demonstrated its confidence in G. Oliver by naming him director of the musical department. This new, salaried position of $150 a month was funded by a local property tax, and it eased G. Oliver's reliance on the financial support of businessmen. The only employees who earned higher salaries were the city engineer/water superintendent, at $250 a month, and the fire chief, at $166.66.[8]

The union musicians, in response, formed their own ensemble, the Bemidji Union Band.

IN JANUARY, ISLEA and her friend Alberta Fisher Ruettell, a soprano soloist from Grand Forks, performed for one hundred and sixty people at a meeting of the Bemidji Women's Civic and Community Club. Leila Stanton Sanborn, an accomplished local violinist, reviewed the event for the *Bemidji Sentinel.* She wrote: "Mrs. Riggs opened the program with 'Rigoletto,' by Verdi-Liszt, which at once played her before her audience as an artist. Bemidji is proud to claim a musician of her excellent technique and expression. Her other numbers were equally enjoyable. As an accompanist to Mrs. Ruettell's songs, Mrs. Riggs made a most capable and artistic showing."[9]

The article also noted that the club's next meeting would feature a talk on public health, a topic much on the minds of Bemidji residents. Teenagers and young adults were especially vulnerable to the ongoing influenza pandemic; it would eventually kill 30 million to 50 million people, including 675,000 Americans.[10] In Bemidji, influenza-related obituaries appeared regularly in the paper, like the February 20 notice for sixteen-year-old Myron Searl:

"Myron was loved by all who knew him, a brilliant faithful student with the bright promise before him of a successful career in dramatic art ... He leaves to mourn his early demise a loving father and mother, his only brother, Percy, having died in France in the service of his country, October 5, 1918."[11]

Cases like Myron's must have concerned Islea and G. Oliver, since Ronald and Percy were in the age group deemed to be at greater risk.

The spread of influenza had declined enough by early February that health officials loosened restrictions on public gatherings. Percy performed with a new men's choral group, the Harmonick Club, and he was a vocal soloist in a school musical that involved fifty students. Islea invited her Sunday school class to the Riggs home for a waffle dinner, and she performed for the new parent-teacher association. The juvenile band presented its first concert on January 14, even though a quarter of the members were ill and unable to play.

As the threat of influenza decreased, another contagious disease reared its angry, red-splotched head. It presented a greater threat to G. Oliver's band aspirations than "Red" sympathizers and clashing egos.

It was measles.

Bemidji's health officer announced on February 25 that the city was imposing new restrictions due to the growing measles epidemic. Dances, private parties, Sunday schools, and prayer meetings were prohibited. Church services could continue if ushers provided adequate space between parishioners; movies could continue if managers kept "coughers or sneezers" out; lodge meetings could continue if people who were ill did not attend; and school could continue as long as the nurse received assistance in monitoring students for symptoms.[12]

By the end of 1920, 469,924 measles cases were reported throughout the United States, and more than seven thousand patients died.[13] In Minnesota, 7,673 cases were reported in 1920, and 159 people died, a majority of them under age ten.[14] A measles vaccine would not be licensed in the United States until 1963.

Further restrictions were imposed in early April. All theaters, Sunday schools, and other places where children congregated (except schools under care of nurses) were closed to all children under age fifteen. For G. Oliver, this meant no juvenile band rehearsals.

While he waited for the restrictions to lift, G. Oliver joined Islea and Ronald in performing for the "best loved woman in Minnesota,"[15] Maria Sanford, one of the country's first female professors and an advocate for women's suffrage. The Bemidji Women's Civic and Community Club sponsored Sanford's evening lecture at the Methodist Church on April 8. By then, Sanford had retired from the University of Minnesota but she continued to give speeches, and her Bemidji appearance came as the country was close to ratifying the 19th Amendment. Women, men, and youth older than fifteen "packed the Methodist church to its doors," and the Riggs family provided the musical entertainment for the event.

Though frail in appearance, the eighty-five-year-old Sanford delivered a spirited talk, expressing optimism that women's fresh approach to voting would result in "a higher plane of political ethics." She advocated electing the most capable men from either party, instead of those promoted by political "fixers," and she predicted women's interest in politics would "not be confined to school matters, children's welfare, etc., as many believe. She will survey the whole structure and set about to remedy the most urgent defects first."[16]

Two weeks later, Sanford died in her sleep in Washington, D.C. Stunned students and faculty at the Bemidji teachers college voted to name the new women's building after her.

When measles cases subsided, G. Oliver resumed juvenile band rehearsals and tried to make up for lost time. The boys gave their first public performance on Memorial Day, joining the Bemidji Union Band in a parade, and the boys were outfitted with uniforms in time for an abundance of summer performances. After school resumed in the fall, the juvenile band performed at two fairs, the Red Lake Indian Fair and the Beltrami County Fair. The Red Lake Indian Fair was a three-day event designed to exhibit Indian products made by tribal members on the reservation. Activities included a baseball game between Red Lake and Bemidji teams, a lacrosse exhibition, and displays of Indian beadwork and handicrafts.

The juvenile band also led a parade from downtown Bemidji to the fairgrounds to celebrate the opening of the Beltrami County Fair. The band performed between sporting events, which included running races for boys and girls and a tug-of-war between farmers and merchants, and it provided music as children formed a "human flag" at the grandstand.[17]

Bemidji residents turned their attention in November to the contest between Republican Warren G. Harding and Democrat James M. Cox. The 19th Amendment had been ratified in August, and perhaps inspired by the late Maria Sanford, Bemidji women turned out to vote in their first presidential election—including eighty-one-year-old Lydia Ward, who "would not miss her chance if she could help it, especially after waiting so many years to aid her party."[18] The newspaper did not interview Islea, who at age forty-four was finally eligible to vote.

Harding had urged a "return to normalcy" following the war, and he won in a landslide. The *Bemidji Daily Pioneer* reported city turnout was higher than normal and said "explanation lies largely in the woman vote, for not only did they go to the polls themselves but they seemed to have been responsible for their husbands getting there as well."[19]

THE FIRST MONTH of 1921 brought a surprise for G. Oliver: he was reunited with the Cowboy Caruso. Bill Pruitt never accepted the Chicago Opera's offer to train in Europe. Instead, he traveled the United States on the vaudeville circuit. That's what brought him to Bemidji.

G. Oliver told the newspaper, "The last we heard of him was when he was playing the Orpheum circuit, until we saw that he was advertised for showing here."[20]

Pruitt performed at the Grand Theatre for two nights, and his songs and stories were said to be "a distinct hit." The newspaper did not follow up with G. Oliver or report on Pruitt's off-stage activities; it's possible he ambled over to the Riggs residence and swapped tall tales with G. Oliver and Islea while enjoying some home-cooked grub.

Islea kept busy that winter with teaching, and in March, she and her friend Leila Stanton Sanborn hosted a recital of their combined piano and violin pupils at the Baptist church; so many people showed up, some were turned away at the door. Percy continued to sing with the men's chorus. He also joined the local Naval Militia and participated in weekly drills with thirty-five other men at the new, $60,000 lakeshore Armory. The facility also housed the local National Guard and was available for community events.

In May, the juvenile band played for the Armory's dedication, and in June, G. Oliver took sixty-five of his advanced players to the two-day state firemen's convention in International Falls, near the Canadian border. The boys accompanied a delegation of Bemidji firemen, and the Bemidji Union Band also performed. The International Falls Fire Department paid for the boys' meals and lodging; Bemidji businessmen raised the additional $300 needed to cover train travel.[21]

The *International Falls Tribune* said the Bemidji boys "have made a great hit in our town, as they have proved themselves musicians of remarkable ability, and at the same time, by their conduct, have reflected credit upon their parents and upon the discipline of their leader G. Oliver Riggs....Bemidji certainly has reason to be proud of her musicians, both small and big."[22]

After the last juvenile band concert that summer, the Riggs fam-

The Bemidji Juvenile Band at the firemen's convention in International Falls.

ily traveled to Iowa and Chicago and attended the Minnesota State Fair. G. Oliver's plans to take the Crookston Juvenile Band to the State Fair had never materialized, and he was eager to arrange the opportunity for his Bemidji ensemble. After meeting with the Fair board, he returned home feeling optimistic.

Islea threw her energies into a new musical venture that fall: she and two dozen other women formed the Bemidji Musical Art Club. It aimed to stimulate interest in music throughout the city, develop local talent, and bring in visiting artists. The members met twice a month to study different composers and styles of music, and they performed for each other. Also active in the group was Islea's friend Leila Stanton (who reverted to her birth name after divorcing her husband). The club became the largest of the city's four women's organizations, with seventy adult members and forty-six student members from the high school and the teachers college.[23]

The juvenile band performed that fall and winter during high school football and basketball games. It also entertained audiences who gathered at the Armory to watch the new Bemidji Teachers College men's basketball team; Percy Riggs was top scorer in several games.

Because of the increasing demands G. Oliver placed on his

young musicians, he likely faced opposition from some parents. Some beginners never made it into the juvenile band; they dropped out or were asked to leave. This may have been why Henry L. Smith of Crookston applied for the Bemidji Municipal Band director job when G. Oliver's yearly contract was almost up. The City Council, after a lengthy discussion, reappointed G. Oliver for another year.[24]

The following month, G. Oliver announced he would form a new beginners band in the fall for boys aged ten to twelve. In a move that seemed to address criticism leveled against him, he said only boys with above-average talent should enroll. The *Bemidji Daily Pioneer* reported:

"Bandmaster Riggs does not consider it a part of his duty to work with boys who are neither talented in music nor ambitious enough to practice every day at home in an earnest manner. Mr. Riggs, however, does consider it his duty to provide a good band to Bemidji so long as he is employed as bandmaster. He is willing to have the results of his work scrutinized thoroughly or compared with other bands, if anyone so desires, but [says] that he must have good material with which to work."[25]

In May, the band boys donned their crisp white uniforms and gathered outside the Armory for a photo. Two boys proudly held two new silver-plated Sousaphones the city had purchased from the Harry B. Jay Company of Chicago. Soon after the band launched its summer concert series, the newspaper printed the photo and an article about the band on the front page.

It said: "The success of this band is largely due to the untiring efforts of Bandmaster G. Oliver Riggs. The boys themselves have shown rare ability and exceptional interest, but even they admit that able direction has done much for them. During the past few years the band has grown rapidly, and at the same time the musical value of the organization has been developed at a rapid pace. If arrangements can be made to have the Bemidji Juvenile Band at the Minnesota state fair this fall, Bemidji will receive a good bit of publicity, both directly and indirectly, and those who hear the band will have an opportunity to enjoy real talent."[26]

Good news came in June: the state fair board offered to pay the band $800 to play at the fair. Bemidji officials accepted, although they had to raise an additional $750 to cover the trip costs. G. Oliver renamed the ensemble the Bemidji Boys' Band, with the boys' unanimous support.[27]

The boys left for St. Paul at half past four in the morning on September 1, in a fleet of vehicles decorated with hand-lettered signs. They stopped for a chicken dinner in St. Albans Bay on Mille Lacs Lake, and by nine o'clock that evening, they were encamped in three large tents at the state fair campground. G. Oliver, Islea, Ronald, and Percy stayed in their own, smaller tent.

The next two days were a whirlwind of activity. Escorted by mounted police, the band paraded in Minneapolis and St. Paul and serenaded the newspaper offices, a public relations move G. Oliver had perfected during his early days in Crookston. The promotion must have worked because the band's two-hour concert on Sunday in Minnehaha Park attracted ten thousand people—three thousand more than the population of Bemidji. The boys were treated to a dinner that evening at the luxurious Ryan Hotel in St. Paul, followed by a picture show at the Metropolitan Theatre. Later in the week, they received an encore dinner at the Ryan, followed by a show at the 2,500-seat Capitol Theatre, the city's showiest movie theater.

It was an eye-opening adventure for the boys. Ten-year-old Basil Britten, the son of a teamster and the youngest bandsman, told a Minneapolis reporter he had never seen a streetcar and had lived all his life in Bemidji, "where I see buses."[28]

Their week of fair performances reached a climax on Friday when the boys played on an elevated platform in front of the grandstand as a special featured act.

Two days earlier, Vice President Calvin Coolidge gave a speech at the grandstand about farming prosperity, using a $50,000, state-of-the-art amplified speaker donated for the week by the Northwestern Bell Telephone Company. Forty minutes into Coolidge's talk, audience members became restless and began walking out, causing the rattled politician to skip to the end. The ninety-eight-degree heat was later cited as the reason for the crowd's rude behavior.[29]

Using this same speaker, Tony Snyder, the fair's director of music, introduced the Bemidji band as "the best boys' band in the world."[30] The crowd responded with a tremendous ovation, and repeated the applause at the close of the band's performance.

The boys returned to Bemidji late Saturday night. G. Oliver had achieved impressive results that were touted far beyond the city limits. An Indiana businessman wrote to the Bemidji newspaper, saying, "The writer, among the many thousands who heard them play and saw them on parade, especially at night under the searchlight, will be a stronger booster for Bemidji and we hope that the Fair association will make arrangements to have the band back next year."[31]

In its promotional literature, the Harry B. Jay Company included a photo of the band and touted G. Oliver as "one of the most successful organizers and developers of boys' bands in the United States." The brochures were mailed to one hundred thousand customers nationwide.[32]

G. Oliver's feat was also noted by ambitious businessmen in St. Cloud, a city in central Minnesota with a long-established band tradition.

Capitalizing on the enthusiasm generated by the State Fair trip, G. Oliver formed a new beginners band of ninety-one boys in October. When he returned from a three-week vacation, the boys threw a surprise banquet for him. Their mothers served a chicken dinner, and on behalf of the band, ten-year-old drummer Eugene Koehn presented G. Oliver with a leather traveling bag.[33]

The gift would have come in handy during his vacation, when G. Oliver traveled to Chicago to pick up his father's violin. The instrument was more than one hundred and twenty-five years old, and Harry B. Jay himself, of the Harry B. Jay Co., had restored it to perfect working order. G. Oliver presented the violin to Ronald, now a junior at the University of Minnesota, as a reward for making it to his 21st birthday without using tobacco.[34]

The year concluded with more good news, when New York instrument company H. & A. Selmer Inc. praised the Bemidji boys in its newsletter. It said: "The Bemidji (Minn.) Boys' Band, 75 strong, was organized by G. O. Riggs, whose motto has been 'The

The Bemidji Boys' Band in front of the grandstand at the 1922 Minnesota State Fair.

best is none too good for the boys.' He therefore points with pride at his solid battery of twelve Selmer saxophones and a large showing of Selmer clarinets. This band recently played at the Minnesota State Fair and surprised its auditors by its proficiency. One of Mr. Riggs' secrets of success is in securing the cooperation of the parents in requiring the boys to practice one hour each day."[35]

IN EARLY 1923, G. Oliver presented a report to city officials highlighting the band's 1922 accomplishments. He also articulated his philosophy about the band-city relationship:

"No city can make an investment that will bring larger returns for the money expended than the support of a Boys' Band under the leadership of a competent Bandmaster. The regular practice and rehearsals builds character in the boys, the citizens derive the pleasure from the concerts and the city gets favorable publicity through the Band."

The report summarized Bemidji's financial arrangement with G. Oliver: through the annual tax levy, the city allocated $2,200 for the band. Of that, $1,800 paid G. Oliver's salary, and the rest covered expenses like music. In return, the band gave fifty-four performances.

"Had the Bemidji people paid cash at a reasonable figure for what they have received during the past year, locally the amount would have been close to $4,000, and it would still have been necessary to have employed a professional bandmaster," G. Oliver asserted.[36]

He showed no signs of wanting to seek work elsewhere. But it's possible that his success at the fair had reminded G. Oliver of yet-unfulfilled goals, because when the St. Cloud band committee approached him with a proposal, he didn't immediately say no. The men wanted him to organize an even larger boys' band in a city twice as large as Bemidji. They were prepared to more than double his salary.

G. Oliver had to think it over.

13

On the Trail of the Cowboy

The visit with Polly Streitz inspired me to look for other former G. Oliver pupils who might be alive. In May 2009, I found Howard Pramann. The Duluth man was in his 90s and belonged to a stamp collecting club (it was this clue that led me to his address). He and my dad would likely hit it off. Dad, too, was—what was the word?—a philatelist. Dad began collecting stamps as a kid, and he still sent me one occasionally—like a two-cent one with Sousa on it, issued in 1940—even though my childhood collection had been gathering dust in the basement for decades.

I sent Howard's address to my dad. My parents planned to be in Duluth in June for Grandma's Marathon; it was Mom's seventh time running a marathon since her ovarian cancer surgery in 1995. Dad, in return, sent me two obituaries he'd found. Sadly, I was several years too late to interview either Lloyd McNeal or Chester "Chet" Heinzel.

Lloyd played in the St. Cloud Municipal Band for sixty-seven years and traveled to China with the band in 1999. He was the original source of the story that G. Oliver once played for Sousa. Lloyd died in 2001 at age seventy-nine, and his obituary revealed no further clues about the G. Oliver-Sousa connection.

Chet, a former assistant US Army bandleader, died in 2003 at age ninety. His obituary contained a wealth of interesting nuggets:

he was a Minnesota aviation pioneer; he served in World War II and the Korean War; and he directed the Army strings ensemble that performed at the White House during the Kennedy administration.

Chet was arguably one of G. Oliver's most famous pupils, second only to trombonist Tommy Pederson. Neither Dad nor I had yet located an obituary for Tommy, although I had found a You-Tube video of him playing "Flight of the Bumblebee" on a 1957 episode of the Spike Jones TV show. One morning, after the kids went to school, I searched again for Tommy's obituary. No luck. But within minutes, I found a 2007 dissertation about him, written by a graduate student at the University of North Carolina–Greensboro. I smiled when I read that colleagues considered his "live performance of *Flight of the Bumblebee* to be a highlight of his career."[1]

The dissertation mentioned nothing about G. Oliver or the St. Cloud boys' band. The author's information about Tommy's early life noted that he grew up in Watkins, Minnesota, where he started playing the drums and viola at age four. It said he started playing the trombone at thirteen and played in the high school band, but most of the paper focused on his life after 1940.

Turning my attention to Chet Heinzel, I discovered that his son Gary lived in Austin, a town about seventy miles from me. When I called him, he agreed to a phone interview on the spot.

"Did your dad ever talk about G. Oliver, and what he was like as a director?"

"My dad had several stories about that," Gary said. "Once he came late to practice. My dad was a good trumpet player; he played first chair. He sat down, and Riggs said, 'What are you doing? You're sitting in the wrong chair,' and he put him in the last chair."

I laughed.

Gary continued. "I remember another story about somebody keeping time with his foot—not my dad—Riggs went over and put his shoe on the guy's toe and said, 'Tap your toe inside your shoe.' He was all about appearance, discipline, being dedicated to what you're doing. I think my dad carried on with those ideas, too. He was pretty much the same way."

After leaving the boys' band, Chet played in dance bands

throughout central Minnesota. He taught in Dassel, Minnesota, after graduating from St. Cloud State. To supplement his income, he directed the local National Guard unit band. Chet served overseas during World War II and traveled from post to post for many years after the war, directing military bands.

"That's how I grew up," Gary said. "He ended his career as one of four commanding officers in the US Army Band, the premiere band at Fort Myer, Virginia. They're the ones that lead the inaugural parade and play at the White House for social functions. My dad was called on to bring a dance group, or sometimes a small orchestra, over to the White House. He played for Jack Kennedy and his wife at several social functions."

Chester "Chet" Heinzel, a pupil of G. Oliver's who became a commanding officer in the US Army Band.

Gary told me his dad liked to tell a story about the time he was at the White House, supervising a group of violinists, and he noticed President Kennedy looked pale. (Chet found out later that the president suffered from back trouble.) Although the First Lady urged her husband to duck out early, "he stayed until all the guests had gone. He came over to my dad and said 'thank you for the performance,'" Gary said.

I wished G. Oliver had lived long enough to hear these stories. It was remarkable that a humble kid from St. Cloud could grow up to entertain dignitaries in D.C., all because of his passion for music.

One of Chet's last events before retiring in 1962 was a parade at Governor's Island for General Douglas MacArthur.

"When he got out of the car, he was a stooped-over old man, but when my dad struck up a march, [MacArthur] straightened up," Gary said.

Chet credited G. Oliver for teaching him leadership skills he used in the Army, and he followed his former director's example in the way he led his band, Gary said. However, Chet discouraged his own son from going into music because it was "too hard a life." Gary pursued teaching instead. He graduated from his dad's alma mater and taught at the high school in Princeton, Minnesota, before joining the faculty at the community college in Austin.

Chet remained lifelong friends with several boys' band members, including John Dinndorf, who ran a paint store in St. Cloud, and Bill Goblish, who became an assistant dean at the college where Gary taught. I smiled when Gary mentioned Goblish; Lennie had called him 'Day-late Goblish' because he'd once shown up a day late for a tennis tournament. Toward the end of his life, Chet moved back to the St. Cloud area. He often visited the Stearns History Museum, Gary said, where the wallpaper in one room depicts a bird's eye view of Chet's National Guard band marching down St. Germain Street in 1941, leading troops going off to war.

"What struck me was they were so self-confident," Gary said of his dad's generation. "They accepted things as they came, they worked hard. They didn't have Social Security then or welfare or food stamps. They were self-reliant—outspoken, too. I think they were very admirable people, like pioneers in a way. They were like Tom Brokaw said, the Greatest Generation."

Gary promised to let me know if he found anything related to the boys' band in his dad's belongings.

I HAD MADE the same request of Lynn Ellsworth, the archivist at Iowa Wesleyan College, and she contacted my dad and me in the spring of 2009—nearly two years after we'd met her—with news. She had not found the cadet march G. Oliver composed, but as she was putting away the 1893 Mt. Pleasant city directory, a page fell open and "Prof. G. O. Riggs, Leader I.W.U. Cornet band" stared back at her. She scanned the line drawing of a young G. Oliver and emailed it to us; we hadn't seen it before.

Nearly a month later, she wrote about a bigger discovery: two 1895 newspaper articles indicating Robert Todd Lincoln's wife, Mary Harlan Lincoln, hired G. Oliver's orchestra to perform at two parties for her daughters. The parties were held at the family's summer home in Mount Pleasant, built by Mary Harlan Lincoln's father, James, a US senator and an early president of the college.

This news sent a jolt of excitement through my body. My great-grandfather performed on his violin for Abraham Lincoln's grand-daughters? I had to re-read the newspaper excerpts a few times to make sure I wasn't making it up.

The first party, in October 1895, was for Robert and Mary's elder daughter, Mary Lincoln Isham, who had turned twenty-six. The article said: "The large library was transformed into a tempting dance hall, and the trained and graceful feet of the initiated kept time to the rhythmic movement of Prof. Riggs' orchestra."[2]

An accompanying story stated that the Methodist school did not permit dancing.

"College students were to leave before the dancing. Two girls stayed and were expelled from class for one week," Lynn wrote.

The newspaper story about Jessie's party in November 1895 was even more descriptive:

"The guests were bidden to come in Domino and mask, which resulted, as expected, in adding gayety to the occasion. The floral decorations of the spacious rooms were of chrysanthemums in great profusion, with vines, palms, and ferns. The long library with its perfectly smooth and polished floor was used for dancing. Prof. Riggs' orchestra in an alcove opening into this room was concealed behind a bower of palms and ferns."[3]

I had to look up domino and mask; domino was a black, robe-like costume worn for masquerade parties in the 1890s. It was worn with a simple black mask that covered the area around the eyes.

What I didn't know was what G. Oliver thought about per-forming for the Lincolns. The elder daughter, Mary, was married by then and was nearly his age; and Jessie attended classes at the college. Had they been friendly to him? Did they request favorite songs? How much did their mother pay the orchestra?

It seemed like the ideal anecdote to tell your children, so it could be repeated for future generations: "I once played for the Lincoln granddaughters." Yet, it had almost remained lost in the archives. I wondered why my grandfather never mentioned the story to my dad. Perhaps G. Oliver never told Ronald about it.

I could tell Dad was tickled about the juxtaposition of the "dance hall" and the college rule against dancing. In his email of thanks to Lynn, he added: "It is actually true that the Riggs orchestra music was so good for dancing that you would risk being expelled. Ha!"

THAT SUMMER WE EMBARKED upon our longest family vacation yet—a two-week rail and car trip through five states, two Canadian provinces, and two national parks. It was no coincidence that it included a two-night stay in one of G. Oliver's former places of residence: Havre, Montana.

Our coach seats on Amtrak's Empire Builder served as rudimentary beds as we traveled overnight through central Minnesota and North Dakota.

As we passed St. Cloud, I felt a tug of connection to G. Oliver; he had likely traveled this route between Minnesota and Montana many times. The next morning, the sun rose over the wetlands of North Dakota, and I marveled at the varying shades of green and yellow grasses.

Later in the morning, while I napped, Steve took the kids to the lounge car for an educational talk about the nearby Fort Union Trading Post National Historic Site, part of an interpretive program offered by the National Park Service. We ate lunch from the lounge car as we crossed into eastern Montana. The terrain was still flat, like in North Dakota, but in a few hours mountains would be appearing on the horizon.

When we got off the train in Havre, we stood outside the depot, blinking in the hot Montana sun. I spotted a statue of the empire builder himself, James J. Hill. A sign listed three quotes attributed to him. One said: "I will make my mark on the face of this earth and no man will ever wipe it out."

He was not subtle, Mr. Hill. I supposed he needed that type of attitude to build an empire.

Once our luggage was stowed in the rental car, we spent the next twelve days exploring Glacier National Park and the Canadian Rockies. Upon our return to Havre, I switched hats from tourist to researcher. While Steve took the kids sightseeing during our one full day in town, I parked myself at the Havre-Hill County Library. Several hours in the archives yielded new information about G. Oliver's exploits in Montana.

We explored the downtown square the next morning before boarding the train. It was difficult to picture how the town looked when the Riggs family lived there. Few early buildings still existed, and some had undergone renovations that obscured their original structures. The landscape was about the only thing unchanged. The Milk River still flowed by on the outskirts of town, and the Bear Paw Mountains hadn't moved. The sky still went on for miles—it wasn't just an advertising slogan—and the nearest towns were still more than twenty miles away.

As the train headed east, I gazed out the window and did the math in my head; when G. Oliver arrived in Havre, he was the same age I was, forty-one. When his family joined him, Ronald was about the same age Sebastian was, eleven. So much of their lives was ahead of them.

The first time he pulled into town, did G. Oliver think he would stay long, or did he expect Havre to be a short chapter in his life? When he moved back to Minnesota, did he have any regrets about leaving?

I had no regrets about leaving Havre, although I would have liked more time in the library.

Back in Minnesota, I dug into the Montana cowboy band story and uncovered a bonanza of information about Bill Pruitt, the Cowboy Caruso. I shared the finds with my dad, who was astonished to learn about this unexpected slice of his grandfather's life.

Then I put the cowboys aside. It was October, when, on a whim, I signed onto eBay and searched for "Montana Cowboy Band." It yielded one notable result, a sepia-toned postcard photograph of a twelve-member band from Helena, Montana. You could have knocked me over with a tumbleweed when I spotted a face I recognized. In the back row, peering out from under a cowboy hat, was G. Oliver Riggs, a.k.a. Ollie the Cowboy.

I had the option to "buy it now," and I did not hesitate. I couldn't believe my luck.

IN JANUARY 2010 I launched a project I had discussed at length with my friend Randy: I started a blog. I hoped it would help me make sense of my research discoveries. I also liked the idea of sharing those discoveries with others who might be interested.

My first post was about Sebastian learning to play the viola. The second was a critique of a podcast about the history of Barden Park. And my third post was about Howard Pramann, the former St. Cloud player my parents met in Duluth the previous summer. Although Dad took notes that day, he suggested I conduct my own interview. So I finally called Howard and discovered he had a lot to say about G. Oliver and tobacco.

Howard played cornet in the boys' band from age ten until he graduated from St. Cloud Tech in 1936. He said G. Oliver gave anti-smoking lectures at almost every rehearsal.

"As a result of all his lectures, I never did smoke my whole life," he said. "He was ahead of his time."

Howard's musical adventures started at the piano bench, at age eight or nine, under Islea's tutelage. After he joined the boys' band, he got to know Ronald and Percy because they occasionally helped G. Oliver. Howard played cornet for two years in the St. John's University band, and for one year at the University of Minnesota, before giving it up to focus on his studies.

When he quit the University of Minnesota band, he told G. Oliver, "I figured I wasn't learning anything there compared to what I did in the St. Cloud band."

Howard said he was in the band when it went to St. Paul to perform for a live radio broadcast.

"Didn't the Minnesota governor, Floyd Olson, make a speech during the show and call the St. Cloud band the 'best boys' band' in the United States?" I asked.

"Well, he did speak," Howard said. "He spoke so long we didn't get much of a chance to play."

This made me laugh. I wondered if I could dig up a copy of the speech. Leave it to a politician to take up valuable airtime when the audience could be enjoying the band music.

My early blog posts were well received by my tiny but growing audience, and this encouraged me. But what motivated me even more was my vanity; I loved seeing my name appear in print-like fashion again, attached to a piece of writing, several times a month. I had not expected to feel this way, but it brought me back to my newsroom days, minus the office politics and paychecks. The blog helped restore my identity as a journalist—a part of me that had withered during the years I'd focused on being an at-home mom.

At the end of the month, during a visit to the history center library in St. Paul, I uncovered stories about the cowboy band's escapades at the 1917 St. Paul Winter Carnival; the more details I learned, the more remarkable it seemed. The cowboy band story exposed a part of G. Oliver that was otherwise obscured by his disciplinarian persona. It helped me see him as someone capable of balancing good-natured fun and hard work, at least for a time.

It was possible we all had a little cowboy in us.

14

AIN'T GOING TO PLAY
NO SECOND FIDDLE

In the early 1920s, St. Cloud experienced an economic boom. Its population grew by fifty percent between 1910 and 1920, and in 1923, with sixteen thousand residents, it was Minnesota's fourth-largest city. Jobs in the granite quarries attracted Swedish, Norwegian, and Finnish immigrants, joining Germans, Italians, Polish, Irish, and Russians. The Granite City placed second worldwide in granite production, and it boasted the longest granite wall in the country. Built by prisoners and completed in 1922, the twenty-two-foot-high wall extended a mile and a half around the state reformatory located east of town.

The city was served by two railroads and an electric streetcar system, its hospital and teachers college continued to expand, and in 1924 it gained a veterans hospital and a Catholic orphanage. To accommodate this growth, the downtown added amenities like the $850,000 Beaux Arts-style Stearns County Courthouse and the elegant 1,700-seat Sherman Theatre and adjoining 180-room Breen Hotel. Newly formed civic and social clubs aided that growth and made St. Cloud an attractive place to live and visit.

In 1923 the commercial club, the athletic club, and the businessmen's association merged to form the St. Cloud Chamber of

Commerce. The Chamber wanted the city to compete for hosting state conventions and regional meetings of the various business, religious, and educational associations. To do this, leaders felt, a quality municipal band was a necessity.

Bands had organized in St. Cloud as early as 1887; the most recent one had lacked a leader since fall of 1922. Leading the effort to find a new director was sixty-year-old Martin Molitor, the ebullient town druggist. Born to prominent St. Cloud pioneers, Molitor played clarinet in the famed but short-lived St. Cloud Bicycle Band. The band claimed to be the only one of its kind in the world—likely with good reason, given the difficulty of playing a trombone while cycling over rough roads. Dressed in striking red and white uniforms, the musicians attracted statewide attention when they performed at the 1895 Minnesota State Fair. Memories of that heady experience, and his trip to the 1917 State Fair with the St. Cloud Military Band, may have played through Molitor's mind as he pursued this latest idea.

Motivated by ambition and a love of music, Molitor and other city boosters sought to put their hometown on the map by organizing a crackerjack band of boy musicians, a brass band so large it would be known as the Largest Boys' Band in the World. It would attract business, it would provide boys with a positive activity during a time of rising concerns about juvenile delinquency, and—as some of the men may have considered—the attention would benefit them personally.

And so in February 1923, the mayor and city commissioners charged five Chamber members with hiring a full-time director to reorganize and direct an adult municipal band and form a mammoth boys' band. The city allocated $5,000 to a yearly band fund created to cover the director's salary and related expenses.[1]

The band committee consisted of Molitor; William Weber, a music store owner; Frank Jung, a municipal band member; Don Freeman, a wholesale grocery manager; and Frank Lee, a war veteran who later owned the popular Lee's Village Inn restaurant in St. Paul. The men considered several candidates to fill the position of band director, and G. Oliver Riggs of Bemidji rose to the top.

When the committee offered G. Oliver the job in late February, he hesitated. He had begun to reap the rewards of four years of hard work in Bemidji. If he went to St. Cloud, he would have to start all over. On the other hand, St. Cloud offered more money and a three-year contract. His year-to-year contract in Bemidji depended upon the politics of the city government.

Bemidji officials scrambled to match St. Cloud's $4,000 salary offer, and came within fifty dollars. However, a provision in Bemidji's city charter prohibited hiring any employee for more than one year at a time. This was not negotiable.

G. Oliver made his decision official on March 9. The *Bemidji Daily Pioneer* broke the news the next day: "Bemidji Loses Bandmaster April 1. Far Better Offer Made by St. Cloud." According to the contract, G. Oliver would reorganize the adult municipal band and form a boys' band of up to two hundred pieces—eclipsing the size of the Bemidji band.

For the next two weeks, Bemidji bemoaned the loss of its bandmaster. People also expressed sorrow about losing Islea and her musical contributions. Meanwhile, Molitor invited musical men from St. Cloud to send him their applications. He would get than band ready for G. Oliver.

Hastily planning for the move, in late March Islea placed an ad in the *Bemidji Daily Pioneer*: "On account of leaving city, will sell new upright piano at cost, on terms to suit. Great bargain. Mrs. G. O. Riggs, phone 623-J."[2] The family sold their Bemidji home but kept their cabin on Grace Lake, southeast of town.

On April 1—the day after Easter—the Riggs family made its St. Cloud debut at a Kiwanis luncheon, with G. Oliver on cornet, Islea at the piano, and Percy on saxophone. Later that week the new bandmaster conducted his first adult band rehearsal week with twenty local musicians in a room above Valet Cleaners, a business owned by band member Bert Papermaster.

During his first two weeks in town, G. Oliver sought to reach every potential boys' band member between the ages of ten and fifteen. He attended a Boy Scouts gathering and spoke to an estimated one thousand boys who were enrolled in the public and parochial schools. Two hundred boys signed up at the first meeting, and a second meeting yielded another one hundred registrations.

G. Oliver assessed each boy's temperament and assigned them instruments. Every Saturday, he divided the boys into smaller groups and taught them how to read notes and how to find notes on their instruments. Playing by ear was prohibited.

"Memory and concentration, to say nothing of strict attention to their conductor, are what the boys must be willing to offer in return for the training they are they receiving without cost to themselves or their parents," a June 1923 *St. Cloud Daily Times* article explained.[3]

It also noted that G. Oliver aimed to instill in the boys a "habit of exactness" and asked parents to compel their budding musicians to practice daily at home for at least thirty minutes.

"Learning music is not a punishment nor a hardship—it is a privilege, and St. Cloud parents whose boys are students under Bandmaster Riggs can easily understand that with cooperation, their boys have the opportunity now to become musicians, an accomplishment which will bring pleasure for all time," the article stated.[4]

An early photo of the band, in front of the courthouse, depicted more than two hundred members wearing dark suits, ties, and newsboy caps. Some boys held bass saxophones that were almost as tall as they were. G. Oliver stood in the center, a black bowler perched on his head.

The Riggs family bought a two-story, three-bedroom bungalow on the city's south side. Islea purchased a new piano and established a home studio where she instructed more than a dozen girls and boys, including a few boys' band members. Percy enrolled at the teachers college.

By the following spring, the St. Cloud boys had mastered the basics of playing as an ensemble and prepared to learn to march and play in parade.

"It was clearly shown last evening that St. Cloud will not be content with a mere 'kids' band. The people want a band that will achieve national reputation and distinction," G. Oliver told the *St. Cloud Daily Times* after the first summer rehearsal.[5]

Privately, though, dissent rumbled through the ranks. Some parents protested the strict attendance policy, and others questioned G. Oliver's methods, which included regularly calling or

visiting moms and dads at home to inquire about their sons' practice habits. A decline in membership over several months may have
raised concerns among band committee members who valued the
band's size, and looked forward to touting the two hundred and
twenty-five musicians as the largest juvenile band in the country
and one of the largest in the world.

The much smaller adult band attracted a loyal following for its
weekly summer concerts. The July 10 concert broke attendance records when four thousand people congregated at Colonial Gardens
Park. The arrival of seven hundred automobiles temporarily held
up the concert, which the *St. Cloud Daily Times* described as the
only annoying feature of the evening.[6]

In August, boys' band members showed off their talents and
their new white uniforms when St. Cloud hosted the sixth annual
state American Legion convention. The three-day event attracted
five thousand visitors. Officials blocked off an entire downtown
block for an evening concert. The boys also marched in a parade
with eighteen Legionnaire bands and drum corps units, and people
began referring to them as "The Pride of St. Cloud."[7]

"The 225 youngsters, immaculate as always, and playing like
Sousa's own veterans, kept perfect formation, perfect step, and
perfect order while playing difficult marches. At the conclusion
of each number, the Legionnaires all along the route and scores of
cars following in the rear emitted sincere applause," the *St. Cloud
Daily Times* reported. "The Boys' band has come to be something
of a favorite in the convention, and at every appearance has scored
a decisive hit."[8]

The convention raised the profile of the boys' band statewide
and boosted civic pride. A *St. Cloud Daily Times* editorial proclaimed, "[It] was the largest and most successful in the history
of the American Legion in Minnesota. And it is a matter of civic
pride that St. Cloud made good as a convention city in every sense
of the word."[9]

IN NOVEMBER, G. OLIVER met with two hundred and fifty band
parents to discuss an exciting opportunity: the boys' band had been
invited to perform at the International Kiwanis Convention in St.

Paul the next summer. It was another step toward G. Oliver's goal of making the band the most outstanding organization of its kind in the country. However, G. Oliver felt some boys were not progressing as quickly as he'd hoped. If they wanted to make a good showing in St. Paul, *all* the boys needed to dedicate themselves to strenuous daily practice. The parents, mostly mothers, agreed to support their sons' efforts.

"If they succeed in this, they will succeed in many of their efforts of the future, but if any of them should fail, it is likely the same influences that caused them to fail now, will cause them to fail on other efforts," G. Oliver said. "They are at that age where they can mold their future for success or failure, and we want success."[10]

Three days later, G. Oliver attended a meeting of the Minnesota Bandmasters Association in Minneapolis. Led by President H. E. Schmidt of Red Wing, who had formed the group a year earlier, fifty band directors gathered at the Nicollet Hotel to discuss the shared goal of supporting and organizing "Better Bands for Minnesota." The group also discussed lobbying for a band tax law like the one Iowa passed in 1921. Created and championed by G. Oliver's friend George Landers, the band tax allowed Iowa cities of a certain size to levy a tax to support community bands. The concept had spread to other states and even inspired a song, "The Iowa Band Law March," which Iowa composer Karl King dedicated to Landers in 1923.

The Minnesota Bandmasters Association members had heard of the growing proficiency of the St. Cloud Boys' band and wanted to learn more about its methods; at the end of the meeting, they voted to hold their 1925 convention in St. Cloud.[11]

NINETEEN MONTHS AFTER G. Oliver began orchestrating the ambitious plans of St. Cloud's business leaders, the city seemed well on its way to achieving its public relations goals.

In December 1924, Ronald graduated from the University of Minnesota with a bachelor of arts degree. He took a salesman job at the Fritz-Cross office supply company in St. Cloud and moved back in with his parents. Percy still lived at home, too, but he spent much of his time with Patricia Anding, a student at the teachers college.

The St. Cloud Municipal Boys' Band in front of the Stearns County Court-house in April 1925.

Through the winter and spring, G. Oliver's band boys progressed, and in April, they gathered at the courthouse for a new photo. The International Kiwanis organization wanted to feature the band in its magazine, which it distributed to one hundred thousand households across the United States and abroad.[12]

Photographer George F. Coan arranged the boys in seven rows and used a wide-angle lens to capture all their earnest faces. Their form-fitting white pants and shirts contrasted with navy blue military-style caps and black ties. G. Oliver stood in the center, a cornet tucked under his arm.

The Kiwanis Convention was not the only focus of that spring's rehearsals. G. Oliver and the band committee were also preparing to host the Minnesota Bandmasters Association. The two-day affair included a public concert by the Third US Infantry Band of Fort Snelling, described by G. Oliver as "easily the classiest band in Minnesota today."[13]

Bandmasters arrived on May 21. The men attended a meeting at the Breen Hotel, where Schmidt encouraged them to strive to make their work more respected. "We must think highly of it, not consider it a little sideline that every Tom, Dick and Harry can do. Music still remains with us, and we are the ones to help to make it better," he said.[14]

The bandmasters' wives attended a reception at the Molitor home, and the men had their own gathering at Valet Hall. That evening, the Fort Snelling Band played to a packed house at the Sherman Theatre. The program followed the typical concert arrangement of the time—a mixture of marches, overtures and popular tunes. The band played numerous encores, mostly marches composed by Carl Dillon, the band's director. During intermission, seven-year-old Louise Schmidt, daughter of the association president, "electrified" the audience with her flugelhorn solo, "Carry Me Back to Ole Virginny."

"It turned out to be no intermission at all because everyone stayed in the theatre to hear the little girl play," the *St. Cloud Daily Times* reported.[15]

The next day, the bandmasters voted to start publishing a monthly newsletter, and they decided to send questionnaires to every Minnesota town with more than three hundred and fifty residents, urging the band directors to become members. In the afternoon, the bandmasters toured the St. Cloud Reformatory and met the director of the prison band, Francis Gonnella.

Gonnella had formed the band the previous year; it aimed to provide inmates with a skill and a positive outlet, fitting with the institution's goal of prisoner rehabilitation. Many of the seventy recruits had never played an instrument before joining Gonnella's class. The band presented weekly public concerts on the reformatory lawn throughout the summer.[16]

The convention concluded with a free "monster open air concert" on the courthouse steps, featuring the St. Cloud Boys' Band. City officials considered the convention a success. A week later, the *St. Cloud Daily Times* printed a laudatory letter G. Oliver had recently received from Faribault bandmaster L. C. Brusletten.

"Never in my life have I enjoyed such a thoroughly good time at a convention, and I have attended a great many," Brusletten wrote. "You certainly have the backing of St. Cloud, and further, you deserve every bit of it. Mr. Molitor makes a most excellent man to be president of your association…He surely worked hard to make the convention a success and a great amount of credit is due him. You two certainly make a wonderful team and are to be congratulated on having the opportunity to work together." He concluded: "The boys of today are the men of tomorrow, and a few years from now they will be very happy to say that you two were instrumental in giving them the right kind of start."[17]

Judging from outward appearances, all seemed well between G. Oliver and the band committee. Behind the scenes, though, tensions mounted over who was in charge, as the band tapered to one hundred and sixty-four players, from the initial two hundred and fifty.

G. Oliver addressed the discord in his annual report to the band committee in June. Rather than expressing apologies or regrets, he defended his policies. He said his system of exactness and responsibility allowed the band to achieve results and provide first-class service to residents, who paid the band's expenses through their taxes.

He commended most of the boys for faithfully attending rehearsals. But he took a harsh tone with parents, asserting that too many of them failed to support his policies.

"It is the duty of every parent to insist on the boy being faithful to his work and to expect him to serve well," he said. "There seems to be a natural law for those who serve well and are faithful to their work to be highly rewarded, and also one for those who disregard their service to meet failure. This holds good in the band as well as in everything else."[18]

It was unclear from what G. Oliver said—and what he didn't say—whether the dissatisfaction stemmed from a small group of parents, or if the problem was more widespread. He concluded by asking for parental cooperation in the weeks leading up to the Kiwanis Convention.

Two days later, the city dedicated the octagonal bandstand in its oldest park. Constructed of local granite and designed by local architect Louis Pinault, the Central Park bandstand snugly accommodated the twenty-member adult band, though it was much too small to hold the boys' band. The adult municipal band played its first summer concert of the season that evening. The following week, Islea held a recital at Cathedral school for eighteen of her piano students. The saxophone section of the boys' band played several numbers, and a young woman demonstrated her ballet skills. The *St. Cloud Daily Times* ran a favorable review the next day. The article concluded, "St. Cloud is, indeed, fortunate in having Mr. and Mrs. Riggs, both artists and leaders in the musical circles and culture of this city."[19]

The ambitious rehearsal schedule during the first half of June proved too much for a handful of boys. G. Oliver told a reporter on June 19 that "several of the weaker boys have dropped out."[20] The remaining one hundred and fifty met for one last practice on June 21. The next morning, they marched in uniform to the Great Northern depot, where railroad officials had arranged for a special train to transport the band, plus eighty Kiwanis members and their wives, directly from St. Cloud to the Twin Cities.

The moment had arrived. The "Pride of St. Cloud" prepared to make its mark in the big city.

First stop was Minneapolis, where an escort of motorcycle policemen greeted the boys. They marched through downtown and serenaded the *Minneapolis Journal* and the *Minneapolis Tribune*. The Kiwanis barbershop quartet contributed its talents to the outdoor mini-concerts.

"One person with the soul of an advertising solicitor made an impromptu speech to the effect that St. Cloud has the greatest boys' band in the world, besides the city being the greatest granite city in the world," fourteen-year-old Bernie Young later told the *St. Cloud Daily Journal Press*.[21]

When the boys arrived at St. Paul's Union Depot, the city already bustled with Kiwanis activity. Special trains from states like Iowa, Michigan, and Pennsylvania arrived at the same time as the St. Cloud train, and a welcoming committee greeted each delegation. Thousands of Kiwanians flooded the downtown streets, where flags, bunting, and Kiwanis emblems adorned the buildings.

The Kiwanis organization had been founded by businessmen in 1915 to exchange contacts, and by 1919 its mission had been enlarged to include community service. Given those ideals, the decision to hold the 1925 convention in St. Paul was an interesting one. Like the rest of the country, Minnesota was under Prohibition. Despite the "dry" laws, St. Paul ranked as one of the two "wettest" US cities, according to *Collier's* magazine (the other was San Francisco).[22] Smuggling, gambling, and racketeering thrived, and gangsters considered St. Paul a haven, thanks to a policy offered by corrupt city officials: in exchange for money and information, police agreed not to arrest gangsters as long as they committed crimes outside the city limits. Officers would meet criminals at the depot and escort them to the police station to register.[23]

The St. Cloud boys likely were oblivious to this as they paraded from the depot to the St. Paul Athletic Club. For them, the trip was a lark and a grand adventure. But at least one St. Paul newspaper warned convention-goers to watch out for the latest innovation in bootlegging: walking bars and bartenders.

"The peddler infests the streets, carrying with him a bottle and glass, always ready to sell a 'shot' or two to his customers, charging from 50 to 75 cents for a drink. The stuff he sells is of the worst quality," the *St. Paul Daily News* reported.[24]

The convention attracted five thousand delegates and visitors. Forty-two bands participated, and although two other youth bands attracted attention that day—the Boy Scout Band from nearby Austin and a group from Joliet, Illinois—the *St. Paul Dispatch* highlighted the arrival of the St. Cloud band on its front page.

"The largest boys' band in the world marched proudly into St. Paul today, letting the world know that it came from St. Cloud, Minn ... As the 150 boys in white trousers and shirts swung through the streets at noon, followed by the marching Kiwanians from their hometown, delegates from all parts of the United States stopped to look and listen in admiration," the article said.[25]

The heat and humidity that afternoon were enough to "wilt the most stubborn collar,"[26] so when the boys arrived at the Athletic Club, G. Oliver gave them a forty-minute break to swim in the pool. Following lunch in the dining room, and after much consumption of water and ice, the young musicians marched to the Capitol lawn, where they performed for the Kiwanis wives. Ruth Christianson, wife of Minnesota Governor Theodore Christianson, hosted the event; she had become known for hosting teas that educated women about exercising their right to vote.[27]

Eight years had passed since G. Oliver's memorable appearance at the Capitol with a different band. It was unlikely the St. Cloud boys knew the story; he rarely talked to them about his past. Even if he had told them, they might have found it impossible to believe their stern bandmaster, who frowned on cursing and smoking, had ever been a cowboy.

There was no chance of history repeating itself this trip; G. Oliver kept the boys focused on the task at hand. That evening, they joined a parade that ended in Rice Park, where twenty bands performed a massed concert. The boys then enjoyed a "big feed" before arriving at the St. Paul Auditorium, where ten thousand people gathered for the event's opening session. St. Cloud residents tuned in to WCCO radio to hear the live broadcast. An estimated one hundred thousand Kiwanis members from across the country also listened to the speeches and the music by the St. Cloud Boys' Band and the Canadian Port Arthur-Fort William bagpipe band.

"Speakers began to speak and it got hot in there, so we left, after playing with the quartet for a little bit," band member Bernie Young said later. "After we got to the depot again, we were dismissed until 10:30. Some of us went back to the athletic club and went swimming again. On the way home, we all made a lot of noise for a long ways, but after a while we got sleepy and tired and tried to sleep ... some of us were so tired that we took taxis home. It was almost 2 o'clock, and we had been up since 5:30 that morning."[28]

The success of the event may have temporarily eased tensions between G. Oliver and certain city officials over the direction of the band program. He told the *St. Cloud Daily Times* the next day he had enjoyed "the fruit of two years of hard work." The paper added that during those two years G. Oliver had built up a popular band "from a group of raw musical recruits. The ovation and cheers and applause given the boys Monday wherever they played or marched were enough to compensate him for his effort."[29]

At the next local Kiwanis meeting, Molitor gave an enthusiastic report about the performance and announced that G. Oliver would start a beginner boys' band in the fall.

"If we can have the moral support of the community,' said Mr. Molitor, 'for the next two years St. Cloud will have a first class band, one that will be second only to the U.S. Marine band.'"[30]

The boys' band clearly made an impression on George Winslow, secretary of the national Kiwanis Club. He sent a letter to the St. Cloud Kiwanis chapter, praising the band's excellence.

"We all enjoyed it very much and hope it will continue to prosper and furnish its delightful music to other thousands who will hear it in the future," he wrote.[31]

The adult and boys' bands concluded the summer with a performance at the first community sing, hosted by the band committee. Community sings had started in Minneapolis as patriotic rallies designed to garner support for US involvement in the Great War. After the war, the events continued to draw thousands of people; the Minneapolis Park Board and the *Minneapolis Tribune* awarded trophies to parks with the highest attendance.[32]

The August 20 event in St. Cloud's Central Park attracted an estimated five thousand people; it was the biggest community sing staged outside of the Twin Cities. Cars lined the streets surrounding the park. Police handled the traffic congestion, and Boy Scouts distributed song pamphlets. A popcorn wagon kept a steady business selling popcorn and Cracker Jack. After numbers by the bands, Harry Anderson of Minneapolis led the crowd in singing tunes like "America," and "My Old Kentucky Home," and in rounds of "My Bonnie Lies Over the Ocean," and "Row, Row Your Boat." The event closed with "The Star Spangled Banner."[33]

Four days later, Islea received sad news: her mother, Flora Bassett Graham, had died of stomach cancer after a prolonged illness. The two women had always been close, and even though the death was anticipated, the loss of yet another family member must have devastated Islea. Ten months earlier, Islea's sister Ethel had gone into the hospital for gall bladder surgery and had died three days later, at age forty-three, of kidney cancer.

Islea traveled to Aledo for her mother's funeral, accompanied by G. Oliver, Ronald, and Percy, and the family stayed for several days.

The St. Cloud Kiwanis club continued to bask in post-convention glory, and in October, it honored the boys with a dinner. It began raucously, as fourteen-year-old clarinet player Sidney Kaufman led the band into the Cathedral school banquet hall to the triumphant strains of Henry Fillmore's "Military Escort" march. The boys mingled with adults, and any prepubescent chatter or baritone guffaws that continued through dinner likely diminished once the program began.

Club president Charles Vasaly, superintendent of the state reformatory, opened by saying that the Kiwanians were immensely proud of the way the boys had represented their city at the convention. Molitor spoke next, and praised the boys for becoming accomplished musicians in such a short time. He also credited G.

Oliver for his hard work and thanked the city commissioners for their financial support of the band.

Mayor J. Arthur Bensen said the bands were a great asset to the city, and he endorsed adding a community chorus to the list of city-sponsored groups. Leslie Zeleny, a teachers college professor, elicited laughter as he delivered a twelve-point list of comedic rules for the boys' conduct, and hardware store proprietor Ebert Johnson foretold that the young men would become community leaders due to their band training.[34]

The good feelings and compliments continued to build until finally, organizers invited G. Oliver to address the room. He rose to his feet, and the crowd gave him a standing ovation. It was an honor granted to no other speaker that evening.[35]

Some attendees may have regretted that act after they heard what he had to say.

G. Oliver's message was brief and blunt. He told the guests that St. Cloud "meant no more to him than any other town."[36] When his contract was up on April 1, he was done. The band committee could find another director.

It was unclear whether G. Oliver planned his speech or if he spoke rashly, provoked by perceived disrespect others had shown him. It was also unclear whether he anticipated that Molitor already had a replacement in mind.

One thing was certain: if G. Oliver's goal was to escalate the discord between himself and the band committee, he had delivered a bravura performance.

15

WIDOWS AND GHOSTS

My productivity soared in the winter of 2010 after I started the My Musical Family blog. In addition to writing a couple of blog posts a week, my *Minnesota Parent* column, and occasional articles for other publications, I signed up for a memoir class. I hoped all the writing would help me figure out whether I should turn the G. Oliver project into a book.

In January, I wrote an essay about growing up on a lake near Alexandria, where our neighbors were like extended family. The essay described how I formed an outdoor exploring club, The Easy Girls, with my friends Sue and Jodi, the summer we were about five years old.

I gathered my courage and submitted the story to a contest sponsored by a Minnesota environmental group. I also sent it to my parents, and Mom shared it with Sue's mom, Linda, who was still one of her best friends. Linda's husband, Paul, was a retired obstetrician with a passion for music, and he and my dad played in bands together for years.

Linda wrote to me, "I cried and cried as you described those days, a time of innocence for sure. I hope you win the contest, but know that we appreciate your words and your memories. I will pass this on to our kids and to Sue's kids and know they will love it too."

Sue died in a car crash in 1993, leaving behind a son and

daughter. Although I lived in Des Moines at the time and hadn't seen Sue for several years, the loss stunned me. She was only twenty-six, and she would never see her kids grow up.

Dad called the "Easy Girls" essay a "blue ribbon winner" and also praised my latest blog post.

"As you know there have been a few tears shed here as well. Partly pride (and joy) and partly awe at your skill to write. I am forever grateful for the journey you have begun. It continues to be such a wonderful story that needed to be written," he said.

My eyes filled with tears after reading the emails. It didn't matter whether my essay got selected for the contest. I had already won. I was writing about things that mattered to me—family and friendships, music and history. It was OK if I didn't know where the G. Oliver project was headed. I had to keep writing.

That winter, Steve threw himself into the character of "Little Mary Sunshine" for a production of the musical *Chicago*. It required long hours of rehearsal most weeknights, which meant he came home from work only long enough to change clothes before heading to the theater, and returned after the kids and I went to bed. As opening night approached, rehearsal intensity increased, which meant my irritability level did, too. (Even the most supportive spouses have their limits.)

Steve's skill as an actor made me proud, and I loved seeing how happy it made him. Having a creative outlet kept him sane while his job at the clinic grew increasingly stressful. But part of me resented the fact that his passion took him away from his family. And from me. There were times when I felt like a bit player in his life. Two days before *Chicago* opened, it hit me: Islea and I could have formed a support group.

How many times did she shoulder the parenting responsibilities while G. Oliver attended conventions or traveled to Chicago? He could not have accomplished all he did without her contributions. She was an accomplished musician, too, yet he usually stood in the spotlight. She may have preferred this, but she may also have longed for more recognition. She may have felt the complicated mix of emotions I experienced as a spouse—love, pride, envy, resentment, guilt. Newspaper accounts of her young adult life showed that family and friends expected great things of her music career, and that she expected much of herself. What compromises did she make because of marriage and motherhood? What might she have accomplished in a different era?

I doubt she regretted for one minute being a wife or a mother—I had no regrets—but it must have been lonely sometimes, being married to G. Oliver.

In March, Steve's paternal grandmother died. We saw lots of cousins, aunts, and uncles at the funeral. After the service, we went to the cemetery. It was an overcast day, and as Steve guided the kids over the slushy ground to the gravesite, he whispered explanations for names he recognized on nearby gravestones. His ancestors had lived in the county since before the Civil War; his three-greats grandfather, Patrick Lawler, moved to Iowa after emigrating from Ireland in 1850.

When we returned to the car, Sebastian said, "Mom, now I know why you pursue your family history so urgently. When I went into the cemetery and saw all the Lawlers, I thought, *my history is here.*"

My eyes, already red from weeping, filled up again. I hugged him.

"I love you, Sebastian. You're a cool kid."

It made me feel proud to know he was learning a lesson some people didn't learn until their 40s or 50s, if ever: Understanding where you came from helps you understand who you are.

Two weeks later, we visited my parents for the weekend. On our last morning there, I asked my dad if I could see the heirloom violin he had inherited from his dad. He brought the case into the family room, where the kids were watching TV, unfastened the metal clasps, and lifted the lid: nestled inside was the violin that once belonged to Jasper. I leaned in for a closer look. It was like opening a musical time capsule; the case contained the violin, the bow, a shoulder rest, a jar of rosin made in Paris, a lavender silk handkerchief with an embroidered letter R, and a tiny key in a little yellowed envelope.

"I had no idea all this was in here," I said.

The violin was made in Germany before 1796. It first belonged to the brother of my three-greats grandfather, and he decided late in life to give it to his ten-year-old nephew.

I tried to imagine Jasper's delight in receiving such a gift. He was the second-youngest of eleven children and likely had few possessions of his own. Did he finish his chores in a hurry each day so he could practice the melodies over and over until his calloused fingers danced over the strings? It made me happy to picture this image of boyhood innocence, knowing what hell was in store for him when he left the farm at age nineteen to fight for the Union.

Dad never studied violin. I hadn't, either, but now I wished I had taken lessons. I tentatively plucked one string. I was afraid it might crumble into dust, but it felt sturdy under the pressure.

"Sebastian, can you come here?" I asked.

I gently handed him the violin and the bow. As a viola player, he knew what to do with them.

"Can I take a photo of you with Jasper's violin?" I asked.

"Sure." By now my children were accustomed to strange requests involving music and old things.

He nestled the instrument under his chin and held the neck in his left hand, then grasped the bow in his right hand and held it up as though he was going to play. He smiled, and I snapped a few photos for posterity, and my blog.

Sebastian was nearly the same age Jasper had been when he received the violin. The connection to those who came before me had never seemed more real.

As a young father, Jasper played this instrument on the Kansas prairie, like Pa Ingalls, and it crisscrossed the Midwest for more than two hundred years as our country expanded, before coming to rest in the hands of my eleven-year-old son.

My history was here. I could touch it with my fingers and feel it in my heart.

I RECEIVED GOOD NEWS that spring: my "Easy Girls" essay was published on the 1,000 Friends of Minnesota website, and my *Minnesota Parent* column received an award from the Minnesota Pro Chapter of the Society of Professional Journalists. It was exciting to know that people who weren't related to me appreciated my work.

Steve was cast as Romeo's father in *Romeo and Juliet,* and Louisa got a part as a nobleman who in one scene wields a sword. Rehearsals would soon complicate the family calendar, so I decided to squeeze in a research trip to Crookston before school ended.

Steve had suggested several years earlier that I take a trip every time he did a show, as compensation for my evenings and weekends as a temporary single parent. I appreciated the idea but it seemed impractical, financially and logistically, especially once he started doing several shows a year. I had wanted to visit Crookston, though, so I invited my parents to go with me.

Dad and I hadn't included Mom in our previous trips, and I was afraid she felt left out, even though delving into her husband's family history appealed to her about as much as undergoing a colonoscopy. To make this trip worth her while, I told her Crookston had a candy shop known for its "chippers"—potato chips made from locally grown potatoes and covered in chocolate.

Yes, I bribed my mom with chocolate. She was in.

The last time I had traveled the stretch of interstate between Alexandria and Fargo with my parents, my brother, Pete, was a senior at Concordia College in Moorhead and I was a senior in high school. Pete got us all tickets for the college's Christmas choral festival, not because he was a fan of choral music—he wasn't—but because he figured my parents would appreciate it. It was my first experience attending a traditional Lutheran college choral concert. I didn't learn until years later that the tradition was established at St. Olaf College in 1912 by an acquaintance of G. Oliver's, F. Melius Christiansen.

Snippets of the concert remained lodged in my brain—the narrator's deep voice, the three hundred-plus choral singers wearing robes—but mostly I remembered the bitter wind that whipped across the flat campus. The trip may have subconsciously reaffirmed my decision to head south for college in the fall instead of north.

This time, my parents and I went farther north, and the land became flatter and flatter as we approached the Canadian border. This was the Red River Valley, known for potatoes, sugar beets, and occasionally for flooding. We planned to visit both Crookston and Grand Forks, which were separated by a state border, a river, and a distance of about twenty-five miles.

The Crookston Juvenile Band in front of the courthouse, 1916. G. Oliver is in the center; son Ronald, with clarinet, is to his left and Percy, cornet, is to his right.

Crookston's downtown was larger than I had expected for a town of eight thousand people. We picked up a walking tour brochure at the Convention and Visitors Bureau, located in the two-story, historic Morris building, designed by G. Oliver and Islea's friend Bert Keck. After lunch at a Chinese restaurant, we ventured next door to Widman's, the chocolate shop, for dessert. It was a delightful step back in time. The long glass counter along one wall displayed a variety of tempting treats, including an assortment of chippers (milk chocolate, white chocolate, dark chocolate). But the real treat was meeting owner George Widman. His grandfather, also named George Widman, opened the store at its present location in 1911. The younger George reminded me of Tim Conway, an actor I grew up watching on *The Carol Burnett Show*. He had a deadpan, earnest way of speaking, but unlike Tim, George was not trying to get a laugh.

I showed him a copy of a Crookston Band program from 1908 that listed Widman's as a sponsor. He told us about how the family business later expanded to Fargo and Grand Forks, and he explained how he made the candy there in the store. We sampled the chippers and bought a variety box to enjoy later.

Another stop on our tour was the Polk County Historical Museum, where my eyes were drawn to a panoramic photo hanging on one wall. It was an old photo of a boys' band, taken on the steps of a building. G. Oliver stood toward the back, with his sons on either side of him. All the boys had numbers printed next to their faces.

When we asked a museum employee about the photo, she said we could take it off the wall and examine it more closely. The numbers corresponded to names listed on the back of the photo. Only a handful of the boys were unidentified. It seemed too good to be true. We also found photos of G. Oliver's city bands from 1899 and 1902.

Before dinner, we drove to Oakdale Cemetery. My uncle Bob had visited the family graves there once, and I meant to get directions from him before the trip, but forgot. All I had were the block, lot, and grave numbers.

Fortunately, I found a number for the off-duty caretaker, and he kindly gave me directions over the phone.

Their graves looked like decorative stepping-stones sunken into the lush green lawn. G. Oliver's included the phrase "Pioneer Minn Bandmaster." Islea's said: "Loyal wife of G. Oliver Riggs" and "A Devoted Mother—a Useful Musician."

"Useful Musician" struck me as odd. Why did he get to be a pioneer, while she was merely useful? I was offended at first; I wondered if her husband and sons had chosen the phrase, or if she had. It was possible that, given her work ethic, being useful was a high compliment. I hoped she was happy with it, since it was indeed written in stone; there was no way for me to know how she felt about it, and no changing it now.

I shivered, despite the June heat, as I stood on the earth above their remains. I was as close to them physically as I would ever be. It seemed important to trace their names with my fingertips, to breathe in the evening air above them, and to listen to the chatter of birds in the nearby trees. It was all so peaceful.

The two younger children were buried there, too: G. Oliver Jr. and Rosalie.

Standing next to my mom and dad, staring down at the small rectangular slabs of stone, I was reminded of another visit to a cemetery with my parents, nearly forty years earlier, on a quiet road outside of Alexandria. I was five or six—old enough to grasp that we were visiting my sister, and old enough to read the words etched into granite: Michele Marie Riggs, August 4, 1965, December 4, 1965. I was much too young, however, to comprehend the weight of sorrow the words and dates represented, or to fully understand one of the first acronyms I ever learned: SIDS, or sudden infant death syndrome.

That visit likely occurred over Memorial Day weekend. I learned later that my parents visited Michele's grave every year at that time and left flowers. We didn't speak of Michele often, but I would think about her when I'd glance at the photo of a baby girl who was *not* me that rested on my parents' dresser. I'd wonder what she and I would have done together, and what it would have felt like to have a living sister.

I would always think of Michele during Advent, when I helped my mom place three ceramic angels on the fireplace mantel. The boy in the blue robe with the trumpet was Pete; the girl in green, playing the violin, was Michele; and the brown-haired girl in pink, singing, was me. Below the angels, Mom and I would hang the red felt Christmas stockings, decorated with glittering snowmen, candy canes, and other Christmas symbols. Michele's would remain in the box, never to be filled, looking as new as the day it was made.

My thoughts of Christmas and angels received a jolt when Dad, ever the gardener, crouched down and started gently pulling blades of grass that obscured the edges of the stones we were visiting. Rosalie died on Christmas Eve, and Islea never again celebrated Christmas.

But my parents didn't stop celebrating Christmas after Michele's death. Two years and nine days later I was born. Nuns at the hospital wrapped me in a giant red felt Christmas stocking; its glittery silver letters proclaimed, "A Star is Born!"

When I was younger, I loved to hear my parents tell this story, and I'd ask them repeatedly to explain why they named me Joy. "Because it was such a joy to have a girl," either my dad or my mom would say. It's what they left unsaid all those years that kicked me in the gut now, as I stood next to them and pictured my own three kids, safe at home with my husband.

How do you go on after tragedy? My parents could have divorced, they could have spiraled into depression, but somehow they kept loving each other, and loving my brother and me.

The next day, we stopped at the two-story house where the Riggs family lived during most of their time in Crookston.

Although it had suffered some neglect, it was a thrill to see it stand-ing. I wondered how many bedrooms the house had, where the kids slept, where Islea placed her piano. I wanted to peek inside, but I couldn't tell if anyone lived there, and I wasn't sure I wanted to find out. So instead I had Dad pose with Big G, our cardboard cut-out, in front of the house while I took pictures.

Later that morning we took a walking tour led by Kay Hegge, a historic preservation advocate I had met through my blog. We took pictures of G. Oliver in front of buildings that dated back to his time, and Kay showed us the parking lot where the Grand Opera House once stood. G. Oliver's early bands often performed there, and Sousa's band had played there twice.

Unfortunately, a fire destroyed the building in the 1980s.

The tour ended at the *Crookston Times*, where the city edi-tor interviewed us about our research visit. She also took a photo of Dad and me holding Big G. It was possible the news coverage would help turn up new photos or sources of information.

After lunch, we drove to Grand Forks and walked around the old part of town. The house where the Riggs family had lived no longer existed, and the block where it stood was all grass; a flood protection levee had been erected between it and the nearby Red River. We did find the sister Widman's location, however, and we discovered that North Dakota chippers tasted just as delicious. Next door to Widman's was the Metropolitan Theatre building where the G. Oliver-led Grand Forks band performed. A developer was turning it into condominiums.

I failed to find any old band photos at the University of North Dakota library or at the Grand Forks County Historical Society, which had a newer bandstand on its front lawn where the current Grand Forks city band performed. Unfortunately, no one at the museum had information about the band's early history. As we headed out of town, I felt discouraged that we'd made no exciting discoveries in North Dakota. If it weren't for newspaper articles I uncovered before the trip, I never would have guessed the Riggs family had lived in Grand Forks. But I shouldn't have been sur-prised. They were gone so quickly they were like ghosts, ghosts that weren't invested enough in the place to linger.

16

BACK IN YOUR OWN BACKYARD

When St. Cloud residents learned in October 1925 that G. Oliver planned to resign, they exhibited a range of emotions, including surprise, dismay, and unabashed pleasure. More than one of those might have applied to Islea; it was unclear when she learned of his decision, and whether she approved, although she must have known about his growing unhappiness.

The *St. Cloud Daily Journal-Press* initially downplayed G. Oliver's announcement, noting that his speech "brought the only unpleasant note of the evening."[1] In the same issue, an editorial stated: "The creation of so fine a musical organization is a great accomplishment, and we do not understand how a man who did it is willing to quit when he has the opportunity to make it the outstanding musical organization of the whole country."[2]

One group of parents presented a petition to the band committee with more than one hundred signatures in support of G. Oliver. The committee tabled it, stating it would not act until it received an official resignation from G. Oliver.

In the midst of the uproar, the Minnesota Bandmasters Association published the first issue of its monthly newsletter, the *Bandmaster*. Written and edited by the association's secretary, Hugo Frey of Minneapolis, it reported on the success of the St. Cloud convention and devoted nearly a full page to Martin Molitor, the band committee chairman.

The *St. Cloud Journal-Press*, in an article about the new publication, also praised Molitor, describing him as "the one man who, more than anyone else, is responsible for the fact that St. Cloud has been always represented by a good band. He is called the sage of St. Cloud musicians."[3]

The *Bandmaster* also lavished praise on G. Oliver, describing him as "one of the outstanding organizers and teachers in the State of Minnesota, if not the United States, especially with juvenile bands. It takes a man with patience, tact, and perseverance to be successful in this line of work. One only has to meet Mr. Riggs to gain an insight into his sunny disposition and to realize why he is successful. The way the convention was put across speaks for his ability as an organizer and the concert spoke for his ability as a teacher."[4]

The same day the article appeared, G. Oliver directed the boys in what turned out to be his last event as their leader. Accompanied by a live goat, the boys led two thousand students, alumni, and faculty members in the first homecoming parade ever organized by the St. Cloud Teachers College. People carried red balloons and marched to the Tech high school athletic field for a football game between St. Cloud and the Winona Teachers College.[5]

While G. Oliver prepared for the parade, Molitor and band committee members Frank Jung, Don Freeman, and Frank Lee decided in a private meeting to dismiss G. Oliver. They did not make the decision public that day, but they must have communicated it to G. Oliver over the weekend, because he appeared before them on Monday, November 2, and submitted his resignation. The committee unanimously accepted it and gave him an additional month's salary.

That evening, more than one hundred parents met at the band headquarters. They questioned the committee's authority to control band expenses, and they elected Martha Redding to lead a new parents association that would lobby for a voice in the operation of the boys' band.

Redding told the other parents, "We have invested $18,000 in instruments, have worked steadily for the band, although we have not been organized, and we have no voice in the matter of retaining or dismissing a bandmaster. We have no voice in the matter ... despite the fact that we have held the job of keeping our boys' uniforms clean for over a year, and that is some job."[6]

The band committee and the mayor declined Redding's invitation to attend the meeting. But G. Oliver accepted. He told the parents "knockers" had made his work more difficult, and the Kiwanis dinner was an example of how "his leadership of the band had not been as completely recognized as it should have been." He said he resigned "only after the Municipal band committee had forced him to do so."[7]

The next day, Molitor told the *St. Cloud Daily Times* that the band committee members did not attend the parents meeting because there was no point in it; they planned to appoint a new man as soon as possible.[8] Parents association officers then discussed their concerns with the mayor, who assured them the committee had the authority to terminate contracts with the director and "act as it believed the best interests of city music directed."[9]

That evening, the entire band committee attended a meeting at Valet Hall, where several hundred boys' band members, parents, and supporters heard G. Oliver give a farewell address and urge the boys "to continue their work under a new director."[10]

Some people accepted the city's response and wished to move forward. The *St. Cloud Daily Journal-Press* adopted this philosophy in a November 6 editorial, which stated: "The fundamental principle of music is harmony. No man is so important that his place cannot be filled."

Although the editorial credited G. Oliver for his work, it said ending the unhappy situation made sense. "The interest of the boys themselves and of the city is paramount to that of any individual. Let the committee find a competent man who can continue the proper teaching and direction of the two bands and give them loyal support."[11]

Others remained upset with the band committee's explanation. A week later, the band parents association passed a resolution in favor of retaining G. Oliver as director, declaring that the committee's criticism of G. Oliver was unjust.

The turmoil must have taken a toll on G. Oliver's energy and confidence. In mid-November, he escaped the drama for a few days and went to Minneapolis for the Minnesota Bandmasters Association state convention. Excitement was high because the association had decided to give John Philip Sousa an honorary membership. Sousa attended the convention, and his band performed an evening concert at the Armory for five thousand people, including bandmasters and spouses. G. Oliver was elected to the board of directors along with Frey, editor of the *Bandmaster* newsletter, and former president H. C. Schmidt of Red Wing.[12]

When G. Oliver returned to St. Cloud, prospects for regaining his job seemed dim. In an article about the search for a new director, an anonymous band committee member took a thinly veiled shot at G. Oliver, saying, "We don't want a man who will let the Boys' Band dwindle from over 260 members to less than 150, without an effort to keep the boys." The man also said, "The band was virtually leaderless for six weeks last summer and it will not break up while we are selecting a new man"[13]—an apparent criticism of G. Oliver's vacation.

G. Oliver may have lost a job, but he had gained a family member. In that same issue of the newspaper, a society page item announced that Patricia Anding, a recent graduate of St. Cloud Teachers College, had married Percy. The ceremony had taken place five months earlier in Wabasha, Minnesota, where Patricia grew up.

The announcement said, "Mr. and Mrs. Riggs are both very well known and very popular among the young people of the city and news of their marriage will be received with pleasure."[14] It did not reveal whether G. Oliver and Islea received the news with pleasure. Had they known about it in June, or had the newlyweds kept it a secret?

The band committee eventually narrowed the field of more than thirty applicants to one man: Albert Koehler of Chicago. Like G. Oliver, Koehler played cornet and had trained under Alfred F. Weldon. Unlike G. Oliver, Koehler had no experience directing adult or juvenile bands. The Germany native had played for symphonies in Chicago and New York, and he played with the Minneapolis Symphony for sixteen years under directors Emil Oberhoffer and Henri Verbrugghen.

Verbrugghen told Molitor "he knew of no finer gentleman nor any musician whom he thought better fitted for the St. Cloud position than Mr. Koehler."[15]

After securing the approval of the parents association, the band committee offered Koehler a one-year contract to direct the boys' and municipal bands beginning January 2. He accepted, and the band committee's announcement made it official: G. Oliver would not return as director. He had no job and no immediate prospects. It was the first time since leaving Tacoma in 1910 that he quit a job without having something else lined up.

IN THE WEEKS SINCE his brief resignation speech at the banquet, G. Oliver may have spent some dark moments considering what-ifs and should-haves. But he couldn't waste much time on such speculations. He needed to earn a living. In January, G. Oliver made inquiries among his band sources. To get the family through the financial drought—and possibly to get away from naysayers in St. Cloud who sided against her husband—Islea took a job at the Grand Theatre in Bemidji, playing accompaniment for silent movies.

In March, G. Oliver accepted a position with C.G. Conn Ltd. of Elkhart, Indiana, the world's largest manufacturer of band instruments. He was hired to represent the company in the northwestern states, talking to civic clubs and fraternal groups about organizing boys' bands, school bands, and orchestras. The position came with a handsome salary, the *Bemidji Daily Pioneer* reported, and offered Riggs "a broad field of activity."[16]

The *St. Cloud Daily Times* reported the news about G. Oliver's job offer two days later. However, nearly all of the band-related items that appeared in St. Cloud newspapers that year were about Koehler and the boys' band.

Early on, Koehler faced difficulty keeping the boys motivated to attend rehearsals; one article reported that only fifty percent of the boys regularly showed up. Koehler made a plea in late January for parents to assist him in encouraging their sons to fulfill their responsibilities.

"By staying away without good cause they appear ungrateful, and show very bad judgment toward their instructor and

G. Oliver and Islea during a working vacation for the C.G. Conn instrument company.

toward the boys who are ready to work hard to gain points without which they cannot make any headway," he told the *St. Cloud Daily Times.*[17]

It became such a problem that on March 3, band committee members attended a rehearsal of the older boys and announced that anyone who missed more than three rehearsals would be knocked down to the beginner band.

If G. Oliver read the St. Cloud newspapers during the first half of 1926, he may have taken a degree of satisfaction in knowing that Koehler and the band committee were facing challenges with discipline. As summer approached, however, he became so busy with his own work that he may not have had time to follow the goings-on of the St. Cloud band program.

In June, G. Oliver drove to South Dakota to visit Conn instrument dealers in the Black Hills. Islea planned to take the train out to meet him for a three-week business and pleasure trip. A few days before she left, Ronald decided to take a vacation from his sales job and join his parents.

Ronald and Islea left St. Cloud on June 13 and arrived in Rapid City the following morning.

"It was raining when we got off the train—as, I might add— had been the case during most of the day before, while we were enroute," Ronald wrote in his trip journal. "As we were somewhat train weary, however, we were glad to spend the day resting while Father attended to his work and had the car checked up for the trip. I bought my trout fishing outfit in Rapid City, and got a complete set for $12.00. We were greatly pleased with the friendly spirit and reasonable prices of the merchants in Rapid City."[18]

They stayed in hotels the next two nights, in Spearfish, South Dakota, and Gillette, Wyoming, because they had trouble setting up their new tent. But after receiving some local advice they got the hang of things and began trying their luck in the Wyoming "tourist camps." Ronald liked the one in Sheridan because it had shower baths, a kitchen, and a city park nearby with plenty of trees. Other camps were of lower quality; upon arriving in Casper, Ronald wrote, "we took one look at the 'Tourist Park' and went to the Gladstone Hotel!"

In Buffalo—"a nice town of 2,500 with a fine tourist park"—the Conn agent took G. Oliver and Ronald into the mountains so Ronald could fish for trout. He had no luck, so the next day, the three men and Islea ventured higher, to an altitude of 7,500 feet. The dramatic views of Cloud Peak, the highest peak within the Big Horns, were unforgettable, Ronald wrote, as were the plateaus "alive with color from the mountain flowers. Purple was the main color, but white and yellow flowers were also plentiful." The fishing was also good: Ronald caught three trout in the first creek, and, after lunch, he caught two in another creek.

Ronald pasted three photos from that day into his journal. One showed Islea and G. Oliver standing on a log bridge. Islea wore a wide-brimmed hat, a long-sleeved traveling dress, and a wide smile. G. Oliver wore a newsboy cap, a cardigan sweater, a white shirt with no tie, and dark pants. His mouth curved into a genuine smile. Vacation—even a working one—agreed with him.

G. Oliver apparently felt relaxed enough to make a joke when they arrived at the geologic oddity known as Hell's Half Acre and gazed at the deep gorge and its jagged spires of rock in shades of red, yellow, and gray.

"It is several miles in circumference and as Father says is, 'a hell of a place,'" Ronald wrote.

G. Oliver Riggs at a tourist camp in Miles City, Montana, June 1926.

Islea's playful and adventurous nature emerged several times during the trip—and possibly at times not recorded for posterity by her son. She convinced Ronald to try a mineral hot springs bath in Thermopolis (he decided it was too hot and put his clothes back on); she threw snow at her husband and son when they stopped at Sylvan's Pass to cool off the car's radiator; and she fed a squirrel a piece of bread out of her hand in Yellowstone Park.

For Ronald, the most inspiring sight of the trip was Artist Point on the south rim of the Grand Canyon of the Yellowstone. "No picture could visualize the magnificent grandeur of the scene. As we looked up the Canyon at the Falls, we were absolutely silent. There was nothing that we could say to express the impression we received," he wrote.

The family stayed in the tourist camp near Old Faithful and watched the famous geyser erupt three times. They saw a black bear at the feeding grounds, they listened to a ranger's campfire lecture about the park's natural history, and they marveled at the springs, the waterfalls, and the bubbling paint pots that reminded them of cooked mush on the stove.

They left Yellowstone Park on June 28 and made their way to Billings. The next day, upon arriving at Miles City, they discovered the Montana town was hosting a big roundup. G. Oliver and Islea drove home the next morning, after the parade, but Ronald stayed for the bare-backed riding and bull-dogging contests before boarding the train back to St. Cloud.

BY LATE FALL of 1926, St. Cloud had an older boys' band of 125 members, a beginners' band of about 163 boys, and a municipal band of thirty-five adults. The band committee and the parents association appeared pleased with Koehler's performance. However, in early December, Koehler resigned due to illness. He entered a Minneapolis hospital after being sick for several weeks with what he thought was rheumatism.[19]

Tasked with finding a new director, the band committee members chose the polar opposite of the dignified, classically trained Koehler: they hired Theodore Steinmetz, familiarly known as "Steinie," from Ashland, Wisconsin.

Steinmetz practically jumped out of the article in the *St. Cloud Daily Times* that announced his arrival. He had led the 32nd Wisconsin infantry band during the Great War, and while encamped at Waco, Texas, he organized all the bands from Wisconsin and Michigan into a 365-piece unit. In Ashland, Steinmetz had directed a 266-piece band known as the World's Greatest Boys' Band, and also the Northwoods Band, made up of adults who performed in lumberjack outfits. Steinmetz insisted that everyone, including the boys, call him Steinie.[20]

His larger-than-life personality aside, Steinie also met the band committee's desire to hire someone who could direct a symphony orchestra and a choral society, thus launching "a new era" for music in the city. Upon arriving in town, Steinie made a cursory survey of the city on foot, spent several hours talking with city officials, and described himself to the *Daily Times* as the "advance guard"—noting that his wife would arrive the next day "with the 'grub wagon.'" The *Times* reported that he retained his good nature throughout the morning and "entertained with several good Scotch stories all of which, by the way, are printable."[21]

While Steinmetz acclimated to St. Cloud, G. Oliver and other Minnesota bandmasters accompanied George Landers to a joint session of the Senate and House committees in St. Paul, where

Landers urged legislators to pass the proposed Band Tax Law for Minnesota.

Landers was known as the Father of the Iowa Band Law, having encouraged the Iowa legislature in 1921 to pass a law that allowed cities to levy a tax to support their municipal bands. Sixteen states had followed Iowa's example, and Landers hoped Minnesota would be next. In his January 28 speech, he emphasized the importance of music in people's lives, calling it "the universal language." The sixty-seven-year-old bandmaster said the law would give girls and boys the chance to study music regardless of family income, and to engage in positive activity that would help them become better citizens.

"You let children blow this energy into horns and you will never have reason to fear they will be blowing bank safes," Landers said. "The child who studies music intelligently becomes a thinker and they apply this to their studies. Recent investigation shows that children in our schools who belong to musical organizations make better grades in their examinations than those who have not taken on this extra work in music."

Landers concluded by praising Minnesota's boys' bands and G. Oliver in particular.[22]

While the Minnesota Bandmasters Association worked to build "Better Bands for Minnesota," Steinmetz built a bigger band in St. Cloud. Whether the band was *better* remained an open question.

In February, the combined band enrollment reached 344, which local officials believed made it "the largest municipal group of its kind in the world."[23] But this didn't satisfy Steinie. He also sought musicians for two new music groups he hoped to establish: a 60-member symphony orchestra and a 100-member chorus.

Although G. Oliver, Islea, and Ronald all still lived in St. Cloud, they shied away from musical events that involved Steinmetz. Percy likely would have done the same, even if he hadn't taken a job teaching in Waukon, Iowa. But G. Oliver did go to the nearby town of Sauk Centre, on behalf of Conn, to help businessmen there start a boys' band. His first meeting attracted sixty-five potential members. At a second meeting, G. Oliver talked about discipline, the need for cooperation between the boys, their parents, and the director, and the necessity of regular practice. He encouraged parents to select quality instruments for their sons, stating that "beginners could not learn on something that a professional could not play."[24]

Two days later, G. Oliver had reason to celebrate. Governor Theodore Christianson signed the Minnesota Band Tax, "making it possible for cities of the second, third and fourth class to levy each year a tax not to exceed three mills for the purpose of providing a fund for the maintenance of municipal bands, orchestras or choruses."[25] This law would spur the growth of bands statewide and also boost instrument sales.

THAT SPRING, WITHOUT the benefit of a tax, the band parents association raised money to buy new uniforms for the St. Cloud boys' band. Each boy was outfitted with white trousers, a white shirt, a white cap, a black bow tie, and a black sash with white tassels. When all 344 boys posed for a photo, they resembled a massive army encamped on the granite steps of the courthouse. Copies of the photo described the group as the "Largest Band in the World."

In May, the boys' band performed a goodbye concert for Koehler, their former director, and members of the Minneapolis Symphony also visited him after their annual tour. The fifty-one-year-old Koehler died of cancer at his home a few days later.[26]

The Minnesota Bandmasters Association celebrated the passage of the band tax law at its spring convention May 20–21 in Duluth. The convention coincided with another Minnesota-related achievement: Charles Lindbergh's transatlantic flight from Long Island to Paris. It was the first solo, nonstop flight across the Atlantic Ocean.

Lindbergh grew up outside of Little Falls, just thirty-odd miles north of St. Cloud, and was only twenty-five, the same age as Ronald, at the time of his historic flight. The feat captivated Americans' imaginations, and people were still talking about it in June, when G. Oliver traveled to Elkhart, Indiana—not by airplane—for a Conn Dealers Convention, where he gave a talk on "How to Create More Bands."

Lindbergh toured the country for several months and even flew over St. Cloud. But for the Riggs family, the most exciting event of the fall was the arrival of a baby girl on September 2. Percy and Patricia named their daughter Mary Jane.

G. Oliver's work for Conn took him as far north as Baudette, on the Canadian border, where he helped the school form a forty-member band. He also kept up with the progress of the Sauk Centre Boys' band, which gave its first concert on October 13.

Any musical progress Steinmetz hoped to make that fall came to an abrupt halt following a finding by the state auditor's office that St. Cloud had exceeded the legal amount that could be appropriated annually for municipal band work, dating back to May of 1923. As a result, the city could only allocate $2,000 to the band in 1928. Once he learned the city could not employ him at his $5,000 a year salary, Steinmetz said he would leave on December 20, when his contract expired.[27] The city asked municipal band members to return their uniforms and informed the boys' band that practices would end December 20.

A statement issued by the band committee said "it would, in our minds, be a waste of money to try to do the impossible and to run the musical activities on such a small sum, nothing would be gained by it as it has been proven time and time again that it costs money to get results and a compromise is poor business."[28]

The band parents called an emergency meeting and decided to push for approval of a band tax in the spring. If it passed, the money would become available on January 1, 1929, and the band program could resume. Until then, they would have to be resourceful. Steinmetz returned to Wisconsin, and the band parents association hired J. E. Rasicot to instruct the boys' band one day a week. Rasicot already directed bands in five nearby towns. He agreed to travel to St. Cloud twice a week if enrollment numbers were high enough.[29] It was a good attempt, but the plan didn't last through the winter.

Dissatisfaction with the mayor and the city commissioners grew, in response to the band situation and other controversial matters, such as the plan to improve Lake George, which the city went ahead with even after residents had voted down a proposed bond issue for the project. At the end of February, real estate agent James Murphy announced his candidacy for mayor. Within two days, Mayor Bensen announced he would not seek reelection. And on March 3, residents filed a petition asking the city commission to levy a one mill tax to support the municipal band. It received more than 1,200 signatures, exceeding the number required.

Given that enthusiasm, it wasn't surprising that the band tax measure passed overwhelmingly on April 2, with 3,130 in favor and 1,959 against. What did surprise many people was that Murphy achieved a political upset. Because he won a majority of votes—3,161 out of 5,794—in the primary election, he became the new mayor of St. Cloud.[30] He took office on May 1, and parents soon approached him seeking G. Oliver's return as band director.

G. Oliver had not actively pursued the idea, but the frequent travel required by his job with Conn may have begun to wear on him. The idea of returning to the podium under new city leadership may have intrigued him, especially knowing the band law tax would provide regular funding. Also, he and Islea still lived in their St. Cloud home. Taking this new job—essentially his old job—would not require a move and would not disrupt Islea's work schedule.

By June 22, the details were resolved. The band parents association hired G. Oliver to reorganize the boys' band, beginning August 1. Also, it formed a committee to raise $1,500 to pay G. Oliver's salary between August 1 and January 1, after which the city would pay for the band. Among the first to donate were parents association president Redding ($25); newspaper editor Alvah Eastman ($25); and Valet Hall owner Bert Papermaster ($10).[31]

While the parents raised money, G. Oliver and Islea spent the month of July at the family cabin in Bemidji. Ronald joined them there for a respite before starting a new job organizing school bands for the Holton Instrument Company of Elkhorn, Wisconsin. G. Oliver returned to St. Cloud on July 31, relaxed and ready to meet with any and all boys who had ever played in the band.

The director of the St. Cloud Municipal Boys' Band was back, on his own terms. And this time, G. Oliver was in charge.

17

A Yankee Family Returns to Dixie

When I returned from Crookston in June of 2010, I resumed my role as appointment secretary and taxi driver for one teenager and two tweens—not a task for the faint-hearted. I kept track of our family schedule on the Google calendar, where we each had a different color.

Louisa (purple) was in *The Phantom Tollbooth*, she was a tour guide at the historical museum, and she was taking French horn lessons. Sebastian (blue) was playing baseball and taking viola and trumpet lessons. Elias (green) was taking piano lessons. All three kids were in theater day camp. Steve (brown) was taking a global health course and working at the clinic. He wasn't much help with kid transportation, but at least I (red) didn't have to drive him anywhere.

My thoughts returned to Crookston in mid-June when the *Crookston Times* published the article about our visit. I clicked on the link: would I sound like a weirdo?

I scanned it and breathed a sigh of relief. I sounded rational, and the writer had included the suggestion Dad was eager to convey—that anyone with information about G. Oliver and John Philip Sousa, or who possessed a photo of the two, should contact us. Two days later, I heard from two men. One had played in the Crookston high school band under G. Oliver's successor. He thought he had a copy of a 1906 band program that listed G. Oliver and Islea and said he'd look for it. The other man was the grandson of Crookston photographer Harry H. Chesterman. He said he would check with a relative who had a box of Chesterman's early photos.

"Hopefully, I will find a picture of John Philip Sousa and G. Oliver Riggs. I would like to think that my grandfather would have wanted to keep a picture of a famous person like Sousa, because I have a picture that he took in 1945 showing Harold Stassen returning to St. Paul after World War II," he wrote.

Weeks passed without hearing from either man. I didn't give up on Crookston, though. I wrote an article about it, emphasizing its history, notable architecture, and the chippers. I pitched it to the *Star Tribune*'s Travel section, and two days later, the assistant travel editor said they wanted to publish it. That same week, at the history center library in St. Paul, I stumbled across a *St. Cloud Daily Times* article in which G. Oliver addressed the importance of practicing.

He said, "Most of the time too many parents have neglected this and have fallen down on their part of the job. It appears that too many parents have never understood and do not at present understand the great importance of daily practice at home for their boy, and that it is the parents' job to keep him at it."[1]

I felt the sting of his reprimand through the newsprint. Although my kids seemed to enjoy practicing their instruments more during the summer than they did during the school year, the time they put into it was nowhere near G. Oliver's standards. However, I found it oddly reassuring that parents in 1925 also struggled with this issue.

The next day, I wrote a blog post about the importance of practicing, and I mentioned another article I'd found, about a recital Islea organized in 1925. It involved her students, saxophone players from the boys' band, and a "toe dancer." I suggested a family recital might be a fun way to motivate kids to practice. My friend Myrna responded that her family would be up for it, and I filed the idea in my mental "to-do-later" folder, along with "research: toe dancing, 1920s."

My travel article appeared on July 18, the same weekend we attended a gathering of my husband's family near Pine City, Minnesota. That afternoon, I drove into town and bought a newspaper. I turned the pages of the travel section until I saw the headline, "Step Back in Time in Crookston," and my byline. My face flushed with excitement.

The next week, I drove to Barden Park in St. Cloud to give a presentation about G. Oliver before the St. Cloud Municipal Band concert. Sebastian and Elias accompanied me. It was a lovely evening for an outdoor concert. Tidy flower beds displayed their late summer colors, and red, white, and blue bunting draped the old granite bandstand. Near the portable band shell where the modern band played, volunteers scooped vanilla ice cream and poured fizzy soda into red plastic cups; ice cream floats were a popular concert feature. A few rows of folding chairs were set up, and some people brought their own lawn chairs. There might have been forty regulars in the crowd.

I began by asking audience members to imagine they had time-traveled to June 4, 1925, when the municipal band first played in the bandstand. Then, I described the scene two months later, when the adult and boys' bands played for five thousand people—nearly a third of the city's population at the time.

"If tonight we had a third of the city's population in attendance, that would be almost 21,000 people, and we'd be a lot more elbow to elbow," I said.

I gained confidence as I spoke, and as I looked out at the audience, I could see that almost half of the people were related to me, including my brother and his kids, visiting from Phoenix.

On that August evening in 1925, I explained, a Minneapolis man led the crowd in singing well-known tunes like "My Old Kentucky Home." When the concert ended, people applauded and honked their car horns until, as the newspaper noted, "the din was deafening."

"This was entertainment in St. Cloud; this was community. This was a big deal," I said. "Residents took great pride in their band, which played at all important community events and also played regular summer concerts in the park, a practice started by G. Oliver. The band was the face of the city when it traveled to parades and conventions in other towns. Having an accomplished band made residents feel like they lived in a special place."

I concluded by noting that when G. Oliver retired, he hoped the band would keep going. "He'd be pleased to see you all here tonight and know that the band has indeed continued, and continues to be an important part of St. Cloud's community, in bringing people together, across generations, to enjoy the common pleasure of a band concert on a summer's evening in the park."

I handed the microphone to Dad. He spoke about growing up next to the park, which he and his siblings considered *their* park. Then he picked up G. Oliver's cornet.

My stomach felt queasy and my armpits felt sweaty. I was more nervous for my dad than I had been for myself. This was a first. I had never been nervous for him, not once in all those years I'd heard him play at concerts, weddings, and church services—especially not on Easter, when the triumphant, invincible notes of his trumpet sounded during the last stanza of the last hymn, and I felt a little closer to God.

My dad did not look invincible, standing amid oak trees that were older than he was. He looked ... vulnerable. Mortal.

Before the event, I hadn't considered how it would feel to stand in the park that held so many Riggs family memories. I would talk, and he would play the cornet. No problem. Now, in the seconds before he lifted the horn to his lips, I felt like a parent waiting for her child to perform at his first recital. I closed my eyes and sent him all my positive energy: *You can do it, Dad.*

He blew air into the instrument. The sweet, mournful notes of the Irish ballad "Danny Boy" (also known as "Air from County Derry") floated out into the park.

Oh Danny Boy, the pipes, the pipes are calling
From glen to glen and down the mountain side
The summer's gone and all the flowers dying
Tis you, tis you must go and I must bide

So far, so good. I forced myself to exhale while I blinked back tears. I was so proud of him. I wished his dad could be in the audience, to see the musician, father, and grandfather his eldest child had become.

But come ye back when summer's in the meadow
Or when the valley's hushed and white with snow

Dad was not used to playing this particular cornet. I held my breath. A high note was coming.

Tis I'll be here

Ooh, that was it. He bobbled the note slightly but kept going.

in sunshine or in shadow
Oh Danny Boy, oh Danny Boy, I love you so.

The last note hung in the air. I exhaled. He wouldn't be happy with that, it wasn't perfect, but most people won't have cared. I loved it, and I loved him for doing it. The audience applauded, and Dad smiled sheepishly. In a voice loud enough for those in the back to hear, he said: "As G. Oliver would say, 'you've got to go woodshed that a little more.'"

In other words, it needed more practice.

After the band concert, we took a picture of three generations of Riggs family members—four if you counted Big G—in front of the granite bandstand. Dana and Bob, my dad's siblings, set off the panic buttons on their car alarms and let the horns honk. It was a fitting end to a perfect evening in Riggs Park.

THE SUMMER ENDED on a multitude of high notes when the four-day Vintage Band Festival filled Northfield with brass band music, performed on antique instruments by musicians from across the country and abroad. It was a band history nerd's dream come true. I introduced Big G to his "contemporaries"—people like Elisa Koehler, a cornet soloist with Newberry's Victorian Cornet Band, and Bill Reynolds, director of the Independent Silver Band, a re-creation of an Illinois town band from the late 1800s. If I closed my eyes, I could pretend I had been transported to the days of G. Oliver's early career.

I didn't have to close my eyes on the third day to feel like a time traveler. I simply had to attend the Battle of the Bands, where festival-goers lined both sides of the river as half a dozen costumed bands—some in blue, some in gray—took turns playing Civil War-era tunes. Our whole family attended that event, and Elias uttered the best line of the weekend: "Back in the vintage times, do you think they had medieval band festivals?"

By the fourth day, Elias had had his fill of vintage music, and he declined my invitation to hear the 1st Brigade Band of Wisconsin perform at Riverside Park. Steve and Louisa also declined; they had a performance of *Romeo and Juliet* that evening. But Sebastian agreed to go.

The sun beat down on our heads as we took our seats. The heat seemed appropriate, since the band was a re-creation of a Wisconsin band that marched through the South with Sherman. Its members wore dark wool uniforms and hats, and I had no doubts that their sweat was authentic.

The concert combined 1860s brass band music with historical anecdotes. One presenter explained that eighty percent of the original 1st Brigade Band's tunes were quicksteps—songs played at 104 to 108 steps per minute, to get troops moving down the road. He also explained that the bells on the over-the-shoulder instruments pointed behind the players because the bands marched in front of the troops.

The modern musicians played more than a dozen songs, including an 1861 version of "The Star Spangled Banner," which we were told we didn't need to stand for, since it didn't become our national anthem until 1931. The program closed with "Marching Through Georgia."

Hearing the 1st Brigade Band heighted my excitement for our fall vacation: we were going to visit the battlefields at Shiloh and Vicksburg. Fortunately, we wouldn't be marching; our travel plans involved an airplane and a rental car.

To prepare for our vacation, Steve pored over guidebooks. I reviewed my notes about Jasper's service and G. Oliver's 1906 trip, and I re-read Tony Horwitz's nonfiction book *Confederates in the Attic*. In one chapter, Horwitz meets tourists whose ancestors fought at Shiloh, and he feels envious, writing: "They had a blood tie to a patch of American soil that I never would."[2]

That statement resonated with me. An odd mixture of pride and curiosity compelled me to investigate the "blood tie" I had to Vicksburg and Shiloh, knowing if Jasper hadn't survived those battles, my kids and I wouldn't exist, and all the lives that emanated from Jasper's would be erased. I could only speculate on what it meant to G. Oliver to visit the military parks some forty years after his dad fought there.

We prepared the kids by watching parts of *The Civil War: a Film by Ken Burns*. I hadn't seen it since it debuted on PBS in September 1990, around the time I started working at the newspaper in Natchez, Mississippi. Louisa and Sebastian both enjoyed it, as I'd expected. Sebastian was a history buff, and Louisa was always interested in a well-told story. Elias, however, spent much of the film lying on the rug under the coffee table, wishing we were watching something else.

He had a low tolerance for complicated historical explanations. He also had a quick, dry wit. He would be the wild card on this trip. Other than the hotel pool, what would interest him?

When I asked him what he was most looking forward to, he said, "The trip home."

Ouch. To be fair, his great-great-great grandfather likely shared that sentiment.

We flew into Memphis in mid-October and drove first to Corinth, Mississippi, once a critical railroad juncture for the Confederacy. The interpretive center had a wealth of interactive displays and an engaging movie about the Battle of Shiloh. It also had a well-stocked gift shop, where we bought a color-coded battlefield map and soldier caps known as kepis. Louisa and Sebastian chose blue, and our wild card child opted for gray. Jasper might have disapproved, but it reflected historical fact: some brothers fought on opposite sides during the war.

We drove next to the actual battlefield, twenty-five miles northeast of Corinth, across the Tennessee border. I'd read somewhere that Shiloh was one of the most pristine Civil War battlefields, and I could see why. Trees were everywhere, and many leaves had started turning various shades of orange and brown. Although we occasionally saw other visitors, we felt like we mostly had the four thousand-acre park to ourselves. We drove leisurely along the twelve-mile paved path and took pictures at famous sites like the Hornet's Nest and the Peach Orchard. We also stopped to inspect stone memorials and cannons scattered along the route. Even with the map, we had trouble finding the memorial for Jasper's regiment. Steve slowed the car to a crawl.

"It should be right there, I think," I said, pointing toward a thicket off to my right.

I saw nothing but tall grass and hardwood trees.

"Maybe we need to get out and look," Steve said. He pulled off to the side of the road.

Feeling adventurous, he and I made our own path through long grass and crunchy leaves, past a cannon, and into the woods. The kids trailed behind. In a hushed clearing that was invisible from the road, a rectangular hunk of white marble stood more than five feet high. Raised letters near its top spelled: "Illinois."

"I think that's it!" I said.

My heart beat faster as we approached. The inscription on the brass plaque said: *Went into battle on this line about 9:00 a.m., April 6, 1862, and maintained this position until 11:00 a.m., when it joined the division on a new line. The regiment lost 1 officer and 22 men killed, 17 officers and 170 men wounded; 3 men missing; total 213.*

We stood in silence. How could bloodshed have occurred in a place of such peace?

The rest of the afternoon, we struggled with this contrast, the evidence of human brutality amid breathtaking natural beauty.

The kids' favorite place was the cemetery. They loved the hills, the trees, and the view of the Tennessee River. The park pamphlet informed me that General Grant spent the night in that spot after the first day of the battle. By the next morning, reinforcements had arrived at Pittsburgh's Landing, which allowed Grant to push the Confederates back until they retreated to Corinth.

I felt an extra connection to the spot knowing that G. Oliver played a concert there. Maybe as he played "Taps," he gazed at the same view of the river we were enjoying.

"This is one of the coolest natural areas I've been to. I wish the dead would let us play capture the flag here—wouldn't they want people to have fun?" Sebastian asked. He gestured toward the rows and rows of white granite tombstones.

I didn't know how to answer. I wasn't sure how to seek permission from the dead. The Shiloh National Cemetery, dedicated in 1889, contained 3,584 Civil War soldiers; 2,359 of them unknown. They played their own cruel version of capture the flag in this area and lost. They probably didn't mind kids having fun there now, as long as it was respectful fun.

Our next stop was New Orleans, a four-hundred-mile drive from Shiloh. Steve and I had both been to New Orleans before, but the kids hadn't, and we spent three days sightseeing. From New Orleans we drove to my old reporting grounds in Natchez. Louisa was two when Steve and I last visited my former boss, Joan Gandy, and her husband, Tom. The Gandys owned a collection of negatives that documented one hundred years of early Natchez history, and they had published several books. After Tom died in 2004, Joan became a minister and moved away.

The town didn't seem the same without them. We ate lunch at Stanton Hall, a former antebellum mansion, where the restaurant's tiny biscuits were as delicious as ever. We also viewed an exhibit of the Gandy photo collection at their former church.

During the seventy-three mile drive from Natchez to Vicksburg, we passed through Port Gibson. I told the kids that Grant admonished his soldiers not to destroy the town because it was "too beautiful to burn." Minutes later, as we passed some rundown mobile homes, Sebastian's voice rang out from the back seat: "Where are we? I thought they said it was too beautiful to burn."

The last time I visited Vicksburg, I was a twenty-three-year-old reporter. Vern Smith, a black journalist originally from Natchez, had been sued for libel by a white county clerk over a story Smith wrote for *Newsweek,* and I was assigned to cover the trial for the *Natchez Democrat.* After seven days of testimony and arguments, the jury found that Smith had not defamed the clerk.

The trial did not take place at the old courthouse-turned museum, distinguished by its clock tower, cupola, and 30-foot Ionic columns. We got out of the car to take photos of the historic structure. Built by slaves and completed in 1858, the courthouse flew the Confederate flag during the battle and siege. Soldiers like Jasper could have seen it from almost any point along the Union line.

When the Confederates surrendered on July 4, 1863, Union soldiers replaced the flag with the Stars and Stripes, and they also raised the flag of Jasper's regiment in recognition of its role in the campaign. Post-war Vicksburg attracted thirty thousand liberated men and women, the US Army built schools for the freedmen, and for a time the city was a model of reconstruction.

I almost got misty-eyed standing there, on one of the highest hills in the city, as I pondered how far our country had come in one hundred and fifty years, and how far we had yet to go. The struggles and accomplishments on civil rights issues felt more personal because of my family's ties to this Mississippi River city. Jasper had fought here to preserve the Union. G. Oliver had visited during the tenure of Governor James Vardaman, when Jim Crow laws erased all the gains black Americans had made during Reconstruction. And here I stood, two years after our country elected its first African-American president.

What societal and political changes would the next one hundred and fifty years bring?

I had been to the Vicksburg National Military Park twice before; once with my parents in 1988, the summer I was a newspaper intern; and once with Steve in 1991, the year I worked in Natchez. On both of those visits, I had admired the impressive Illinois monument and wished the park's Minnesota monument had been more interesting—or at least as interesting as Iowa's. So it blew my mind when I discovered, early in my G. Oliver research, my direct family connection to the Illinois Memorial. When I learned that the names of all 36,325 Illinois soldiers who fought at Vicksburg were listed inside, I knew I had to find Jasper's.

During the siege of Vicksburg, Jasper's regiment was positioned near the Shirley House. The house was also near the site where Jasper's regiment made three failed attempts to seize a major Confederate fortification, the Third Louisiana Redan. During the June 25, 1863, attack, when the 45th exploded a mine, splinters struck Jasper in the face and arm, injuring his left wrist. He also suffered permanent hearing loss.

While we sat near the Shirley House, the park's only surviving wartime structure, and ate a picnic lunch. I contemplated these now-remote events.

"Jasper probably had a few meals around here," Steve said.

I nodded. I was thinking that too.

"Not Sun Chips, though," I said.

"Probably hardtack," he guessed.

Louisa, who was listening to the conversation, chimed in: "They had that on the Mayflower!"

After lunch, we stepped inside the Illinois Memorial. When we found the bronze plaque for the 45th Regiment, my eyes traveled down the list until I saw the name. I handed Louisa a piece of white paper and a black crayon, and she traced it: Jasper Riggs. It was the cheapest souvenir in the park, but it was priceless to me. I couldn't wait to show it to my dad.

Our last stop in the park was the Iowa Memorial. I stared at its bronze relief panels and thought about G. Oliver, the poet soldier S. H. M. Byers, and the journalist Ernest Sherman. I thought about the ladies of Vicksburg, "who do not use water in their punch." I thought about invisible connections between generations, and I wondered how often we unknowingly follow in the footsteps of our ancestors.

Before we flew home, we spent a few hours at the National Civil Rights Museum in Memphis. It was built around the old Lorraine Motel, where Martin Luther King Jr. was assassinated in 1968, the day after giving his "I've Been to the Mountaintop" speech. I was three months old when King was shot outside Room 306, and Steve was not yet born.

Seeing the room frozen in time gave me chills. It also inspired me.

Our country might never overcome the stain and scourge of slavery. But we had no choice but to keep moving forward. We had to hope that, with each new generation, we moved closer to becoming a United States of America that was worthy of all those who died for its highest ideals.

18

On the Sunny Side of the Street

G. Oliver returned to his job in St. Cloud when the national economy was booming. By the end of the 1920s, Americans had more leisure time and more money to spend on entertainment than ever before. More than twelve million households had radios,[1] and the diverse array of programs they could listen to included baseball games and live performances of the latest music sensation—jazz. Record player sales skyrocketed, and an estimated fifty million Americans attended the movies each week.[2]

When President Calvin Coolidge opted not to run for a second term, the strong economy helped boost his commerce secretary, Herbert Hoover, into the White House. Hoover defeated Democrat Al Smith in a landslide election on November 6, 1928. In Minnesota, Republicans also triumphed, as voters overwhelmingly reelected Governor Theodore Christianson.

But it was a smaller-scale election two weeks later in Minneapolis that affected G. Oliver's life more directly for the coming year, when members of the Minnesota Bandmasters Association unanimously elected him president for 1929. He quickly identified his priorities: helping more communities pass band levies, preparing for the first state band tournament, and boosting membership.

The January 1929 issue of the *Bandmaster* ran a photo of G. Oliver wearing a suit and tie, dark round glasses, and a serious expression. The accompanying full-page article about the new association president said, "We feel safe in saying that Bandmaster Riggs is one of the most successful organizers and developers of Boys' Bands in the United States."[3]

One challenge G. Oliver and other band leaders faced was that with the advent of radio, music-lovers suddenly had far more performance options to choose from. Why drive your Ford Model A to the park to hear an amateur band play Sousa's "Minnesota March" when you could listen to Sousa's band on the Victrola in your living room? It was all the more reason for bandmasters to improve the profession.

Teacher Erwin Hertz formed the first band at St. Cloud's Technical High School in the fall of 1928.

The overall growth of bands in Minnesota in the 1920s was aided by the development of school band programs. Before 1920, only a handful of schools had them, but during the 1920s, as teachers and instrument dealers promoted their social and educational value, bands became a common feature of high school music programs.[4]

One school with a new band was practically in G. Oliver's back yard—more specifically, four-tenths of a mile from his house. The new social studies teacher at Technical High School in St. Cloud, Erwin Hertz, formed a band that fall. Composed of one girl and twenty-three boys, the student band was soon performing at sporting events and assemblies.

Hertz had worked as a missionary in China and studied at the University of Chicago before moving to St. Cloud with his wife, Katherine, and their two daughters. He stood 5 feet 7, had a receding hairline, and wore round glasses that made him look studious. His arrival would have a noticeable effect on G. Oliver's career in years to come.

The St. Cloud Teachers College also got its first band that fall, directed by Loren L. Maynard. He also directed the college orchestra, and his wife, Lela, taught music classes at the college.

The St. Cloud Municipal Boys' Band spent the winter rehearsing for the summer state band tournament, and parents raised $2,500 for new uniforms. In February, when temperatures dropped and a storm dumped three inches of snow on the city, only thirty-three boys showed up for a rehearsal, and G. Oliver complained to the *St. Cloud Daily Times.*

"If a little boy of 10 years could walk 16 blocks to and from rehearsal and return again to practice on Thursday night and not even have a cold, why should older boys, who may have only a few blocks farther to walk, stay away from band practice because 'it's too cold.' It is quite evident that this little boy who walked the 16 blocks will be a successful man."[5]

That spring, Percy, Patricia, and Mary Jane returned to St. Cloud so Percy could seek work as a musician. They moved in with G. Oliver and Islea. Ronald still lived there, too, but he spent most of his time on the road organizing school bands for the Holton instrument company.

In June, G. Oliver's top ninety-six players traveled to St. Paul for the first state band contest, joining thirty other bands. Attired in natty French blue uniforms trimmed in red piping, the St. Cloud boys led the kickoff event, a one-mile evening parade through downtown. The esteemed judges—Iowa Bandmasters Association President Karl King and University of Illinois Band Director A. Austin Harding—sat on an elevated platform in front of the St. Paul Hotel with other officials, including Governor Christianson and Mayor Laurence Hodgson.

Traffic was so backed up before the parade, hundreds of motorists abandoned their cars mid-street to search on foot for a viewing spot. Some onlookers perched on fire escapes. An estimated sixty thousand people watched the parade, which was broadcast by the KSTP radio station.[6]

G. Oliver managed dual roles at the event; as the organizer, he wanted it to run efficiently, and as a director, he wanted his boys to shine. He must have been pleased when the *St. Paul Pioneer Press* described the St. Cloud band as "one of the most colorful organizations in the parade, with its bright blue uniforms and meticulously polished instruments. The sinking sun peeped out from behind a cloud for a moment as the band came into view. The effect stimulated the crowd and the St. Cloud band was given a tremendous ovation."[7]

Other audience favorites included the Brainerd Ladies' Band, wearing striking scarlet skirts and white coats trimmed in gold; the Crosby Ore Diggers, sporting yellow slickers and matching hats; and a St. Paul novelty band of twenty-five boys and girls who played "The Battle Hymn of the Republic" on harmonicas. When all the musicians reached Rice Park, King and Harding led them in Sousa's "Stars and Stripes Forever."

"The music from the hundreds of instruments welled up and outward in a blast which reverberated against the buildings in the vicinity," the *St. Paul Pioneer Press* article said. As thousands of spectators pushed forward hoping for a better look, "they pressed so hard that the bandsmen were jostled about while playing."[8]

Following the concert, band members and their families attended a dinner at the Masonic Temple. *St. Paul Pioneer Press* music critic Frances Boardman interviewed King and Harding, both friends of Sousa's, amid the clatter of dishes and the clamor of admiring fans. She noted that they appeared calm in the midst of "bedlam" and attributed it to their experience—Harding was used to managing seven hundred college students, and King was a former circus bandleader.

The men talked about the important role brass bands played in providing music education for the masses, and the benefits of band tax laws, before the interview was cut short by the appearance of G. Oliver, who "made it a trio by pressing the visitors to get food and drink while food and drink were still to be had, and they decided to call it a finale and let it go at that."[9]

The second day was devoted to competition. Bands were divided into three classes based on experience. St. Cloud placed second of fifteen bands in Class B, with a score of 91.9. Sleepy Eye High School placed first with 93.5, and the Bemidji Boys' Band placed third with 90.75. The top three finishers in Class A were the American Legion Band, the Working Boys' Band, and the Pillsbury Flour Band, all from Minneapolis. The top three bands in Class C were the Elk River Band, the Brainerd Ladies' Band, and Pederson's Concert Band of Hallock.

No St. Cloud boys participated in the solo contest. But the top two soloists in Class B were Bemidji boys trained by G. Oliver: saxophone player Clayton Ebert, who took first, and French horn player Basil Britten, runner-up. G. Oliver must have taken pride in their proficiency.

Given his competitive spirit, it's likely he also enjoyed seeing St. Cloud finish ahead of the Bemidji boys. Judges said of the St. Cloud band: "This organization as well as its conductor deserves a great deal of commendation for what has been accomplished with so many very young players. Much can be expected of them in the future."[10]

Before the trip, G. Oliver tried to tamp down the boys' expectations about how they would score against more experienced players. After the contest, he told the *St. Cloud Daily Times* that he was completely satisfied with the performance. The St. Cloud Boys' band received a silver loving cup and performed with all the other winning bands on Sunday afternoon for nearly eight thousand people gathered at Highland Park.[11]

But the St. Cloud boys weren't done. They traveled to Minneapolis that evening for their final event of the trip—a concert for fifteen thousand people at the Lake Harriet Park Pavilion.

"The applause and honking of horns which followed the selections by the boys was something to throw credit on the city of St. Cloud," the *St. Cloud Daily Times* reported. "In spite of their good conduct during their three-day sojourn, the boys had the time of their lives, especially while bunking at the St. Paul armory. Among the notable events there was the winning of an unexpected foot race by Joe Bettendorf, a St. Cloud snare drummer. While the band was encamped at the armory, a kind gentleman entered and advised them that he had a dollar bill for the fastest runner in the crowd."[12]

Less than a week later, G. Oliver called the band into special duty. His former band committee adversary, Martin Molitor, had died of a heart attack. The boys' band and the St. Cloud Legion band escorted Molitor's body from the funeral home to the

Cathedral of St. Mary, where mourners remembered the sixty-seven-year-old Molitor as a successful businessman dedicated to community service. The *St. Cloud Daily Journal-Press* also noted his keen sense of humor and said, "He was a lover of music, and for many years was one of the effective leaders in the band organizations, as player and manager of the municipal bands."[13]

During their month-long summer vacation, G. Oliver and Islea took an auto tour of northern Minnesota and visited family in Illinois. After the break, the boys performed at the National Letter Carriers Convention in Minneapolis. The August 28 event featured eighteen letter carrier bands from across the country and attracted an audience of eight thousand people. Several days later, local letter carriers treated the boys to ice cream and cake and gave them a $100 check.[14]

G. Oliver, meanwhile, helped guest director J. W. Wainwright of Fostoria, Ohio, organize the first Minnesota State Fair High School Band. Two hundred and twenty-five boys were selected from seventy-four counties throughout Minnesota to perform at the fair for a week.[15]

St. Cloud sent four boys: Herbert Jung, Ben Whittinger, and brothers Joe and John Tessari. All four were in Hertz's St. Cloud Tech band—although, as G. Oliver may have pointed out, Jung got his start in the boys' band.

G. Oliver wrapped up his term as president by attending the fall convention in Windom, in southwestern Minnesota. Entertainment included solos by Clayton Ebert, the saxophonist who placed first at the state band contest; and twelve-year-old cornetist Edmund Walter Lienke of Windom. Islea accompanied both boys on the piano. Carl Christiansen, dean of the music department at South Dakota State University, was the featured speaker.[16] The bandmasters granted him a year's honorary membership, and they granted a lifetime honorary membership to George Landers, who was in Iowa recovering from abdominal surgery. G. Oliver was elected to the association's board of directors for 1930, and he agreed to serve as chairman of the 1930 band tournament planning committee.

Landers later thanked the bandmasters for the lifetime membership and the get-well wishes.

"Sickness surely draws one's friends close to them," he wrote. "Now that I am on the road to recovery, I realize how close I came to 'Crossing the Bar.' I hope to be spared many years yet that I may be of service to my fellow-men."[17]

BUSINESS ACTIVITIES ON Wall Street seemed worlds away from musical activities in Minnesota, but people throughout the country noticed when the stock market crashed at the end of October. Billions of dollars were lost, and thousands of investors were affected. However, at the close of 1929, the economy showed signs of recovery. Ronald continued his work with Holton, and Percy found work directing a youth band in Watkins, a town of five hundred people near St. Cloud.

That winter, G. Oliver's work was interrupted by distressing news: his eighty-four-year-old mother, Rebecca, was ill. G. Oliver traveled to Illinois to be with her. A few days after he arrived, Rebecca died. She was buried in the New Boston cemetery next to her daughter Loie.

Rebecca had been a widow for almost twenty years. An article in the St. Cloud newspaper about her death noted that she had lived through the Civil War and that she had married G. Oliver's father, Jasper, while he was home on an Army furlough in 1864.

"Recollections of those stirring days were very clear in Mrs. Riggs' mind and she was a very interesting conversationalist when she told of her early experiences," the article said.[18]

G. Oliver had always been close to his mother, and her death may have caused him to contemplate his own mortality, and his unfulfilled career goals. He was fifty-nine—nine years younger than Jasper was when he died.

In the spring, all 163 St. Cloud boys' band members gathered in front of the courthouse for a photo. It was used to publicize the 1930 state band tournament, although G. Oliver only took his top 78 players to the competition. Percy's band also made the trip to St. Paul, joining an estimated eleven hundred musicians from around the state.

Led by a police motorcycle escort and a hundred members of

Members of the St. Cloud junior and senior boys' bands pose outside the courthouse, June 1930. Standing in the back row are assistant director Percy Riggs, left, and director G. Oliver Riggs.

the St. Paul Musicians Union, twenty-seven ensembles paraded through downtown on June 20. The *St. Paul Pioneer Press* estimated that fifty thousand people "delayed their dinner" to watch the parade, including numbers of "urchins" who found prime seats along the sidewalk curbs.[19]

Three Fort Snelling officers judged the bands in categories of best marching, best drum major, most novel band, and best uniforms. The St. Paul Police Band took first place in the marching contest with a score of 93. The St. Cloud Boys' Band placed second with 90, and the Brainerd Ladies Band and the Sleepy Eye High School Band tied for third with 89.5. The St. Cloud Boys' Band placed sixth out of eighteen bands in the uniform contest.

The 200 participating female musicians stayed overnight at the Ryan Hotel, while the men and boys bunked at the armory or the St. Paul Auditorium. The boys from Sleepy Eye had the ironic distinction of being the last group at the armory to "turn in" for the evening.[20] The next day, performances by twenty-three bands and fifteen soloists were scheduled from morning into the late evening. The Brainerd Ladies' Band, directed by Winifred Cronk Ziebell (the only female director in the tournament), also performed at the Gillette State Hospital for Crippled Children and the Shriners Hospital for Crippled Children.[21]

191

Judges for the concert portion of the contest were Carl Christiansen, from Brookings, South Dakota; S. E. Mear of Whitewater, Wisconsin; and Fred Griffen of Hartley, Iowa.

G. Oliver voluntarily moved the St. Cloud band into Class A, which had the most difficult music, to increase the number of bands in that smaller category. Bands were judged on general appearance, intonation and balance, expression, and interpretation of the music. When his band finished in fourth place with 92 percent, G. Oliver must have been disappointed, although the scores were close: The top three were the Eveleth Band (93.66); the Pillsbury Flour Mills Band (92.6); and the Minneapolis Working Boys Band (92.33).

G. Oliver pointed out to the St. Cloud newspaper that his boys scored higher than Bemidji, which placed first in Class B with a score of 91, ahead of Sleepy Eye and the St. Paul Police Band.[22] The top three bands in Class C were Pederson's Concert Band of Hallock; the Ortonville Kid Band; and Elk River High School. Percy's band, Watkins Junior, took fourth.

In the bandleader contest, G. Oliver placed sixth out of twenty, behind younger men like Bemidji director A. K. Lekvold—a result that could not have pleased him. Christiansen called G. Oliver an excellent director "which, of course, shows up in the work of this splendid band." Griffen said, "I don't just agree with you on all points in conducting, but you get good results, and that, after all, is what counts." Mear wrote: "This is a remarkable demonstration by a young band doing worthwhile things. Your community can be justly proud of such an organization."[23]

G. Oliver may have taken greater interest in comments received by Percy, who placed twelfth. Mear called Percy's band "splendidly trained" and said: "You handle your band like a veteran."[24]

When the tournament ended, G. Oliver took a break from bandmasters association responsibilities. He attended the annual convention that fall, but he was not elected to any office.

ONE YEAR HAD PASSED since the stock market crash. The number of bank failures continued to rise as more farmers defaulted on their loans and more investors withdrew their money. An estimated four million Americans were out of work. Although President Hoover maintained that the economy was fundamentally strong, Minnesotans decided on a different approach. They elected Hennepin County Attorney Floyd B. Olson as the state's first governor representing the Farmer-Labor Party, a coalition of farmers, union members, and small businessmen. Olson's win ended the Republican party's fifteen-year streak of executive office dominance in the state.

G. Oliver achieved a different level of fame in early 1931; he was featured in the *Northwest Musical Herald,* the monthly magazine produced by the Minnesota Music Teachers Association and the Minnesota Federation of Music Clubs. The article's introduction said, "There are band leaders and band leaders. Some simply wield a stick; others are educators, disciplinarians as well as musicians, who occupy a high place in the educational and cultural life of the communities in which they reside. In the latter category is G. Oliver Riggs."[25]

In the three-page article, G. Oliver said he believed a band's success depended upon having a leader who studied music seriously and received training in band organizing—not, for example, someone who taught Latin or geometry well and directed bands on the side.

"For a boy or girl to play in a band under unfavorable conditions is not only a waste of time and money but it is likely to wreck his chance of ever getting back on the right track in continuing the study of music," he wrote.[26]

In describing the ideal conditions for a bandmaster, G. Oliver cited a sufficient budget, a liberal salary, and adequate rehearsal rooms—a topic he would return to in later years. He said a community with a successful band was willing to pay a small tax to support the band because it was a source of pride for everyone. When he started his first boys' band in Crookston, he noted, he gave individual lessons, but he soon adopted the method of larger group practices. Members of that first band went on to successful careers in farming, medicine, and the law, and he said several of them later told him their band experience helped them learn self-control and poise.

Two other early bands he started, the Burnham Creek Band and the Bygland Band, were made up of boys from Norwegian farm families. This was during the time of horse-driven transportation, he said, adding, "These boys and the bandmaster were forced at times to drive over snow drifts several feet high to get to the country school house for band practice. My efforts in these two communities were as highly appreciated by the band boys, by their parents and friends as in any work that I ever engaged."[27]

The ways in which bands were financed changed several times during his forty-five years as a professional musician and band leader, he explained: in the early days, band members bought their instruments, uniforms, and music and paid a weekly fee to their instructor; next came the time when directors sold yearly concert subscriptions and used the proceeds to pay band expenses; and after that, a system developed in which chambers of commerce supported bands.

In what seemed like a reference to his early experience in St. Cloud, he noted that the latter method "did not last long as in some cases it divided the authority into too many groups and had a tendency to destroy the unity between business men and the band which had existed formerly."[28]

This led to the current system of the band tax, he said, which he believed was the most equitable yet devised.

ECONOMIC CONCERNS CAUSED the Minnesota Bandmasters Association to cancel the 1931 state band tournament. But G. Oliver had other plans, anyway; his Senior Boys' Band was invited to the twelfth annual National Junior Chamber of Commerce Convention in Des Moines, Iowa.

Because G. Oliver now faced competition in St. Cloud for community support and players, he counted on his boys to make a favorable impression. The band boarded a special train in St. Paul on June 10 and headed south with three hundred business leaders and one brown bear.

The businessmen hailed from Duluth, St. Cloud, Sauk Centre, St. Paul, and Minneapolis. Because St. Paul hoped to host the 1932 convention, the St. Paul chapter president, Leslie Farrington, wanted to impress delegates who leaned toward a vote for Pasadena, California. That's why he invited the band and the bear.

The bear, as far as anyone knew, had no concerns about impressing anyone.

"Junior" lived at St. Paul's Como Zoo, and this was his first gig as a mascot. Anticipating the damage a three-hundred-pound bear cub could inflict upon persons and property, Farrington secured an insurance policy on Junior before departing St. Paul. He also arranged to have the cub tethered in the baggage car for the six-hour trip to Iowa's capital city.[29]

It was a wise move. Junior proved to be a poor insurance risk.

When the train reached its destination that evening, the Minnesotans received a rousing welcome from Des Moines businessmen, and the boys led a parade to the Hotel Fort Des Moines, the convention headquarters.

During the three-day convention, the need to stimulate the economy was much on the minds of the two thousand delegates. Empowered by the growing feeling that it was their generation's turn to take a crack at fixing the older generation's mess, the young businessmen addressed the issues of the day with rowdy enthusiasm.

While the men debated issues like the economic effects of Prohibition, the band played numerous concerts, "serenaded the mayor and other city officials at city hall, and serenaded the governor and state officials at the State Capitol. The stenographers at city hall decorated the band boys with flowers."[30] From the time they stepped off the train that first evening until they re-boarded the train to Minnesota, the boys' clean-cut behavior—drilled into them by their director—was noticed.

The same could not be said of Junior the bear.

Junior made a big splash early in the convention when he got away from trainer Ray Gravelle, jumped into the decorative pool in the Hotel Fort Des Moines lobby, and scattered goldfish on the expensive rugs. He also took a friendly swipe one afternoon at "Hamlet," a Great Dane that the Pasadena delegates used as their mascot.[31]

But Junior's most notable escapade took place at the Hotel Savery, where Gravelle had booked a room with two twin beds.

"Gravelle kept the cub in his hotel room. He awoke one morning to find the mattress of the cub's bed torn to shreds. Later the

195

bear broke loose to gambol in the corridors while chamber maids screamed and fought him with brooms. Gravelle has been tethering the cub in the hotel basement since," one newspaper noted.[32]

The band's most prominent performance came on Friday when the boys serenaded the convention hall, the delegates gave a thunderous cheer, and the St. Cloud men distributed a thousand free samples of granite. On the last day, California delegates handed out free oranges and orange marmalade, and Pasadena defeated St. Paul in the bid to host the 1932 convention. But the Minnesotans did not leave empty handed. The St. Paul delegates won a trophy for best attendance, and the St. Cloud band members, heralded by convention-goers "as the outstanding musical organization of the country,"[33] left knowing they brought national fame to their city. Percy went home with a job offer to direct the school band and orchestra in Manilla, Iowa. The *Des Moines Tribune-Capital* ran a photo of him, flashing a dimpled smile as he held his band hat over his head. The caption read: "I'll take off my hat to Iowa!"[34]

On the return trip, G. Oliver extended the publicity tour with a stop in Mason City. Although the town would later gain fame as the birthplace of Meredith Willson (who wrote the famous musical, *The Music Man*, in 1948), its music man of note in 1931 was Gerald Prescott, who had recently led his high school band to a national competition. G. Oliver paid tribute to Prescott at the depot, and the St. Cloud boys played a few numbers. Junior must have been tuckered out; according to the *Mason City Globe*, the bear cub "sat solemnly on the platform to listen to the music."[35]

When they returned to St. Cloud, G. Oliver received a letter from George Landers, who had attended part of the convention. Landers wrote:

> *I must congratulate you upon that very outstanding meritorious band, the best organization of its kind that I have had the pleasure of listening to … That band of yours cannot only play well, but their general gentlemanly appearance, discipline, and all make the organization conspicuous. Not a boy did I see smoking a cigarette, wonderful in a way, considering the "jazz-age" we*

are going thru when little attention is given the true philosophies of life by our youth.

I wonder if your citizens realize what publicity St. Cloud receives at the hands of this band? The organization is a credit to their instructor, their hometown and state. I wish we had more of such bands over the country.

Remember me to the boys when you have them assembled. Tell them the old bandmaster loves them all.[36]

As summer turned to fall, the band's success was a sunny spot of hope amid gloomy economic uncertainties that weighed heavily upon St. Cloud residents. In the coming years they would need all the boosting they could get.

19

CATCHING GRASSHOPPERS

Shortly after we returned from our battlefield-based vacation in October 2010, we adopted a sweet one-year-old apricot poodle/dachshund mix and named him Waffles.

I shared the latest dog stories with my parents over dinner in St. Cloud one night in early November, and then holed up in my hotel room, tweaking the slideshow for a talk I was giving the next day. The journalistic "high" of working on deadline sustained me until 2 a.m., when the need for sleep won out over the desire for perfection. As a forty-two-year-old mom, I had no business pulling an all-nighter. Several hours later, running on nervous energy and weak hotel coffee, I arrived at the Stearns History Museum with my parents.

Amid the gathering crowd, I recognized Francis Schellinger and his wife, Karen. Francis looked professorial in his cable-knit sweater vest and khaki pants. He walked with a cane, which he hadn't needed in 2008, the last time I saw him.

"Francis, you look great! It's so nice to see you," I said.

His manner of speech, which had been deliberate and thoughtful before, seemed a few beats slower. He said he'd had a stroke but was doing better.

"You haven't aged a day," he added. "You look—vivacious."

I beamed at him. I remembered why I liked him so much.

During my talk, I discussed the accomplishments of the St. Cloud Boys' Band. I also cited examples of members who served in World War II and continued in music as performers or teachers—for example, Lennie Jung, Herb Streitz, and Adrian Opitz, who had died the previous July at age ninety-four.

I had communicated with Adrian's daughter Pamela earlier that fall, after I found Adrian's obituary. He joined the boys' band in 1923 at age eight, played drums in the band until age twenty-one, and assisted G. Oliver until 1944. After serving at Iwo Jima, Adrian returned to St. Cloud and played in bands until he was in his sixties. He later developed Alzheimer's disease, so if I had found him before he died, it's unlikely I could have interviewed him.

Fortunately, Pamela shared one of his stories: when Adrian was twenty-one, he and other former band members met G. Oliver for a drink and a jam session, and G. Oliver told them how nice it was that they were finally old enough to socialize with him. It made me happy to know they had experienced G. Oliver's sociable side. I loved imagining G. Oliver jamming with them.

When I mentioned Adrian in my talk, a voice called out, "His widow is right here!" A younger woman in the audience pointed to an elderly woman with a soft cloud of silver-white hair, who smiled at me. It was Adrian's wife, Dorothy.

I almost burst into tears, I was so pleased to see her.

"Thank you so much for coming," I blubbered.

I was off-script now, and it took me a minute to recover. The next slide showed Francis with his brothers. Knowing he was there ramped up my emotions even more. I took a breath and told myself to keep my eyes dry while I read a quote by Francis about how G. Oliver influenced his life.

After the presentation, I hugged my parents and thanked them for their help. Mom wrote later to say that Dad was "walking on air, bustin' his buttons, thoroughly ecstatic about the morning."

I imagined him telling his coffee friends about it, and it made me smile. The friends also, no doubt, would hear about the latest accomplishments of the three grandchildren in Northfield and the four in Arizona.

It was surprising my dad had any buttons left.

In December, I began writing articles for *Northfield Patch*. *Patch* sites were springing up all over the country, in many cases staffed by print journalists who had lost their previous jobs due to the Great Recession and the decline of the newspaper industry. I continued to pitch travel ideas, too; my latest was on Mantorville, a historic town near Rochester with a surprisingly vibrant arts scene. And I heard from the daughter of Howard Pramann, the stamp collector from Duluth. She thanked me for writing the blog post about her dad, which she had forwarded to relatives. It was gratifying to know readers were enjoying my posts months after I wrote them.

Two days before Christmas Eve, in a post about my great-aunt Rosalie, who had died so young, I wrote: "I will think of Rosalie this week as we prepare to celebrate Christmas with family. Instead of feeling stressed about holiday tasks, I will try to take a breath, enjoy the moment, and treasure those around me, grateful for their presence in my life. We all can learn from Rosalie's example, and strive to live in the spirit of an unbroken rhythm."

I included a photo of Rosalie at about age five, wearing a dress, her hair in a bob. Its ethereal beauty charmed me. It showed her silhouette, her body and head turned slightly away from the camera. Her arms reached forward, above her head, and her face tilted toward the sky.

At the bottom of the photo, Islea had written "Rosalie catching grasshoppers."

More than two dozen friends and relatives responded to the post; some were moved to tears. My second cousin Pete in Massachusetts said he wished we could have met our great-aunt.

My dad wrote:

All your blogs recently have caused reflection, and perhaps I need to start some annotation so I can remember my thoughts and feelings better. Your latest one on Rosalie is powerful and an emotional experience for me. Dad did not talk about it a lot but it changed Christmas for him completely and I think it changed Islea and G. Oliver as well.

[Dad] told me several times how hard Mom had worked and prepared to make his Christmas celebration positive and

fun. How much he had appreciated it because there was no Christmas celebration ever after 1917 for him at home.

He loved celebrating Christmas. I do too!

I know that the death of Michele was a huge loss for Dad and for us and of course it came just before Christmas. Nana and I have worked hard to keep Christmas positive and fun but her death changed us too.

Thanks for being such a Joy and surrounding us with such powerful and fun times all year.

Tears welled up in my eyes. I knew Dad was proud of me, and I was grateful that the project continued to stimulate important conversations with him.

Digging into the past had taught me more than I'd expected to learn about how people are shaped by loss and pain; how grief can affect a family years and generations later; and how the desire to love and be loved propels us forward, even in those moments when we can't seem to find the rhythm in our daily existence.

EARLY IN THE new year, I decided to visit an eye doctor. I had hoped to put off getting glasses until after Louisa graduated from high school. But I was done in by laundry tags.

Why, oh why, had clothing manufacturers decided to shrink the print on those pesky tags? What devilish mind concocted the latest innovation in washing instructions, printing them directly on the fabric, ensuring that the letters rubbed off after one or two wash cycles?

I could have asked for help with the laundry. Or started washing everything in the cold, gentle cycle. I could not assign anyone else to do my writing and editing, however. For that, I needed the letters on the computer page and in the pages of books and newspapers to be sharp and clear. The doctor suggested I start with readers, so I bought a pair of plastic frames with a helpful level of magnification. I consoled myself with the idea that they made me look more writerly.

The other health concern on my mind was heavier and less easily addressed. But I resolved that in 2011, I would seek an answer to a question that lurked in the dark corners of my mind while I focused on travel stories and parenting columns and band history: Had I inherited a genetic mutation that greatly increased my risk of developing breast and ovarian cancer?

The "Yes" chances were 50/50—I had known this since 2005. That's when my mom—then a ten-year ovarian cancer survivor—learned she had a BRCA1 mutation, which she'd likely inherited from her father, who likely inherited it from his Irish mother, who died of breast cancer. That's also when I learned that an estimated 750,000 Americans had a mutation of the BRCA1 or BRCA2 gene, which accounted for the majority of hereditary breast and ovarian cancers (and about five to ten percent of all breast and ovarian cancers).

I got tested in March 2010, but my blood sample was thrown out due to a paperwork mix-up, so I redid the test in January of 2011. While I was in test limbo, Steve and Louisa were cast in another play, and I jumped at the chance to go to San Francisco with friends for four days. The day after I returned, the genetic counselor called with the report: I had the dreaded mutation. My stomach dropped. I'd come to expect that answer, but it was not what I wanted to hear.

"The risk was there before you took the test, and now you can do something about it," she said.

My airway felt clogged. "It's good to finally know," I managed to say, my voice quavering.

She said it was OK to feel sad, and she reminded me that many options existed to reduce my risks, options not available to my aunts or my mom.

"You're in the generation creating the change in mindset. It will be easier for your kids, and for your nieces and nephews," she said.

Ah, yes. It was one of the reasons I'd wanted to know. Did my kids have it? They each had a 50/50 chance. I thanked the counselor, got off the phone, and spent an hour crying so hard that my nose dripped and my eyes turned red. I wanted to tell Mom, but I was afraid I'd start crying again. So I wrote to her instead:

Hi, Mom. I love you and I'm proud to be your daughter. I hope

I have inherited your strength, because I learned about an hour ago that I have the BRCA1 mutation, too.

I had a nice talk with the genetic counselor. She told me it was OK to be sad about it for a while, but that in the long term it's great to know, especially at my young (!) age. There are so many things they can do now, things that weren't known or available for you and your sisters.

I am glad I know, for me and for the kids, especially Louisa. I've always operated under the assumption that I had it, but it feels a little different to get confirmation of it. I'll just let the news sink in for the next few days, and then I'll think about future steps … Might get rid of those ovaries—don't need 'em anymore, anyway. :)

I am sorry to deliver less than happy news on this snowy Monday. I did have a great time in San Francisco!

Love, Joy

Mom wrote back:

I don't quite know how to respond. In my mind you did not have the BRCA1 mutation. I do know that you will be able to deal with it—you have tons of strength that you don't even realize you have! I believe the genetic counselor is right—so much has changed since Mary and Marge and even I were diagnosed. Lots of progress has been made.

Have some chocolate. Hug your puppy!

I love you—so sorry to pass on the stupid mutation!

Bisous, Maman

I told Steve the news, but I decided not to tell the kids until I knew what I planned to do with the knowledge. While I sorted it out in my head, I threw myself into writing. I signed up for two writing classes and embarked upon a long-overdue project to organize my research files.

In early March I drove to Mankato for another travel story. I was excited to explore the city. I felt like I had lived there in a past life, thanks to the Betsy-Tacy books by Mankato author Maud Hart Lovelace. Mom introduced me to the series when I was in elementary school, and I fell in reader-love with the character of Betsy, who had pigtails, like me, and wanted to be a writer, like me. The books progress through time, as Betsy and her friends grow from little girls into young women in early 1900s Mankato (called Deep Valley in the books).

When I paged through my set of the books before the trip, I realized the years depicted in the first eight books, 1898–1910, coincided with G. Oliver's first stint in Crookston. Maud's stories included details about how children played and dressed, and they gave me a new perspective on what everyday life had been like for my grandfather and his siblings.

The next day, I tried to see Mankato through Maud's eyes. So-called improvements over the decades had destroyed or disfigured buildings that once graced the downtown. But the two places I most wanted to see, the houses where Betsy (Maud), and her best friend Tacy (Frances Kinney) lived, had been preserved by the Betsy-Tacy Society. I'd have to return with my mom in the summer so we could sit on the bench at the end of Hill Street and have a picnic.

Such idle thoughts were dashed a few days later when I received bad news from my parents. They had taken a lengthy vacation with friends on the west coast of Mexico, and while they were there, one of their friends had died of a heart attack, and a tsunami warning had delayed their return home.

A few days after they arrived in Minnesota, Dad sent me an email. "Nana and I are overwhelmed [he wrote] by the events of the last few days. This morning has not been easy. It had been one of our best trips … Both of us know that it could have been one of us. So we are reviewing what we have learned again about unexpected death. It probably means that I really do have to deal with the treasures in the garage."

He told me the positive news of the day was receiving the latest issue of *Minnesota Parent*, which contained my column about camp, a subject close to his heart. Dad's job as a summer camp counselor helped him pay for his college tuition and books.

He concluded: "The pay/costs picture has changed but the life skills I learned are getting me through this latest round of helping all of our friends and ourselves through this loss. Nana learned them even better in both English and Spanish! It will be a tough week."

A spark of Mom's humor emerged a few weeks later. She and her friend Kathy had become legendary figures in Alexandria: a story of their ride in a motorboat during the emergency in Mexico had been transformed, as stories often are in small towns, and people now believed the two petite women had rowed a boat all the way from Yelapa to Puerto Vallarta.

"Someone told my haircut lady," she wrote, "that it didn't surprise her because Anne Riggs is the queen of kayakers in Douglas County. Well, should I dispel that rumor, or go with it? We have to laugh a little to get through this all!"

That same week, I inserted myself into a smaller-scale crisis: the fate of the school district's orchestra program. A proposal before the school board called for eliminating the elementary orchestra teacher position. Although the superintendent recommended that the board cut other areas instead, the proposal raised concerns among many parents and students.

I spoke up for the program at a school board meeting, and the next day I wrote a blog post and emailed it to the superintendent and the school board. The core argument of "My Musical Manifesto" asserted: "Music belongs in the public schools, especially at a time when instruction is so focused on testing. All students should have the chance to pursue a passion for music—whether it's through band, orchestra or choir programs—regardless of gender, race and income level. It makes them better students and better people. It makes our communities better places to live. If a school district loses its commitment to educating students in the arts, it loses its soul."

A week later, families packed the high school gymnasium for the annual all-district orchestra concert. Students in grades four through twelve participated, including Sebastian on viola and his cousins Hannah on cello and Franny on violin. Steve's parents came from Iowa to see their three grandchildren perform. The concert concluded with all 271 musicians performing an excerpt from Tchaikovsky's *1812 Overture*.

Three weeks later, the school board voted to keep the elementary orchestra program intact. I wrote a follow-up blog post about the decision, and my uncle Bob responded, "I think they are just trying to string you along for another year!"

His pun made me laugh, and it raised a good point. Northfield was an above-average community when it came to supporting the arts, but it was unwise to take that support for granted. As the parent of three student musicians and the great-granddaughter of a music man, I could advocate for music education. My voice, and my writing, could make a difference.

Before I took on another cause, though, I needed to focus on my health. My parents' experience in Mexico showed me how quickly the ground could shift. I wanted to increase my odds of being in the concert audience for many years to come.

20

RHYTHM IS OUR BUSINESS

In the fall of 1931, commodity prices plunged, banks continued to fail, and the number of unemployed Americans kept rising. Nothing President Herbert Hoover did seemed to help—not even his $49 million dam project on the border of Nevada and Arizona that provided thousands of jobs. He became the butt of jokes. If you pulled your pants pockets inside-out, showing a lack of cash, you waved your "Hoover flag." When the soles of your shoes wore out, you replaced them with pieces of cardboard called "Hoover leather." Millions of homeless families lived in shantytowns known as Hoovervilles.[1]

In St. Cloud, officials anticipated that more than four hundred families and three hundred single men would need help from the city's poor fund that winter.[2]

Despite the economic conditions, G. Oliver reorganized the senior boys' band, formed a new beginners' band, and started an eighty-five-piece marching band—a decision that may have been influenced by the fact that the rival band at Tech High School marched in parades. Music seemed to buoy residents' spirits, and the city received a dose of excitement in September when the world-famous US Army band, "Pershing's Own," stopped in St. Cloud.

More than a thousand residents gathered at the Northern

Pacific depot on September 7 to greet the forty-piece band and its director, W. J. Stannard. The St. Cloud Boys' Band and a police escort led the touring musicians to the Breen Hotel for an official welcome. The Army band presented an afternoon concert for hundreds of schoolchildren, and it returned to the junior high auditorium for an evening concert, which the newspaper billed as "one of the outstanding musical events in the city's history."[3]

Stannard directed the St. Cloud boys in the first number, "The Montana National Guard March," and G. Oliver directed the Army band in "The Merchant Prince." The Army band, under Stannard's direction, then performed a dozen additional pieces.

It must have been a thrill for G. Oliver to direct a professional organization as well known as the Army Band. A post-concert newspaper article did not interview him about the experience. It did, however, scold residents who greeted the band at the depot but failed to shell out $1 per adult or 25 cents per child to attend the concert.[4]

This lack of support for a quality touring group did not bode well for an effort launched later in the month—the St. Cloud Civic Music Association—but organizers went ahead with their plans, anyway. The association aimed to bring at least three high-class music groups to St. Cloud each year. People could buy a yearly membership for $5, which guaranteed admission to at least three concerts. Only those with memberships could attend the concerts.

Fred Schilplin, publisher of the *St. Cloud Times-Journal*, said the effort would help St. Cloud maintain its prestige as the fourth-largest city in the state.

"Factories and payrolls follow things of this character," he pointed out, "such as music, schools, churches, institutions of cultural character. Such features make St. Cloud a desirable city, extending a cultural appeal to others to come here."[5]

Others cited different reasons for their support. The Rev. Roy Olson of Bethlehem Lutheran Church, for example, expressed the belief that "good music" would tend to counteract the "jazz" music that had become so popular. "It has been said," he declared, "that music is the language of the soul, and jazz is its profanity."[6]

Islea served as assistant director of the membership drive, and

208

she and G. Oliver were among the eighty-seven charter members. One St. Cloud resident bought five memberships to give to people who couldn't afford them. When the campaign ended, about four hundred and fifty memberships were sold.

The boys' band played for the St. Cloud Junior Chamber of Commerce annual meeting in early October, and it ended the month by performing for the Chamber-sponsored "St. Cloud Days," a two-day event that encouraged people to shop downtown and support local merchants.

While the American boys entertained shoppers, across the ocean, German youth also paraded in the streets. They carried flags featuring a black swastika in a white circle on a field of red. On October 31, a photo of Adolph Hitler and the flags appeared on the front page of the St. Cloud newspaper. The caption called him "the fiery young leader of Germany's nationalists."[7]

When economic conditions worsened in November, Mayor James Murphy proposed a two-pronged approach to supporting the city's poor and unemployed. Voters soundly defeated the first component—a $25,000 bond issue for city building projects, which would have provided hundreds of jobs—but he pressed forward with the second part, raising $25,000 for the poor fund. City employees like G. Oliver pledged to donate one day's salary per month for five months. Employees of the city's businesses and industries also pitched in, and by early December, the fund contained nearly $30,000.[8]

However, budget-trimming was still necessary. One casualty was the American Legion Band, which had filled a void created when the adult municipal band disbanded under Steinmetz's tenure. Now the city was no longer willing to pay the salary of Legion Band director Hubert Gans.[9]

THE BARRAGE OF UNSETTLING international and national events continued that spring; the country was gripped for months by the twists and turns of the Lindbergh baby kidnapping case, and John Philip Sousa died of a heart attack, at age seventy-seven. The balm of music again provided St. Cloud residents with some relief. The Civic Music Association concluded its first season with a concert by the St. Olaf College Choir, directed by F. Melius Christiansen, and—with Islea as co-chair—the association launched a second membership drive.

Two days after the choir concert, G. Oliver's ninety-member marching band debuted. It led a parade from downtown to the junior high auditorium, where two thousand residents listened to speeches by candidates running in the city primary elections. The city's League of Women Voters sponsored the public forum.[10]

In April, residents upset over the addition of a city golf course and the construction of a new fire station voted in a new mayor, Phil Collignon, and two new commissioners. The newly elected officials reappointed G. Oliver as city band director at a reduced salary of $250 a month (down from $300).[11]

Soon after his contract was renewed for another year, he enjoyed a weekend vacation on Lake Minnewaska in Glenwood with Islea, Ronald, and Percy's four-year-old daughter Mary Jane; they were the guests of George Landers, who had retired from his music business in Iowa and was spending the summer at the lake. At the end of the month, the Riggs family hosted Landers at their St. Cloud home, and Landers directed the boys' band in the "Star Spangled Banner" during the Memorial Day program.[12]

That fall, Percy started his second year of teaching in Manilla, Iowa, and Ronald took classes at St. Cloud Teachers College, where he played in the band and served as its assistant director. Islea continued to teach piano students and participate in local music groups.

G. Oliver took the St. Cloud Boys' Band to St. Paul on September 9 for the final day of the Minnesota State Fair. Ten years had passed since G. Oliver's trip to the fair with the Bemidji Boys' Band. His current band was not as strong musically, and because finances were tight, the St. Cloud boys didn't even stay overnight. They performed during the afternoon and evening of the fair and gave a special concert in front of the grandstand before returning home by train.[13]

In early November, three days before the election, incumbent Governor Floyd B. Olson came to St. Cloud and had dinner at the Breen Hotel.

"Olson interrupted his dinner long enough to go out and fraternize with Director G. Oliver Riggs and the band boys, who gave him a warm welcome," the newspaper reported.[14]

Later that evening, Olson delivered a two-hour speech to twenty-five hundred people at the junior high auditorium, and he endorsed Franklin D. Roosevelt for president. Both men ended up winning; Roosevelt received 472 electoral votes to Hoover's 59; and in Minnesota, Olson received 50.57 percent of the vote.

THE *ST. CLOUD DAILY TIMES* kicked off the new year with an editorial titled, "What has 1933 in store?" It expressed optimism that the worst days of the Depression had passed, and it asserted confidence in the new president's ability to bring economic relief to the nation.[15]

For G. Oliver, the new year meant a salary cut, from $250 a month to $175. The band parents association protested this action and requested a hearing. However, parents dropped that request after the commissioners met with G. Oliver and announced "Mr. Riggs was 'perfectly satisfied' with the salary reduction made in common with other city employees."[16]

Roosevelt was inaugurated in early March, and much of the local news that month focused on the new president's actions in imposing regulations on banks, taking steps toward repealing Prohibition, and establishing the Civilian Conservation Corps. But St. Cloud newspaper readers also received nearly daily updates from Germany, reporting on Hitler's consolidation of power as the new chancellor and dictator of Germany, his Nazi party's takeover of the government, his crackdown on dissenting parties, and the launching of policies curtailing the rights of Jews.

By the end of the month, despite international outcry and protests in places like London and New York, the situation in Germany grew more dire. Hitler instituted a nationwide boycott on all businesses and professional work conducted by its Jewish residents, declaring it the "beginning of a war on the entire Jewish race of the world."[17] Nobel Prize-winning physicist Albert Einstein, who had been in the United States when Hitler came to power, gave up his German citizenship. Meanwhile, on April 4, the St. Cloud Civic

Music Association welcomed the Minneapolis Symphony Orchestra and its Jewish, Hungarian-born conductor, Eugene Ormandy. It was the orchestra's first time performing in the city.

Three weeks later, shortly after Germans celebrated Hitler's 44th birthday, fifty Jews from Minnesota and neighboring states gathered in Minneapolis to discuss forming a Jewish advocacy organization. Bert Papermaster, the unofficial leader of St. Cloud's Jewish community, was named to the group's board of directors.[18]

G. Oliver devoted time that spring to organizing a regional band festival on May 21 in St. Cloud. The boys' band and the Tech band were among the twelve participating groups. Judges were Gerald Prescott, director of the University of Minnesota band (formerly of Mason City); Loren L. Maynard, director of the St. Cloud Teachers College Band; and Captain Otto Rupp, commander of the St. Cloud National Guard unit. The bands did not compete against each other, but they received performance ratings from the judges.

Festival events included a parade, a banquet, an evening concert by the St. Cloud Boys' Band, and a massed outdoor band concert. Prescott directed the 514 participants in two numbers and G. Oliver directed the final number.

"It was probably the largest band ever heard here," the *St. Cloud Times* reported.[19]

Competition between G. Oliver and Hertz continued after the festival ended. Hertz scheduled an outdoor band concert for the same day and time as a senior boys' band concert. The May 25 concert by the boys' band was at Central Park and was the opening concert of the summer season. Three miles away, the Tech high school band performed at Roosevelt school and demonstrated marching maneuvers on the playground. G. Oliver did not comment publicly on Hertz's move, but he likely had some choice words for Hertz that remained unpublished.

Both bands participated the following week in the city's Memorial Day observance at Central Park, attended by a thousand people. It marked the debut of a new city musical group, the Veterans of Foreign Wars drum corps, and it was the first public parade for the Cathedral High School Girls' Drum and Bugle Corps, which

G. Oliver directs the St. Cloud boys at the National Junior Chamber of Commerce Convention in St. Paul, June 1933.

had formed in the fall of 1932. In the keynote address, attorney Harrison Sherwood noted that the United States had fought seven major wars, each time to defend its policies, principles, or rights.

"America never has been adequately prepared for war when war was thrust upon her, [Sherwood said], and he set forth as a warning the unsettled conditions of the world today, which may at any time precipitate a war which can again involve the entire world," the *St. Cloud Times* reported. "He warned that this nation must maintain an adequate defense army and navy, not one for aggression."[20]

Despite concerns about budget-tightening, many St. Cloud residents remained advocates of the school music programs and pointed to frequent public performances as evidence of their value.

But St. Cloud residents weren't the only ones who appreciated quality band music. When the ninety-piece St. Cloud Boys' Marching Band appeared in St. Paul on June 21 for the 1933 Junior Chamber of Commerce National Convention, it impressed delegates from all over the country. The entire St. Cloud Junior Chamber membership also traveled to St. Paul for the convention, where they mingled with 900 delegates from 125 cities.[21]

Two weeks after the band's vacation in July, G. Oliver and Hertz reached an agreement over scheduling conflicts. The terms of the one-year agreement spelled out how and when boys could participate in both organizations, and which organization took priority.

For example, boys' band members could temporarily enlist in the Tech band to perform at football and basketball games, but they had to play with the boys' band whenever the two groups had conflicting performances. Also, both bandmasters agreed to consult each other before adopting any policies or taking actions that could cause misunderstandings between them.[22]

A few weeks later, G. Oliver announced plans to form an adult municipal band in the fall. The news item did not indicate whether he had discussed this idea with Hertz, who had formed an adult community orchestra earlier in the year. G. Oliver invited adult musicians to rehearse Monday evenings with the boys' band, and he said the instruction method would accommodate eight different degrees of difficulty, allowing a wide range of players to rehearse together.[23]

That week, G. Oliver asked the city commission to increase his monthly salary from $175 to $200. He reminded commissioners that he had accepted a 16 percent cut earlier, followed by a 26 percent cut, with the understanding that his pay would be restored when economic conditions improved, and he argued his salary had been cut more than that of other department heads. He also asked the commission for money to pay adult members of the marching band for their time and equipment.

The commission took the requests under advisement.[24]

IN SEPTEMBER, RONALD started a job in Farmington, Minnesota, teaching history and directing the high school band, and Percy moved back to St. Cloud to complete his degree at the St. Cloud Teachers College. Percy assisted Alf Harbo, the new director of the college band and orchestra, and he assisted G. Oliver with the boys' band. Islea hosted a birthday party for her six-year-old granddaughter Mary Jane; seven friends came to the Riggs house for cake and games. Islea and Patricia, Percy's wife, made plans to co-teach a piano class that fall for kindergarten and primary school students.

G. Oliver took the marching band back to St. Paul in September—this time with three hundred St. Cloud Eagles members—for a celebration honoring St. Paul legislator George Nordlin, president of the Eagles national organization. The band marched up Wabasha Street to the Capitol in a parade led by Nordlin and Governor Olson. The highlight for G. Oliver appeared to be leading the band up the Capitol steps.

"Playing a march up the hill is a hard task, but playing while marching up the steps is an outstanding feat. Mr. Riggs is wondering what other bands in the state have attained the same distinction," the *Times* reported.[25]

It was unclear whether this was a veiled dig at Hertz. It was true that the Tech High School band could not claim this particular feat.

Both G. Oliver and Percy took on additional responsibilities that fall as directors of newly formed pep bands. G. Oliver organized a group of thirty-one boys' band members from Cathedral High School to play at the school's football and basketball games, and Percy formed a pep band at the Teachers College.

G. Oliver spent most of December preparing the St. Cloud Boys' Band for an exciting event in January: performing for a National Junior Chamber of Commerce radio program.

The band traveled to St. Paul on January 22 and received a police escort to the St. Paul Hotel; the hotel's twelfth floor housed the KSTP studio. Percy went along as assistant director, and Ronald played clarinet in the band. The half-hour broadcast was aired live over the NBC Blue Network to thousands of listeners in more than thirty US cities, including New York, Boston, Chicago, and Detroit. It included speeches by Governor Olson and Leslie Farrington, the National Junior Chamber president. G. Oliver prepared a program of six songs. But because both Farrington and Olson spoke longer than planned, the last song was cut short.

The governor called the band the "best boys' band in the United States," and he said it "reflects the trend in youth development ... which at the present time is coming into its own because the economic adjustment necessary for the country cannot be accomplished by those people of the older schools, but rather by the youth which is now plastic and ready to adjust itself to the scale of living which present conditions demand. This youth will carry through and blend itself to the various changes which a new philosophy will decree."[26]

The next day, Congressman Harold Knutson sent G. Oliver a letter from Washington, D.C.

"My dear Mr. Riggs," Knutson wrote, "Last evening I broke a longstanding rule and sat up until midnight to hear the St. Cloud boys band, and I am happy to say to you that I was well repaid. I do not recall ever having heard a program over the air that pleased me so much ... I was both proud and thrilled to think that that splendid musical organization came from my hometown. The boys surely put St. Cloud on the map last evening. Please extend them my congratulations and thanks."[27]

G. Oliver didn't let the boys rest for long: they gave a concert for St. Cloud Teachers College students, followed by a concert at the junior high that was hosted by the public school music department (a sign, perhaps, of a detente between G. Oliver and Hertz). In March, the boys' band played before a speech by Minnesota politician and noted orator Anna Dickie Olesen. Two weeks later, G. Oliver and Hertz both planned to attend a three-day clinic for band and orchestra directors at the University of Minnesota, sponsored by the Minnesota Bandmasters Association. But G. Oliver fell ill at the last minute, and Ronald filled in for him.

Growth in the Minnesota Bandmasters Association had slowed during the Depression, and the association officers hoped the clinic would stimulate interest and membership. It featured three well-known guest directors: Harold Bachman, of Bachman's Million Dollar Band of Chicago; Glenn Bainum, of the Northwestern University Band in Evanston, Ill.; and James Gillette, of the Carleton College Symphony Band in Northfield. The clinic was such a success, officers decided to make it an annual event.

G. Oliver recovered from his illness and directed his energy toward preparing the boys' band for a major event at the end of the summer: the sixteenth annual Minnesota American Legion Convention in Duluth.

IN EARLY JUNE, Percy directed the boys' band at a rally for *St. Cloud Times* publisher Fred Schilplin, who entered the race for governor as a Democrat. Led by Bill Goblish, band members took a unanimous vote and declared Schilplin "governor of Minnesota by acclamation."[28] If Governor Olson learned of this vote, by the group he had called "the best boys band in the United States," his reaction was not printed in the *St. Cloud Times*. But the newspaper did run a letter of thanks from Schilplin, placed prominently on the front page.

Two days after the St. Cloud rally, Schilplin held rallies in Minneapolis and St. Paul, and the St. Cloud Boys' Marching Band and the Cathedral Girls' Drum and Bugle Corps accompanied him.

The excitement generated by the band wasn't enough to secure the nomination for Schilplin, however; he lost in the primary to John Regan of Mankato. Governor Olson easily won the nomination of the Farmer-Labor Party, and Martin Nelson of Austin won the Republican party nomination.

Percy graduated from the teachers college in July with a bachelor's degree in music, and he accepted a job as director of instrumental music at Riley High School in South Bend, Indiana. He planned to stay in St. Cloud through August, partly to help his father with the boys' band, and partly because his wife was due with their second child. The baby girl arrived two days before the band left for Duluth. Her parents named her Islea Anne, after her paternal grandmother.

The band's ninety members reported for duty at 4:45 a.m. on August 6. Ronald and Percy helped load equipment into the vehicles that transported the boys to Duluth, where they were among the thirty thousand convention participants. Upon arriving, the band performed at the Shrine Temple, took a boat trip on Lake Superior, and performed at the St. James Orphanage. The boys then enjoyed a few hours of free time before the Forty and Eight Torchlight Parade.[29]

The Forty and Eight was an organization of Legion members who were veterans of the Great War, and the name came from box cars used to transport troops—forty men or eight horses—in France. In a nod to this history, the parade included "box car" floats. St. Cloud's box car featured "an engine that displayed a flow of beer where the coal should have been."[30]

The evening parade featured twenty-six bands, including five American Legion bands. That day, the *Duluth Herald* called the

St. Cloud band one of the three outstanding state musical organizations in attendance, and it ran a large photo of the band and the other two groups: the Hibbing auxiliary drum corps, composed entirely of women; and the Fifth District drum corps and drill team, composed of Legionnaires from all the posts in Minneapolis.[31]

More than fifteen thousand people lined the streets of the city to hear the bands and to marvel at the colors and designs of their uniforms, amid the red glow of torchlights. The St. Cloud boys took first place as the best band. Mankato won for best men's drum corps, Aitkin for best ladies drum corps, Pelican Rapids for most comic band, and Crookston for the band with the most comic drum major. St. Cloud also won for largest delegation.

The St. Cloud band boys gave a concert at the courthouse square on the second day and marched in a three-mile parade that attracted seventy-five thousand spectators.

The *Duluth News-Tribune* said the St. Cloud band "of 92 pieces, marching nine abreast, again was a favorite," and that its appearance the previous year inspired Legion posts in other cities to organize youth marching and music units for the 1934 event.[32]

A few days later, G. Oliver and Islea went to Bemidji for a well-deserved vacation. The year had been filled with musical successes, and their St. Cloud house had been filled with the spark of a granddaughter and the excitement of a new baby's arrival. With Percy's eminent departure, they would have to readjust to being a family of two. And although G. Oliver likely had goals for the band season ahead, he would find it challenging to top the highlights of 1934.

21

BUILDING MY WINGS

Steve and I faced a parenting challenge in April of 2011 when Louisa received crushing news: she was not cast in the Northfield Arts Guild production of the musical *13*.

Louisa had experienced prior theatrical rejection, and she'd survived without too much drama. But she felt especially passionate about this show and was inconsolable for days. It didn't help that her almost thirteen-year-old brother *did* get cast. In an act of loyalty, Sebastian declared, "She can have my part." His words warmed my heart, even if Louisa didn't appreciate the gesture.

Mainly known among theater nerds, *13* was the first Broadway musical with an all-teenage cast and band (including future pop star Ariana Grande). Louisa looked older than most teens who tried out for the Northfield show, and this likely worked against her.

I considered pointing out that even G. Oliver had overcome disappointment, only to find greater success—but I doubted that would improve her mood. Fortunately, Liz Shepley, the director of the Northfield Youth Choirs, offered an alternative: Louisa could fill an open spot in the touring choir that was performing in a prestigious choral festival that summer in Oregon.

Unlike G. Oliver, Liz was warm and encouraging. She believed strongly in the organization's founding principle: All Children Can Sing, and All Children Should Sing. Louisa had not originally signed up for the tour because it conflicted with *13* rehearsals. The trip made sense for her now, and we accepted the offer.

Later that month, I met my parents in Sauk Centre, halfway between St. Cloud and Alexandria. I was combining research for a travel story and for the G. Oliver project. On my way into town, I stopped at the Sinclair Lewis interpretive center. I had passed signs for it on the freeway countless times growing up but had never visited. On display were items such as the author's writing desk, his collection of kaleidoscopes, and the maps he drew of his fictional town, Gopher Prairie. I had never read any of his novels, but on the strength of the displays I vowed to read *Main Street*—soon.

After lunch, Mom and I explored the Palmer House Hotel, while Dad visited a friend. Lewis had worked briefly at the hotel as a night clerk, and it was said to be haunted, although not by him. We also stopped at the local historical society. The executive director was out, so I left a note, asking if the archives contained a photo of the 1927 Sauk Centre boys' band.

Then my parents and I drove to the town of Melrose to interview Laverne Jung. She was the sister-in-law of Lennie, whom Dad and I had visited in D.C. a few years earlier. Laverne's husband, Richard, had played cornet in the St. Cloud Boys' Band and had died in 2006.

Laverne met us at the Meadowlark Country Club, where she tended the flower gardens. She had short, wavy brownish-gray hair, and her aqua cardigan sweater brought out the blue in her eyes. We sat at a table inside the clubhouse, and Laverne and Dad reminisced about St. Cloud's earlier days.

Richard was eleven years older than Laverne, and she didn't date him until after the war. As a Cathedral High School student, she "went with" classmate Bill Sherin, who also played cornet in the boys' band. (Apparently Laverne had a thing for cornet players.) Sherin joined the 217th Coast Artillery Band in 1941 and later joined the Air Corps. During a solo training flight in California in 1943, he died in a plane crash.

"He was one of the first Cathedral students to die in the war," Laverne recalled. "If he had lived, I would have a different last name."

She stared into space for a second, and my heart ached for the young girl she had been and the loss she had suffered.

Dad dug into his satchel and pulled out a concert program from February 11, 1940. Laverne's eyes widened as Dad pointed to Sherin's name; he was listed as a soloist. She said she used to watch the boys' band march in parades, and although she didn't know G. Oliver, she once sat next to him at the Paramount Theatre.

"Everyone in St. Cloud knew who he was. The boys really respected him," she said.

Laverne said her husband, Richard, considered himself the black sheep of his family because he didn't go into a music-related career. He served in the Navy, became a photographer, and had a studio in Melrose for twenty years.

The next day, the Sauk Centre Historical Society's director called to say she had a band photo from May 1927. She mailed me a copy, and when I shared it with my dad, he spotted the name Pullman Pederson Jr. in the caption. Dad wondered: Was this Pullman related to Lennie's friend Pullman "Tommy" Pederson?

"He has to be related, doesn't he?" I responded. "Or would it be Tommy himself—is it possible he moved to St. Cloud from Sauk Centre?"

As usual, an answer to one question led to more questions.

THAT SUMMER LOUISA went on her trip with the choir, and Steve and I spent a few weeks on a Mediterranean cruise. One week after we all returned from our travels, I cleared my throat and announced to the kids after lunch, "I have some bad news that I've been meaning to tell you."

Three pairs of eyes stared at me with concern. Their questions came on top of each other:

"Are you and Dad getting a divorce?"

"Are you having another baby?"

"Are we losing our house?"

"Are we moving?"

I had not anticipated these particular questions. If I hadn't been so nervous, I might have burst out laughing. Faced with the alternatives they presented, the actual news was not so bad.

"No, it's nothing like that. I wanted to tell you that I took a test and learned that I have a genetic mutation that makes it much more likely that I could develop breast or ovarian cancer."

Relief spread across their faces.

I took a deep breath and continued.

"I inherited the gene from Nana Riggs. And the good thing is, now that I know, there are things I can do to protect myself and reduce the chance of getting cancer. I am planning to have a surgery later this summer to remove my ovaries, which would make it almost impossible for me to get ovarian cancer."

I fast-forwarded through the speech I had rehearsed in my head to get to my last point: because they each had a 50/50 chance of inheriting the gene, they might want to get tested when they were older.

"That's all I wanted to say. I love you all very much."

"We love you too, Mom," they said in chorus. They hugged me, took their plates to the kitchen, and dashed off to their various afternoon activities.

As I placed dirty dishes into the dishwasher, I felt slightly miffed that they didn't seem more worried about me, even though I knew that was silly. The whole point was to present them with facts so they didn't fear the unknown. Knowledge was power. Besides, they had good reason not to be upset. Their maternal grandmother survived ovarian cancer and went on to run marathons, kayak across lakes, and paddle across an ocean during a tsunami, as some legends told. There was no reason to think their mom wouldn't be OK, too.

When the day arrived for the surgery, we made record time driving to the hospital; hardly anyone else was on the freeway at 5:30 a.m. A woman ushered me into the bustling pre-op area, where overhead TV monitors tracked incoming patients like airplane flights. Steve stayed with me through the pre-op procedures, and the oncologist stopped by to reassure me, "You're the healthiest person here."

I awoke a few hours later to find Steve and my best friend from high school, Maria, chatting in my recovery room. The surgery had gone well, as expected. Steve drove me home, and my parents and the kids greeted us with a sign that featured a picture of ovaries and fallopian tubes. It said, "Welcome Home, Mom! We Missed You!"

That evening we ate a meal delivered by our cruise friends Lee and Laurel, and I went to bed feeling loved and grateful.

That fall, *Northfield Patch* discontinued its use of freelance writers. For my last assignment, I covered a visit to St. Olaf College by King Harald V and Queen Sonja of Norway. A crowd of polite but enthusiastic fans waving Norwegian flags welcomed the royal couple to campus for an afternoon tour. The fun of witnessing history and the rush of filing a story on a tight deadline reminded me of my old print newspaper days. I wasn't too disappointed about losing the *Patch* gig because a few weeks later, I landed a part-time job copy editing the *Voice*, the Carleton College alumni magazine.

Steve also made a job switch. He left the Allina Clinic in Northfield after thirteen years as a family practice doctor to work for another division of Allina that managed nursing home care. Although he did not look forward to a longer commute to the south metro area, he was eager to leave behind the frantic clinic pace. Best of all, perhaps, the new job allowed plenty of time for community theater.

I didn't devote much time to G. Oliver research that fall, but a new topic of inquiry found me anyway. Dad discovered that G. Oliver once provided musical help to a group of nuns called the Benevolent Beethoven Benedictines. Dad learned this from Dick Egerman, whose family had operated the popcorn wagon in St. Cloud's Barden Park. Dick's late mother had played tuba in the group, but left the order after a short time. She later married and had eight children.

According to Dick, the nuns, "hearing of the fame and generosity of G. Oliver, approached him explaining their dedication to teaching, preaching and prayer; they expressed a need for fun and culture. Music was the answer," he wrote. "It is reported that G. Oliver agreed to teach them the rudiments of music, provided they furnish their own instruments. The nuns from capable families got instruments, and the others got to sing in the choir."

Dick said his mother left the order for three reasons: "Female tuba players were not respected on the same high level as trumpets and other horn players; Mother had no rhythm; and she did not look good in black."

I loved the mental picture of G. Oliver directing a group of nuns. If an actual picture existed, I would snap it up in an eBay second. I hoped I could find other sources to corroborate the story.

INSTEAD OF CUTTING BACK on activities as the holidays approached, I joined the board of the Northfield Fine Arts Boosters, which supported the high school's fine arts programs. I believed strongly in its new project: collecting new and used musical instruments and putting them into the hands of kids who wanted to play. If I learned one thing from my great-grandfather's directing career, it was the importance of making instruments accessible. It was step one of building a quality music education program.

Early in the new year, Dad compiled articles and photos about Percy's career and mailed them to Percy's grandchildren. He heard back almost immediately from Mary Jane's daughter Patricia. She had photos of G. Oliver and said she would send us copies. She also thought she had a photo of G. Oliver's band playing for President Roosevelt.

"Do you have that one? If not, I can try to dig it out and forward it," she wrote from Arkansas. "It is great to know both of you have taken such an interest in recording this important history of our musical ancestors for all of us to enjoy."

Mention of a Roosevelt photo puzzled me; I wasn't sure when or where that would have happened, or which Roosevelt it involved.

The second grandchild to respond was Chris Duncan, from Texas. He had a pocket watch that once belonged to Percy (who later went by Pete), and he suspected it had been G. Oliver's.

"According to the serial number of the watch, it was manufactured in 1892, long before Pete was born, but would have been an expensive watch for a man in his early 20s just starting his working career," Chris wrote. "Possibly a gift to G. O. for what would appear to be his first adult job at IWU? Either way I would be happy to see this watch somehow stay with someone in the Riggs family as it did belong to Pete, regardless of its origin."

He also sent me photos of it. It was manufactured in Illinois by Elgin and had no inscriptions.

"It was working before it got packed away for around five years, and now would need to be serviced as it only ticks for about 20 seconds if you shake it a little, then stops. If y'all would like to have it, just give me an address to send it to and I will do so," he wrote.

I thanked him for his generous offer.

"I think your guess is a good one, about G. Oliver receiving it as a gift—maybe from his parents, who were living in Illinois at the time," I responded. "Since G. Oliver gave his dad's violin to my grandfather, Ronald, it's quite possible he gave his watch to Percy (Pete). Too bad the watch can't tell us more about both of them and all their adventures."

I could hardly contain my excitement. When I told Dad, he said, "It's no wonder we keep working on this project."

Even if we didn't learn more about the watch's origins, we had forged a connection between branches of the family tree that had grown apart since Percy and Ronald died.

I had never met any of Percy's grandchildren, and I hadn't known anything about them until I started the G. Oliver project. Now, in addition to sharing great-grandparents, Chris and I shared a family mystery.

22

LET'S FACE THE MUSIC AND DANCE

During his first eighteen months in office, Franklin Delano Roosevelt transformed the federal government's role in the economy and, in some cases, tested its constitutional limits. With the help of Congress, he restored consumer confidence in banks, ended Prohibition, put more than 250,000 men to work in National Parks and Forests, provided financial assistance to one-quarter of the nation's unemployed workers, and imposed regulations on Wall Street. He reduced the likelihood of bank failures by creating the Federal Deposit Insurance Corporation, created the National Industry Recovery Act and the related National Labor Relations Board, and established the Federal Housing Administration, which provided loans for home construction and repair.

But despite these efforts to revive and strengthen the economy, the devastating effects of the Dust Bowl still posed grave challenges for US agriculture. In 1931, after decades of misguided farming practices, blizzards of black dust began blowing across the plains. By May of 1934, drought had spread to more than 75 percent of the country.[1]

In Minnesota, Governor Floyd Olson continued to advocate for farmers and workers as he campaigned for a third term; the Farmer-Labor leader believed government should be "an agent for social and economic change."[2] Olson and his two challengers traveled to St. Cloud within weeks of the November 6 election, and

226

the boys' band performed at rallies for each candidate.

First to appear was Olson. The band serenaded him in front of the Breen Hotel on October 16 and led a parade to Central Junior High, where four thousand people filled the auditorium. An amplification system was set up so people standing outside could still hear Olson's words.[3]

Ten days later, fifteen hundred people heard Republican Martin Nelson call for tax reform and criticize government control of industry; and on November 2, three thousand people welcomed Democrat John Regan.

Olson won handily, with 44.6 percent of the votes; Nelson received 33.7 percent, and Regan 16.8 percent. After declaring victory, Olson announced that he planned to push for an increase in the old age pension allowance and maternity insurance for families "where married women find it necessary to work because of inadequate family income."[4]

G. OLIVER AND ISLEA may have welcomed the pre-election excitement that fall. Their home had been quieter since Percy moved to Indiana and Ronald returned to Farmington for a second year of teaching. As band directors, both sons implemented techniques learned from observing their father, but each also adapted his style to suit his own personality; Ronald was steady and low-key, while Percy was more gregarious and driven. People undoubtedly compared them to their father, and to each other, which increased the pressure on them to succeed.

Percy's job attracted more public notice (and praise from G. Oliver) than Ronald's. Located ninety miles from Chicago, South Bend had more than 100,000 residents, and the school had 2,300 students. The Studebaker Automobile Company was a major industry, a fact that did not escape Percy's notice—the son of the Studebaker president played in Percy's band.

Farmington lacked any major industry, other than what its name implied—agriculture. It had 1,300 residents, and the school enrolled four hundred students in grades five through twelve. Farmington had five Johnson families, and of the eighty-five students in band, eight had the last name of Johnson. One of those students, a fifteen-year-old flute player named Eleanor, would later play a key role in Ronald's life.

Ronald rented a room in a house owned by Eleanor's parents, Charles and Alice. "Charlie" Johnson had emigrated to the United States from Sweden in 1889 at age nine—the year G. Oliver directed his first band in Kansas. Charlie met and married Alice Nelson in Waseca, and they moved to Farmington after the Great War. During the Depression, hungry and broke residents discovered that if they knocked on the back door of Charlie's grocery store, he would send them home with free groceries—much to his wife's dismay.

Even though Farmington was ninety-five miles from St. Cloud, G. Oliver still called upon Ronald to assist with band tasks. In mid-December of 1934, he wrote to Ronald and asked him to pick up a clarinet that had been in for repair, "as soon as convenient," and deliver it when he came to St. Cloud for Christmas.

In the same letter, G. Oliver also provided a candid assessment of the musicians he was currently working with. "My beginners band and Junior Band both doing fine," he wrote. "The remnants of last year's marching and concert band are getting worse and fewer in numbers." He signed the letter, "Father G. Oliver Riggs."[5]

That winter he scheduled three performances for the junior band in February: a concert of "popular music" for hundreds of farm boys and girls at the annual seed show; a performance at the Cathedral High School boys' basketball game; and a "complimentary" concert for all the Catholic nuns in the area.

March was a busy month for his seventy-five-member concert band. It gave two concerts at the Paramount Theatre on March 10, scheduled before and after the movie *David Copperfield*. An estimated five thousand people, including two thousand children, attended the afternoon performance, which featured a cornet duet by Bill Goblish and Howard Pramann. A newspaper review said: "Persons who heard these concerts heard the group at its best. It was one of the finest programs played for the people of St. Cloud."[6]

G. Oliver received more positive press when he was profiled in that month's Chicago-based *Educational Music Magazine*. It noted he had "50 years successful experience with bands, 23 of which have been with boys' bands," and it included his quote: "I tell my boys that the only way to win success is by hard work and thorough preparation."

The article also said G. Oliver had inspired many men to become directors of successful school bands and orchestras, including "his son, H. P. Riggs, now 31, who plays on as many instruments as any man known and who is the clever and noted bandmaster of the Riley Junior-Senior High School in South Bend, Indiana."[7]

The article did not mention Ronald. It concluded: "St. Cloud acknowledges the success of their bandmaster as due to his promptness, sincerity, determination and frankness, and know him to be a firm believer in the old adage: 'Anything worth doing at all is worth doing well.'"[8]

Bill Goblish, a cornet soloist with the boys' band in the 1930s.

G. Oliver announced the following month that he planned to organize a new beginners band in the fall, and he encouraged boys to enroll only if they possessed musical talent and had a B minus or better average in school.[9]

The St. Cloud newspaper mentioned Percy again at the start of the summer, when he and his family came to Minnesota on vacation. The story explained that in his first year, Percy expanded the school band from thirty to one hundred members, it won first prize out of twenty-five bands at a festival in Michigan, and it performed at two Notre Dame football games.[10]

The newspaper also ran an editorial that summer about G. Oliver and the land he owned between Bemidji and International Falls. It explained that G. Oliver had considered abandoning the land during the Depression, when a Swedish man and his three sons made him an offer: they would pay "in muscle" to rent the land. "It was a mutual effort to give these men a chance to keep off the relief rolls, and in time to bring some compensation to the owner. They had a pair of horses, and a cow or two. There were only trails, and what milk they sold had to be carried on the back of one of the men to the nearest settlement," the editorial said.

"The three-year lease expired last fall, and far from being discouraged they asked for another three-year lease, and purchased 40 of the cleared acres at $20 an acre, to be paid partly in work on the other acres. From this 40 acres last year they raised crops that brought them $900. Today they have a good herd of stock, hogs and poultry, and are going ahead with thrift and energy. In a few years, they will each have a fine farm. Mr. Riggs will receive compensation for his long years of waiting and his kindly spirit in giving these men a chance. What these four men did others can do if they have the same spirit of self helpfulness."[11]

IN DECEMBER, PERCY's band achieved another honor: it played for President Roosevelt. The President arrived at the South Bend train station on the morning of December 9, and his motorcade drove down Michigan Street, which was festooned with flags. Percy's band was one of several ensembles stationed along the route to the University of Notre Dame, where nine thousand people gathered to hear Roosevelt speak.[12] The experience must have given Percy something to talk about over the holidays. It also may have caused G. Oliver to reflect upon his own experience thirty-six years earlier of performing for President McKinley.

G. Oliver's band boys maintained a full schedule before Christmas, amid apparent rumblings about his job security. No specific complaints from parents or city leaders were reported in the newspaper; however, at a December 17 band rehearsal, the boys adopted a resolution: "We, the members of the St. Cloud Municipal Boys band, wish to express our deep gratitude and appreciation to our band director, Mr. Riggs, for all the capable instruction he has rendered us in the past. We feel that he has been the nucleus of our success as a band, and we sincerely hope that our organization will be untouched by any political action and that Mr. Riggs will always remain our leader and instructor."

The newspaper article about the situation said, "The boys expressed their desire to cooperate with Mr. Riggs in every respect in order to make it easier for him and the entire band. After the discussion, Mr. Riggs stated that he has a great pride in all his band members, and he expressed a word of thanks to each and every one. A short and informal social meeting followed."[13]

After Christmas, G. Oliver wrote to his architect friend Bert Keck, who had moved to Florida. G. Oliver said he expected to retire in five years, when he turned seventy.[14]

IN EARLY 1936, G. Oliver called a meeting of band parents to discuss a proposal: he believed St. Cloud needed to build a new band rehearsal hall. One reason such a facility was necessary, he explained, was that students were not practicing enough at home.

"The present day boy or girl, it seems to me, does not wish to practice at home, and most parents do not care, or are too busy at something else to see that the child does practice daily. There cannot be anything of any merit accomplished without work. This holds good in learning to play a musical instrument," he said. "Considering it as a fact that these young people of today, who are members of our bands and orchestras, cannot, or will not practice at home enough to get good fundamentals and advance enough to have a fairly good command of technique ...the only way I see for us to make further advancement in this wonderful work is for the teachers to have facilities where supervision of personal practice may be given by the teacher or an assistant."[15]

He had toured school and municipal music facilities in four states the previous fall to get ideas, and he recommended building a sixty-foot by sixty-foot facility that would contain a large rehearsal room, offices, several small rehearsal rooms, a restroom, and a music library. It could be located on city property near Tech High School, he said, where it would be accessible to all schools and the municipal band.

"The study of music is here to stay ... we should keep abreast of this great movement and encourage its continued success and advancement. I believe we should think more about developing the young mind to do more good, clean thinking with the understanding that by diligent work and sensible living only, good results can be obtained," he said.[16]

Parents formed a committee to work with G. Oliver on the proposal. The next month, the *St. Cloud Times* extolled the lifelong benefits of teaching music to youth and advocated for a new facility that could serve as a rehearsal hall and bandstand.[17]

The day after the editorial ran, the city commission discussed remodeling the unoccupied Unitarian Church, which the city purchased in January. Plans called for converting the main floor into a municipal auditorium and using other rooms for a library expansion. The proposal did not include using the space as a band headquarters.[18] However, that option continued to percolate among some residents.

In February, when the temperatures hovered at 25 degrees below zero for several days, causing water pipes to freeze across the city, G. Oliver took the extraordinary step of canceling two rehearsals. But the weather didn't prevent the band boys from performing for one thousand visiting grocers, and it didn't keep eighty high school musicians from traveling to St. Cloud for a two-day band festival that received extensive newspaper coverage.

G. Oliver's nemesis, Tech band director Erwin Hertz, organized the festival, with the assistance of a newly formed parent group, the Music Boosters of the St. Cloud Public Schools. The musicians came from eleven nearby towns, and they attended a clinic led by Gerald Prescott, the University of Minnesota band director.[19]

Another St. Cloud music ensemble that received press coverage that month was the St. Cloud Cathedral Girls' Drum and Bugle Corps. Six hundred people braved the weather to attend a fundraiser at the Breen Hotel to raise money for equipment for the girls' group. At the end of the month, the girls' group and the boys' band traveled together to Brainerd—along with five figure skaters and the college hockey team—to represent St. Cloud at the Paul Bunyan Winter Carnival.

That spring the older boys presented afternoon and evening concerts at the Paramount Theatre, featuring soloists Bill Goblish on cornet and Tommy Pederson on trombone. The newspaper said, "It was as fine an appearance as the band has made in its long history, and the audience appreciated the fine entertainment given them by the group. They are musicians."[20]

Not to be left out, Islea received newspaper coverage for her talk about Polish pianist and composer Ignacy Jan Paderewski. The first talk was so well received by the Music and Drama Club, she repeated it for the Reading Room Society. Islea reviewed the book *Paderewski: The Story of A Modern Immortal* by Charles Phillips, and performed a few Paderewski pieces. At the end of her talk, she quoted from the book:

"In a story Paderewski's one truth is surely brought home: that art is life; that the artist, be he musician, painter, writer, sculptor, is not remote from life nor antagonist to it, but a living and illuminating part of it. Better still we learn another truth, that life itself is an art, a fine art which we all may practice, in which every one of us may perfect ourselves no matter what our work or our station may be."[21]

G. Oliver traveled to Ronald's school in Farmington in April to serve as guest director at the third annual Mississippi Valley League Festival. It featured 250 musicians from the six schools in the conference, and Ronald was one of the organizers. The bands and choral groups performed separately that afternoon, and in the evening they performed as massed groups. Both concerts featured a solo by cornetist Louise Schmidt of Red Wing, daughter of the first Minnesota Bandmasters Association president. She had wowed audiences eleven years earlier during the bandmasters convention in St. Cloud. Now a high school student, she had recently won an amateur contest sponsored by the *Minneapolis Journal* and the KSTP radio station.

The Farmington newspaper reported, "There was no competition between schools, no prizes; hence all the schools went home feeling they had gained—and not lost—something. We who attended the grand festival caught the spirit of cooperation from the young artists, and we came away with a feeling that it was fine and good to have been there."[22]

A few days later, St. Cloud Mayor Phil Collignon and Commissioner of Streets Nat Fish were reelected. After the swearing-in ceremony, the new commission reappointed all city officers at their current salaries, including G. Oliver as municipal band director.

At the end of April, fifteen thousand people gathered downtown to mark the end of an era: a bus line was replacing the thirty-year-old streetcar system. The St. Cloud Boys' band led a mammoth parade on the last day of streetcar service. Other participating groups were the Cathedral Girls' Drum and Bugle Corps, the St. Cloud Tech band, the Teachers College band, and the six-member Old Heidelberger Little German Band.[23] Although his band led the parade, G. Oliver may have felt the pressure of the other ensembles following closely on his heels.

THE ST. CLOUD MUNICIPAL Boys' Band opened its summer concert season with a twist; G. Oliver invited the St. John's University Band, which contained many boys' band graduates, to play in Central Park on May 28. In exchange, the boys' band would hold a concert at the university later in the fall.

Because the number of band members exceeded the performance space in most parks, G. Oliver kept them divided into two groups: the seventy-five-member concert division, made up of older, more experienced boys; and the ninety-five-member junior group. But the entire band led the Memorial Day parade on May 30. G. Oliver felt so strongly about the boys participating in Memorial Day activities, he required 100 percent attendance, with no excuses granted.

Ronald stayed in Farmington in June and July to direct the high school band. It was his last hurrah with that ensemble, which had grown from forty-two to eighty-eight members under his tenure. He had accepted a job teaching history and directing the band at Lincoln High School in Thief River Falls, a town seventy miles south of the Canadian border.[24]

Granddaughter Mary Jane spent most of the summer visiting G. Oliver and Islea. Her parents and sister arrived in late July, and G. Oliver invited Percy to co-direct a band concert in Central Park. The concert included "Bride of the Waves" performed on trombone by fifteen-year-old Tommy Pederson. The St. Cloud newspaper printed a lengthy review of the concert accompanied by photos of Percy and G. Oliver.

"Pederson can entertain that audience anytime he wants to," the St. Cloud newspaper reported. "Perhaps he knew what his director expected of him, and he proceeded to produce. Mr. Riggs believes Pederson is the best trombone solo player in a far reaching area.

Percy Riggs, commenting on this solo and the playing of it, said he had heard high school champions who could not have presented this cornet solo on a trombone."

Percy, who directed the concert's second half, "paid a tribute to his father, declaring the band to be especially alert and rapid at sight reading ... One good turn deserves another, so the elder Riggs made some comments about his conductor son. He has shown vast improvement, he said, as a director and conductor during his two years of experience in the South Bend school.

Pullman "Tommy" Pederson wowed St. Cloud audiences as a teenager and later became a famous Hollywood trombonist.

His conducting of the band in the second part of the program indicated that he is 'at or near the top' as a band conductor, and he either has improved, or he has been up for some time,"[25] the newspaper article said.

After the concert, G. Oliver wrote a note to Ronald on the back of a concert program: "Your turn is next so get ready. We expect you soon."[26]

Two weeks later, Ronald co-directed the concert boys' band at East Side Park. A brief article noted that Ronald was directing the program's second half, but the newspaper did not run a story afterward or a photo of Ronald.

The junior boys' band concluded the summer by participating in the American Legion state convention parade in Brainerd. The ninety-five-member junior band traveled to the event with the Cathedral Girls' Drum Corps, and G. Oliver said afterward that he was pleased with the how the younger boys performed in "their first big assignment."[27]

Governor Olson had been scheduled to appear at the American

Legion convention, but instead he went to Rochester to receive treatment for severe abdominal pain. He died in the hospital on August 22 at age forty-four. (It later was revealed he had pancreatic cancer).

President Roosevelt said the country lost "a personality of singular force and courage," and the *St. Cloud Times* said, "he might have been president, the second Minnesota man with that possibility, both to be cut down in the prime of life—John A. Johnson and Floyd B. Olson. In his passing we pay him sincere tribute as a man of great ability, courage and personal charm."[28]

A week later, Ronald started his job in Thief River Falls. He continued to correspond with Eleanor Johnson, who was finishing her senior year of high school. Eleanor played flute in the band, but piano was her passion, and she was taking lessons at St. Olaf College that fall.

Islea approved of the deepening relationship between Ronald and Eleanor, despite their difference in age. In October, while G. Oliver was in northern Minnesota with Ronald, Islea wrote to Eleanor:

I have been intending to write to you for some time—but the days go by so fast—of course I am busy with my many duties. I think about you, though, and would be glad to hear from you.

Ronald tells me that you are carrying quite a heavy program at school and with your piano practice—so I know you are busy too.

This has been a beautiful day—a quiet one for me, as I've been alone—and have passed the day practicing for an hour this morning—then to church—back home for a dinner alone—a nap—and to a show this afternoon. I saw "The General Died at Dawn"—and did not care for it. I kept wishing dawn would come, so I could leave! That is not my type of picture.

I expect Ronald and his father have had a nice time at the lake—they were to spend yesterday at the farm. I hope Ronald was able to sell his hay—but perhaps he will have to hold it till the price gets better. Isn't his car radio nice? I am so glad he has it—it helps a lot on his long drive.

I notice by a little item in the St. C. paper that Sup't Bye has announced to his school board that there are 122 enrolled

*in Band work. That seems rather a large number for Ronald to
instruct—but perhaps he can get time to do it. I am confident
that he can make good—if anyone can, aren't you?*

Islea mentioned upcoming trips to Crookston, and to Minneapolis, where three of her piano students were competing in the
state music teachers' contest. She closed the letter:

*My love to you, Eleanor, and do write me. I'll be very glad to hear
from you.*
    I am
    Yours Sincerely,
    Islea G. Riggs[29]

Two weeks later, President Roosevelt was reelected, and Elmer
Benson was elected governor of Minnesota. Islea's piano students
advanced to the state finals but did not place in the top ten.

Ronald spent Thanksgiving with his parents, where, according
to his mother, he "rested a lot, and listened to the radio." The holiday fell on G. Oliver's sixty-sixth birthday, and Islea cooked a huge
turkey. After Ronald left for Thief River Falls, Islea wrote another
letter to Eleanor:

*… I always hate to see him go—especially when I know there
is such a long drive ahead of him. It would be nice if he were
nearer, wouldn't it?*
    *I had such a good time in Crookston—it was the first real
visit I'd had there since we left in 1918. Many of my old friends
are gone—but many are left—and they were so very nice to me.
I had several nice trips—one to Grand Forks, and one to Thief
River Falls. It was nice to see where Ronald was teaching—and
to get a glimpse of the house where he lives. Thief River Falls is
such a nice town—it does not look much like the little country
place it was when I played there years ago.*
    *My three pupils who won the right to play in the finals at
the University on Nov. 7th did not get a place in the finals,
altho their grades were very good. They all say that they wish
to try again next year—and perhaps I'll let them—altho much*

depends on what the contest pieces are, and how well they work. ... There were 22 in each division—and only 10 could pass. These 10 are to play in a Piano ensemble—10 pianos—under Percy Grainger's direction at the Music Teachers Convention in Dec.

We had a lot of fun in Minneapolis that day—it was the day of the Homecoming game, so there was a big crowd—and the girls were all so thrilled to be there.

We are hoping very much, Eleanor, that you and your mother will come to visit us a few days during the holidays. It would be so nice to have you here and we would try to show you a good time. Ronald is counting on it. Won't you try to come? I shall write to your mother soon. Ronald can drive down for you and take you back.

It is nice to hear about your Piano study—you are doing some nice work and I am sure that you have a good teacher and will improve a lot. Ronald tells me you are doing the Moonlight Sonata. It's a fine one—lots of hand work in the last movement.

I am still working on the Bach Chromatic Fantasie & Fugue—but get so little time for practice.... I am getting ready to have a Pupils Recital here in about 2 weeks. Will have my usual Christmas treat for the youngsters—candy and pop-corn balls. I ask the mothers, too, and have a lunch for them so it makes a little extra work.

Ronald tells me you are having a birthday this week. I am wishing it may be a happy one for you and that you will have many more of them!

You will try to arrange to make us that visit won't you? It will be something to look forward to.

Give your mother my kindest regards.

Love to you, and a happy birthday—

Your Sincere Friend
Islea G. Riggs[30]

Ronald came home to assist his father with a band rehearsal on December 23, and the younger Riggs introduced the boys to five challenging pieces chosen as contest numbers by the Minnesota Public School Music League. The band boys expected to see G. Oliver again a few days after Christmas, which fell on a Friday. But on December 29, they learned that their bandmaster was hospitalized after a "rather sudden attack of illness."[31]

As city residents said goodbye to 1936, it remained unclear how much G. Oliver's illness would affect his ability to lead the band in the new year.

23

FINDING TED

In January of 2012, Elias became a vegetarian. It wasn't a huge surprise, since he had never been fond of meat. He would occasionally eat a cheeseburger or a handful of chicken nuggets—which weren't really meat anyway, let's be honest—but he had never liked pork, fish, or seafood. What did surprise me was the catalyst for his decision: the unlikely duo of long-dead author Upton Sinclair and modern documentary filmmaker Morgan Spurlock.

Louisa was reading Sinclair's *The Jungle* in English class, and Sebastian was watching the movie *Super Size Me* in health, which meant our dinner conversations that month covered everything from slaughterhouse conditions in the early 1900s to America's obesity epidemic.

When I asked Elias about his decision, he said he liked animals and didn't want to eat them, and he thought being a vegetarian would be healthier. He was eleven and was exploring his identity as someone different from his siblings, who were not easy acts to follow. I didn't try to talk him out of it; I only asked that he explore culinary possibilities beyond buttered spaghetti—because being a "noodle-tarian" was not a thing.

Elias still took piano lessons, but he disliked practicing. As I pondered how to encourage Elias to practice without nagging him, I thought back to my own piano days. My teacher for nine years, Beverly Rolfsrud, was a combination of G. Oliver and Islea.

She was strict, but she also loved dogs, and her Saint Bernard would often hang out in the studio during my half-hour lessons.

I was scared of disappointing Mrs. Rolfsrud, especially when I hadn't practiced enough and knew she would be able to tell. She liked me, though, and under her tutelage I competed for several years in the state piano contest, the same one Islea's students once entered. When I was Elias's age, I reached the pinnacle and performed on a grand piano at the University of Minnesota's Northrup Auditorium.

Elias didn't seem to be motivated by competition, but he might be open to performing at a "house party," like the ones G. Oliver and Islea once attended. Newspaper descriptions of those events made them sound delightful:

"Miss Islea Graham gave a party and musical entertainment at the home of her parents, Mr. and Mrs. W. N. Graham, last evening. It was one of the finest affairs of the kind ever in the city. The musical program was of exceptional merit and was a real treat to lovers of fine music. Miss Florence B. Wright of Burlington and Prof. G. O. Riggs of Mt. Pleasant, Iowa, the eminent violinist, contributed to the enjoyment of the evening. There was a large attendance of Aledo's most fashionable people."[1]

I proposed my idea to Elias: we'd host a party and encourage guests to play an instrument, sing a song, or read a poem or essay. When he didn't object, I invited two families we knew to join us for the first-ever My Musical Family recital.

At the start of the evening, once everyone had gathered in our living room, I announced that "G. Oliver used to do this kind of thing all the time, back at the turn of the last century—that's what people did. They'd get together and they'd play their instruments and they'd sing and read poetry. Tonight, people are welcome to do anything they'd like to do, and there is no pressure to do anything at all."

Steve interjected, "There's a little pressure.'"

Everyone laughed.

"So, who would like to go first?" I asked.

Elias stood up, driven by enthusiasm or possibly a desire to get it over with quickly. "I'm going to be playing a song called 'Andante,'" he announced.

He walked over to the piano in our adjacent dining room and played the two-minute piece, and everyone applauded. The recital was launched.

An hour later, we had enjoyed solo and group performances on instruments that included guitar, mandolin, trombone, ukulele, and violin; one poetry reading; and a demonstration speech on how to make a clothespin catapult. After the recital, we dined on two types of chili (one vegetarian and one with meat), salad with roasted pears, homemade soda bread, and for dessert, ice cream sundaes and French macarons. My friend Myrna made a special flavor of macarons, black licorice, and arranged them on the plate to look like music notes on a staff.

I considered the event a success, especially when Myrna told me the next day it inspired her kids to start playing the ukulele.

A few weeks later, I received the pocket watch in the mail from my cousin Chris in Texas. The heirloom timepiece fit snugly in my palm. I pried open the case and peered at the dial; the thin black hands had stopped at twenty-two minutes to six.

"Hopefully you have a local watch repair person that knows about 150-year-old watches," Chris wrote. "If I remember correctly the watch kept almost perfect time."

Steve had the next day off from work, and he and I took Sebastian out of school to attend a talk by Shelton Johnson, a National Park ranger who spent fifteen years telling the story of the Buffalo Soldiers who once worked at Yosemite and Sequoia National Parks.

The story of these African American soldiers had nearly been lost. Now Johnson was using it to address a greater cause—getting more African Americans to visit and feel connected to the parks. He even convinced Oprah to go camping, he explained.

During his talk I jotted down several themes that related to my own investigations: You know the people you came from enabled you to become who you are; What happens if you don't tell your story? Your story disappears; Stories aren't just stories. Stories can change the world; Don't let the people who came before you ever be forgotten.

In late February an envelope arrived in my mailbox addressed to G. Oliver. What a surprise! It was from Google. Either the ubiquitous technology company was not as omniscient as some people feared, or it knew something I didn't. Since my great-grandfather had been dead for sixty-six years, I took the liberty of opening his mail.

The form letter offered $100 in free advertising to "help promote" G. Oliver's small business.

"You might be surprised at the number of people who are searching Google for exactly what you have to offer," it said.

I laughed out loud. Yes, he would be quite surprised. Perhaps Google would consider hiring him as a pitchman. He had extensive public relations experience, and the right initial.

A few days later, I started working on a new G. Oliver presentation. Lynn Ellsworth, the archivist at Iowa Wesleyan, had invited Dad and me to participate in the college's Friends of the Harlan-Lincoln House historical lecture series. Although she couldn't provide a speaker stipend, she offered a free two-night stay at the Van Vorhies Haus, a Victorian home that had been converted into an assisted living facility.

"The Van Vorhies Haus was originally the Beckwith home. Jessie Lincoln, daughter of Robert Todd Lincoln and Mary Harlan Lincoln, scandalously eloped with Warren Beckwith Jr., who grew up in the home," Lynn explained. "It was also a retirement home until 10 or 15 years ago when it was sold to the present owners."

It sounded intriguing, and I accepted.

With the name Warren Beckwith in my short-term memory, I prepped for my talk by sifting through programs and clippings from G. Oliver's Iowa Wesleyan days, and I made a startling discovery: listed among the members of the 1893 Cadet Band was a W. Beckwith on snare drum.

Did Jessie Lincoln's sweetheart play in G. Oliver's band? The question tantalized me. I became more convinced it was true after I read about Beckwith's background and his ill-fated marriage to Jessie in 1897. I told Dad about the discovery, and I emailed Lynn. She responded that, indeed, Beckwith studied at the college during G. Oliver's tenure, between 1890 and 1895, and he was listed in the conservatory band of 1893.

I made one other discovery before the Iowa trip that had nothing to do with Beckwith. It did relate to Google, though. A woman from New Jersey emailed me about a blog post I wrote in 2010 that included names of the Crookston Juvenile Band members.

"I was Googling my family name and found your music blog with the Crookston band, and there are my great-grandfather, Ole Fylling, and my great-uncle, Pete Fylling. How fun!" Marni Fylling wrote. "Pete played/sang for years with the Anson Weeks big band in San Francisco in the '30s. My dad was born in Crookston, and was a musician his whole life. My grandfather worked at St. Olaf in Northfield for a while, and my sister went to college there."

She concluded, "The internet is a strange and amazing place. Thanks for posting this."

I did a quick online search for the Anson Weeks band and examined the Crookston band photo before responding.

"Hi, Marni. That is so great! I listed all those Crookston band members for that very reason, so their relatives could find them. How neat to know that your great uncle continued in music—playing with the Anson Weeks Band must have been quite an adventure. What instrument did your dad play, and what did your grandfather do at St. Olaf?

I continued, "It looks like your great uncle is standing next to my great uncle, Percy, in the photo, and your grandfather is not quite in the version of the photo that I posted on the blog. I could make a better copy of the entire photo and send it to you, if you'd like one. Let me know!"

Marni responded that she would like a copy. (I discovered later that the Ole Fylling in the photo was not Marni's great-grandfather, but another relative named Ole.)

"My grandfather went to St. Olaf for college," she wrote. "He was a student conductor at one point, and received a beautiful baton that we still have. My dad played trumpet in the Navy band, and played trumpet and upright bass in some of his own bands, but mostly he played piano. He really considered himself a composer, but played piano for a living—jazz as a young man, then popular music in the 70s and 80s (just because that's what people wanted); then played jazz up until his death three years ago."

She concluded, "Having music in the family is truly a gift. As much as I miss my dad, it's amazing how much of him is still here in his recordings, and we'll always have that music. Thanks again!"

Because I was traveling to Iowa, I pitched two new travel story ideas to the *Star Tribune,* on Des Moines and Iowa City. The editors approved them, so I added those stops to my itinerary. I drove to Des Moines on March 24 and spent the night at the eleven-story Renaissance Des Moines Savery Hotel. It was built in 1919 and was on the National Register of Historic Places, but I chose it for two other reasons: it was where Junior the bear stayed in 1931, and it was where Steve and I stayed the night after our wedding in 1993.

It was Steve's only regret about our wedding (or so he said): he decided to cut costs by getting a deal on the hotel room. He hadn't anticipated that the room would be dark, cramped and unromantic, and he hadn't realized that the hotel did not offer room service—a problem for newlyweds who were too busy to eat at their reception. Like all unpleasant experiences, it became one of our favorite stories to tell later—when we could laugh about it.

The hotel was renovated in 2011, and I was glad I gave it another chance. It offered a variety of food options, and its spacious, well-lit guest rooms were bear-free. The second night I stayed at the 1900 Inn, a bed and breakfast near Drake University, my alma mater. My parents met me in Des Moines the next morning, and we drove to Mount Pleasant in two cars.

We made two G. Oliver-related stops along the way. First was Albia, where G. Oliver directed a concert band and a small orchestra in 1890–91. It had a quaint town square, a friendly Chamber of Commerce employee, and a bandstand built in 1995 that was reminiscent of an earlier era. We took photos of Big G and moved on to Centerville, where George Landers once directed the regimental band. It also had a bandstand in the town square.

That evening, after dropping off our bags at the Van Vorhies Haus, my parents and I went out to dinner and took a driving tour of Mount Pleasant before returning to the house. It had space for about fifteen residents, each with his or her own room and bathroom. It was clean, and the staff seemed capable, but I soon realized I had romanticized what it would be like for us to stay there.

I had focused on the historic and "complimentary" parts of the offer, and less on the fact that we would share space with people who needed living assistance—like the woman who gave my dad the stink eye when he attempted to fit some pieces into a puzzle displayed on a table in one of the common areas.

When I went to my room for the night, I discovered the door didn't lock, and my bed had plastic sheets underneath the fabric ones. I couldn't decide if I should laugh or cry. Saving on hotel costs had seemed like a good idea—the money I'd receive for the travel stories would barely cover the cost of two nights in Des Moines. I should have known it would be like trying to save money on your wedding night.

As I fell asleep, I decided I would politely decline the invitation to stay a second night. I doubted Warren Beckwith would be offended. I just hoped my parents would forgive me for prematurely checking them into an assisted living facility.

Thirty people attended the talk the next morning, including the college band director, who said he would keep looking for the elusive cadet march G. Oliver composed. Afterward, Lynn gave us a tour of the Harlan-Lincoln House. It was exciting to see the alcove where G. Oliver's orchestra played during the parties for the Lincoln granddaughters. I took photos of Big G in the space, which seemed too small to comfortably fit a three- or four-person orchestra—with or without the palms and ferns.

We also visited the chapel, which opened in 1893. As I stood on the auditorium stage, I tried to imagine G. Oliver performing in that larger space. Had he stood where I was standing now? What were his dreams for his career then, and how many did he fulfill?

We spent that night in Iowa City, where Steve had attended medical school, and we stopped in Mason City on the way home the next day. The Meredith Willson museum had closed by the time we arrived, so I took a photo of G in front of Willson's boyhood home and statue. I had no reason to believe the two men ever met, but they did know some of the same band directors.

IN AUGUST, WE TOOK a family vacation. We traveled to Crookston, where we bought chippers at Widman's, and continued on to the

Canadian border, where the agents asked us where we were headed.

"Winnipeg."

"Why?"

"We're going on a vacation."

"To *Winnipeg*?"

I didn't appreciate the agent's tone.

"We're going to Folklorama," Steve said. This was true. Winnipeg hosts an annual event billed as Canada's largest and longest running multicultural festival. While we were in the city, we planned to sample the food and entertainment at several of the forty "pavilions" that represented the cultures and ethnicities of the city's residents.

The men looked skeptical, but they let us continue.

During our stay in Winnipeg, we visited half a dozen Folklorama pavilions and the Manitoba Museum, but my research in the public library produced only a few rather generic comments about G. Oliver's visit there in 1899. One in the *Manitoba Free Press* said the band "was present at the exhibition both in the afternoon and evening and by its capital music made itself very popular with the Winnipeggers. They played an excellent programme of music in the evening and then massing with the Citizens band played for the various platform attractions."[2] The article also said many residents went to the train depots to see off the visitors.

The next leg of our trip included stops outside Lincoln High School in Thief River Falls where Ronald had directed the band, and Bemidji where we walked along Lake Boulevard in search of G. Oliver and Islea's old house. I was dismayed to discover it had been replaced by a Bemidji State University parking lot. What was it with Riggs houses and parking lots? The only consolation was that the lot served the fine arts building.

A few days after we returned home, a package of black and white photos arrived from my cousin Patricia. One of them depicted a 1930s-era car in front of a hotel decorated with patriotic bunting. On the back, someone had written: "G. Oliver Riggs, South Bend, Ind., La Salle Hotel, playing for President Roosevelt."

South Bend. This was a helpful clue. Through online searching, I learned that Franklin Delano Roosevelt traveled to South

Bend in 1935 to receive an honorary degree at Notre Dame. I wasn't sure "who" played for the president; I guessed it was Percy's high school band, and G. Oliver had assisted Percy. But a scouring of the St. Cloud newspaper turned up no mention of G. Oliver traveling to Indiana.

I set aside the mystery because I had other work to do. The *St. Cloud Times* published a story that summer about the municipal band's 125th anniversary, and its timeline contained several inaccuracies. I agreed to help Dad prepare a corrected version for the band before the concert in November. Despite our exhaustive efforts to gather and disseminate a factual historical account, people were still getting basic facts wrong. Giving talks and blogging wasn't enough; I needed to write a book about G. Oliver and his St. Cloud Boys' Band.

I attended the St. Cloud band concert with my parents, and one week later, I took out my files from G. Oliver's early days in St. Cloud. When I reviewed the list of band members from 1923, the name "Theodore Papermaster" jumped out at me. *Cool name!* I thought. An hour later, I examined a 1924 article about a piano recital Islea organized. Among the students listed: Theodore Papermaster. I located a list of band members from 1930, and there again was Theodore Papermaster.

An online search for Theodore Papermaster yielded several nuggets of information: he had been a pediatrician in the Twin Cities, he was a flight surgeon during World War II, and he was Jewish. His parents, Bert and Sonia, owned the Valet Cleaners in St. Cloud; and he had siblings named Ralph and Adele. I found an obituary for Ralph, but I didn't find one for Theodore.

With each discovery, my heart beat faster and my cheeks flushed. When I learned his daughter Gail was a doctor in the Twin Cities, I found a listing for her office and began rehearsing a speech in my head. Then I dialed the number. I told the receptionist I was working on a book about my great-grandfather, and I believed Gail's father played in my great-grandfather's band. The woman didn't hang up—a good sign—and she took down my contact information.

The next day, Gail left me a voice message: her ninety-eight-year-old father was still alive. He lived in a nursing home in

St. Louis Park, a suburb of Minneapolis. She also gave me her email address. I wrote to her and said I would love to talk to her dad about his memories.

That evening, Gail called me from her dad's room and handed off the phone.

"I was very well acquainted with G. Oliver Riggs," Ted said in a strong, clear voice. "He came to St. Cloud in 1923, when I was 9 years old, and I was the No. 5 clarinet player in a band of 240. I stuck with him. He was kind of an abrasive guy, but the two bandmasters—no, three—that followed him, they were not very satisfactory, so they hired him back. He directed another generation of the band, and I was among that, too."

I opened my laptop and typed quickly as he spoke. It was as though he had waited years to release this rush of information: He rose to the position of No. 1 clarinet player and played in the boys' band until he graduated from high school. He took piano lessons from G. Oliver's wife. He knew Percy and Ronald. He took care of Ronald's twin grandchildren when they were babies.

This last tidbit was unexpected. He had to be talking about my cousins Scott and Brent.

Before he ended the conversation, he added: "The happiest days in my life were when I was playing in the band."

I felt so energized after the call, I could hardly sit still. Dr. Theodore C. Papermaster lived only forty-five minutes from my house. I had to visit him as soon as possible. Although he sounded lively and lucid, I couldn't trust he would be alive next week, or next month. The hands of the pocket watch could stop at any time, for any of us.

24

DO I WORRY?

Through the first three weeks of January 1937, G. Oliver remained hospitalized, recuperating from what may have been a bleeding ulcer. During that time he put his assistant director, Earl Bohm, in charge of the band. Bohm was only nineteen, but as a boys' band alumnus, he had proven his leadership skills. He was in his second year at the Teachers College, studying to be a public school instrumental music teacher.

Band members Bill Goblish, Tommy Pederson, and Leonard Jung helped Bohm with the younger players, and a series of adult directors took turns rehearsing the senior boys. Ronald was first, followed by boys' band alumnus Phil Thielman; St. Cloud Reformatory Band director Francis Gonnella; William Allen Abbott, director of the Minneapolis South High School band; and Gerald Prescott, director of the University of Minnesota band.

During G. Oliver's hospital stay, President Franklin Roosevelt delivered his second inaugural address. The three-minute speech ignored displays of unrest in other parts of the world—Germany's occupation of the Rhineland, Italy's victory in Ethiopia, civil war in Spain—and focused on Roosevelt's first-term economic accomplishments and his concern that one-third of the nation's men, women, and children still lived in poverty.

Roosevelt said, "The test of our progress is not whether we add more to the abundance of those who have much; it is whether we provide enough for those who have too little. If I know aught of the spirit and purpose of our Nation, we will not listen to comfort, opportunism, and timidity. We will carry on."[1]

It was unclear whether G. Oliver heard the speech, but "we will carry on" summed up his philosophy regarding his health and work. He left the hospital on January 25, and while he rested at home for another week, he wrote a glowing letter of recommendation for his former pupil Herbert Jung, who applied to the US Navy Band in Washington, D.C. Jung was accepted and began his training in March.

G. Oliver also wrote a letter that winter to the *St. Cloud Times-Journal.* The St. Cloud school district was seeking voter approval to build an addition to Tech High School that would provide rehearsal and practice rooms for its band and orchestra. In his letter, G. Oliver expressed his support for the bond issue and proposed that the municipal band be allowed to use the rooms during certain hours in the evenings and on Saturdays. The letter did not say whether he had discussed this possibility with Erwin Hertz, the Tech band and orchestra director.

"For the past three years the City Commission have had tentative plans drawn for the building of band quarters and band shell on the Lake George property near the Tech High school building, which would have given the Tech Band and orchestra and the Municipal Boys' Band suitable quarters and a wonderful place for concerts," he wrote. "The uncertainty of building the foundation without considerable extra cost caused uncertainty as to when any of the structure will be built. I believe that if the Bond Issue carries it will not be difficult for the School Board and City Commission to work out an agreement that will be satisfactory to all concerned."[2]

G. Oliver also mentioned he planned to add girls to the municipal band—an idea spurred, perhaps, by a desire to boost enrollment and compete with Hertz for members.

Voters approved the bond issue the following day by a 2-to-1 margin.

Rehearsal space wasn't the only issue that plagued G. Oliver when it came to Hertz. His nemesis had become active in the Minnesota Bandmasters Association, and in April, the Tech band performed at the association's spring clinic in Minneapolis. For the first time, the clinic included choral groups in addition to bands and orchestras.

The bandmasters held the event in conjunction with the North Central Division of the Music Educators National Conference. Three thousand music teachers and directors from ten states attended, and many bandmasters association members joined the national group.[3] Membership of the state bandmasters association in 1937 reflected a nationwide trend that began in the early 1930s: school band directors gained influence as school bands grew in number and improved in quality. Meanwhile, municipal bands continued to decline.

Ronald attended the conference and was appointed to the bandmasters nominating committee. His father, who may have felt alienated by the association's shift in focus, stayed home and prepared for the annual spring concert at the Paramount, a joint effort of the boys' band and the Cathedral Girls' Drum Corps.

The two groups presented afternoon and evening concerts on April 11 for four thousand people. G. Oliver dedicated the first song, Henry Fillmore's "Gifted Leadership," to the men who rehearsed the band when he was hospitalized.

The newspaper praised the boys and said of the girls: "Their ease and perfection in marching and playing, and the striking appearance of the trim and effective group, as well as the blue-uniformed band in the background formed a harmonious yet contrasting picture."[4]

The image of the municipal band "in the background" did not bode well for G. Oliver's hopes of boosting its membership and influence.

Percy received accolades that spring for his own endeavors. The St. Cloud newspaper ran a photo of him with his South Bend band on May 6. One week later, the seventy-five-member band placed first out of twelve high school, municipal, and regimental ensembles in a statewide Knights Templar Convention in Indiana.[5]

The St. Cloud newspaper did not run stories about Ronald's accomplishments that spring. But the Thief River Falls newspaper occasionally mentioned the band's activities, and the school

newspaper ran a photo of Ronald and other teachers performing at a pep fest, dressed in "old-fashioned," turn-of-the-century
costumes.[6] Like his mother, Ronald was serious about his work,
but he did not take himself too seriously.

Before the summer concert season started, G. Oliver announced he would only accept up to forty young men in the municipal band (formerly the concert band). Members had to be between sixteen and twenty-three, but experience in his beginners
or boys' bands was not required—players from school bands were
eligible. He cited transportation difficulties and "rickety," cramped
area bandstands as reasons for the membership cap.[7]

Mary Jane Riggs returned to St. Cloud in June, and Islea invited fifteen children to the house on July 17 to celebrate her granddaughter's tenth birthday.[8] The rest of Mary Jane's family arrived a
week later.

Toward the end of July, the band performed "Ragazzazzamo,"
which G. Oliver had written in 1912. He had misplaced it several
years earlier and found it while cleaning his office. The newspaper reported, "It is characteristic of a great many 'rags' that were written from
1900 to 1910, just before the fox trot era. Most of these 'rag' tunes of
this period have fallen by the wayside, but a few, such as 'Alexander's
Rag Time Band,' have stood the test of time. Mr. Riggs is modest
in his claims for his composition. 'It is just a plain rag,' he says."[9]

Percy later said it dismayed his father that his compositions
were never published, though Percy also admitted that they were
"so difficult as to be almost unplayable."[10]

The following week, when G. Oliver invited parents and
friends of the boys to attend the final summer concert in Hester
Park, he was uncharacteristically complimentary.

"Though I admit that I am a hard bandmaster to please, I am
proud of these boys who have shown such a fine spirit of cooperation through the storm and stress of the past two years or more,"
he told the newspaper.[11]

A large crowd attended the concert, and G. Oliver praised the
work of Bohm, his assistant, predicting that "in a very few years he
will be at the head of an instrumental department in a large high
school system."[12]

Bohm proved G. Oliver right; he became a celebrated music teacher in St. Louis Park, a Minneapolis suburb. But G. Oliver didn't live long enough to see that happen.

Stress over band issues likely intensified for G. Oliver in September when the Tech High School band placed first out of fourteen school and city bands at the Minnesota State Fair. The *St. Cloud Times-Journal* ran a front-page article about the band's success.

G. Oliver could not have missed the prominent coverage, and it may not have pleased him, but he was perhaps more upset when an editorial said Hertz "has the patience and the good will toward the pupils to develop a high grade of efficiency. He is a modest gentleman, seeking no honors for himself, but those he serves."[13]

Patient and modest were not adjectives St. Cloud residents used to describe G. Oliver.

Nothing his bands did that fall matched the excitement generated by the Tech band's achievement. However, Ronald attained a noteworthy honor: his sixty-four-member high school band performed in Grand Forks for President Roosevelt.

The performance resembled the one Percy had given two years earlier in South Bend. The Lincoln High School band was one of seventeen ensembles stationed along the parade route as the President toured East Grand Forks and Grand Forks. Roosevelt concluded his visit by dedicating the new fairgrounds grandstand in Grand Forks, a federal Works Progress Administration (WPA) project. More than forty thousand people attended the event. Ronald's students marched past the reviewing stand where the President was seated, and they were treated to a free lunch afterward.[14]

A few weeks before Thanksgiving, Islea got her own moment in the spotlight—although she had to share it with Harvey Waugh, head of the Teachers College music department. The *St. Cloud Times-Journal* ran an article about Waugh, the director of the St. Cloud Civic Chorus, and Islea, the group's accompanist, in advance of a concert featuring the chorus, the WPA Minnesota Symphony Orchestra, and piano soloist Guy Maier. The article referred to Islea as "Mrs. G. Oliver Riggs" and said she had "given much of her time and talent toward the cultural and artistic life for the people of St. Cloud and vicinity."[15]

A capacity crowd filled the junior high auditorium for the concert. Maier later told the newspaper he was impressed by the number of youth in the audience. "St. Cloud is to be congratulated for encouraging its young people to study and appreciate music," he said.[16]

Two weeks before Christmas, Ronald finally received a mention in the St. Cloud paper. It wasn't for a musical achievement, though—it was for a romantic one. He and Eleanor Johnson, his former band student, eloped on December 11 at the Little Brown Church in the Vale, a historic church in Nashua, Iowa. The newlyweds traveled to Farmington afterward to celebrate with the bride's parents, and to St. Cloud the next day to celebrate with the groom's parents.[17]

What the newspaper didn't mention was the reason thirty-six-year-old Ronald and eighteen-year-old Eleanor eloped. The couple feared Eleanor's older sister Helen would object during the ceremony if she were invited; she did not approve of the age difference and was jealous because she had not yet married.

Two months later, G. Oliver and Hertz attended the 14th annual Minnesota Bandmasters Association conference at the University of Minnesota in Minneapolis. It was also the "last Minnesota Bandmasters Association conference"; members voted on the first day to change the organization's name to the Minnesota Music Educators Association.[18] Whether G. Oliver voted for this is unclear; his friend George Landers later expressed regret to Ronald about the change.[19]

G. Oliver led a discussion on "Municipal Band Problems," and Ronald assisted him. Topics included the band tax and the need for better rehearsal rooms. G. Oliver was elected chairman of the association's municipal band division and named to its board of directors.[20] Hertz's band performed on the last morning of the conference.

The rivalry between G. Oliver and Hertz continued into the summer. In June, the St. Cloud municipal band performed at the state Eagles convention in Winona, and in July, it performed at Paul Bunyan Days in Brainerd. Meanwhile, Hertz prepared his band for a return to the State Fair. In July, he asked the school board for $2,000 to buy new band uniforms and instruments. The

Times-Journal expressed support, saying the expense was worthwhile because band participation enriched the lives of young people. The editorial suggested Hertz be allowed to instruct students in the junior high as well as the high school, as some parents were requesting. It also praised the Teachers College music program, the Cathedral Girls' Drum Corps, and the boys' bands.

"As long as we have these bands," the editorial stated, "we should have enough self respect to see that they are well uniformed for the credit of the city. Every child having an aptitude towards music and the determination to profit by opportunities should be given all reasonable aid. That is the stairway of good citizenship."[21]

Talk of expanding Hertz's role as a director could not have been well received by G. Oliver. Perhaps sensing a need to further ingratiate himself with the newspaper staff—and divert attention away from Hertz—G. Oliver devoted one July rehearsal to having the band serenade the *Times-Journal* and other downtown businesses. Whatever his reasons, the gesture paid off: the newspaper ran an editorial the next day, in which it praised the boys and their director.

"It is an organization of which our citizens can be proud, and in time it should give them adequate quarters and some modern shell bandstands. Boys so well started and who have the love of music and the skill to produce are on the right road to good citizenship and useful and admirable gentlemen," the editorial stated. "When we know the crime cost to this country is 15 billions—not millions—a year, to develop law abiding and respected citizens is worth more than the comparative few dollars we are providing for their training and healthful recreation."[22]

IN SEPTEMBER, THE Tech band again took first place at the Minnesota State Fair, and the *Times-Journal* devoted much of its front page to the event. G. Oliver, who was vacationing in Bemidji, sent Hertz a telegram that said: "Accept my congratulations on your success at the state fair. You and your players worked hard and intelligently and deserved to win."[23]

He may have hoped his overture to Hertz would reap benefits, as city officials considered a Chamber of Commerce proposal to build a new municipal auditorium that would include space for the band. However, citing concerns about debt and the lack of a pressing need, the city commission rejected the idea. The newspaper agreed, saying the new Tech auditorium could handle most of the city's convention and event needs. It did not mention the municipal band's space needs.[24]

G. Oliver also sent a telegram that fall to the newspaper in Crookston. Given the situation in St. Cloud, it was perhaps not surprising he waxed nostalgic about the days before schools had competing band programs. The telegram said:

> *Forty years ago Friday, September 23rd, I located in Crookston as bandmaster and orchestra leader. Mrs. Riggs and I were married soon afterward and spent many happy years in Crookston. We both feel a strong attachment for that locality and its people and wish everyone a healthy and happy life.*
>
> *The old bandstand, built on wheels, and the Grand Opera House, which was located on Main Street, brings back many happy thoughts.*
>
> *Mrs. Riggs is teaching piano and I am teaching and directing the St. Cloud Municipal Band of 40 players and boys' band of 100.*
>
> *Best wishes to all. G. Oliver Riggs, St. Cloud Municipal Bandmaster.*

The *Crookston Daily Times* said G. Oliver was "recognized throughout the state as the originator of municipal juvenile bands." It further explained: "Bandmaster Riggs conceived the idea of a juvenile band under his direction as a feeder to the municipal band. The results were astonishing. Hundreds of embryo musicians passed through his hands for musical instruction. As they developed and passed the juvenile stage they were inducted into the regular band. In another few years his juveniles had surpassed the majors in ability and attendance and Mr. Riggs was called to greener fields to repeat his achievements."[25]

The article also applauded the musical contributions Islea had made to the city, and it included an early photo of the Crookston band.

In late October, G. Oliver's St. Cloud boys performed for Republican gubernatorial candidate Harold Stassen. The municipal band joined with bands from Sauk Rapids and Foley, and the Litchfield drum and bugle corps, in a parade from downtown to Tech High School. Nearly four thousand people attended Stassen's rally, the first event held in the new auditorium, and the address was broadcast over statewide radio.[26] The next Tuesday, Stassen won by 240,000 votes, defeating incumbent Governor Elmer Benson, of the Farmer-Labor party, and Democrat Thomas Gallagher. Thirty-one-year-old Stassen became the third youngest man elected governor in the United States.

Minnesota election results figured prominently in the St. Cloud newspaper's coverage, but alarming events overseas soon overtook the headlines after Jewish teenager Herschel Grynszpan murdered a German diplomat, Ernst vom Rath, in Paris. Grynszpan had retaliated for the Nazis' treatment of his family in Germany. Hitler used the assassination as a pretext for launching what became known as *Kristallnacht*, or Night of Broken Glass.

Beginning on November 9 and continuing through the next day, angry mobs throughout Germany, Austria, and other Nazi-controlled areas plundered Jewish shops and torched and vandalized synagogues. Officials rounded up thousands of Jewish men and sent them to concentration camps. President Roosevelt publicly condemned the events and recalled US Ambassador Hugh Wilson from Berlin "for consultation."[27]

A *St. Cloud Times-Journal* editorial on December 2 described the increasing persecution of Jews in Germany and cited reports that sixty-three thousand were taken to concentration camps, where they likely faced cruel treatment or death. Although the newspaper called it a "most heart-sickening situation" and predicted Hitler's action would in time bring "a terrible punishment on his country,"[28] it did not call upon the United States to intervene.

Disturbing reports from Germany continued almost daily through December as the Nazis imposed additional restrictions upon its Jewish population, such as forbidding them to run businesses, expelling them from universities, seizing their money and property, and dissolving marriages between Jews and Gentiles. The Gestapo-controlled Jewish newspaper *Juedisches Nachrichtenblatt* called upon President Roosevelt to offer 100,000 German Jews temporary refuge in the United States. The request went unheeded, although the president did allow thousands of visiting Germans with expiring visas to stay in the United States.[29]

Meanwhile, St. Cloud residents prepared for the holiday season. Islea enjoyed a visit from her friend Lela Stanton Langley of Minneapolis (formerly of Bemidji), and five days after their fortieth wedding anniversary, Islea and G. Oliver received exciting news: their first grandson, William Johnson Riggs, was born in Thief River Falls.

Early 1939 brought more good news for G. Oliver: the city transformed rooms at the community center into a band rehearsal space.

For its first gig of the new year, the municipal band performed for one of its own: Lawrence Hall, a boys' band alumnus who had become speaker of the Minnesota House of Representatives. The thirty-year-old legislator returned to St. Cloud on January 13 for a banquet hosted by the Chamber of Commerce. Governor Stassen also attended, and the boys' band played before the dinner at the Breen Hotel.[30]

The next month, the band performed at a music clinic in Minneapolis. The Minnesota Music Educators Association sponsored the event for band, orchestra, and choir directors from five states. G. Oliver again led a discussion on municipal music problems, and Ted Thorson, the Crookston director (and younger brother of G. Oliver's friend Nels), presented a paper, "Entry of high school graduates to municipal bands."

Before the event, G. Oliver wrote Thorson a letter and described his experience of organizing the first Crookston boys' band in 1907:

"My sons, Ronald and Percy, who at present are very capable band leaders and music educators, were just little boys then. They were with me a great deal of the time when I was teaching and directing this group of young boys, and I have often thought that perhaps my sons were greatly influenced by their association with the band boys and its director, and who knows but what a part of their success of today was being founded at that time."[31]

His St. Cloud band performed that spring with the Civic Chorus, and for the Knights of Columbus state convention. But its experiences didn't match the excitement of the Tech band's field trip in May: Hertz and his band of seventy-five girls and boys went to Winnipeg to play for the King and Queen of England, accompanied by one hundred St. Cloud residents and *St. Cloud Times-Journal* staff photographer Myron Hall. The band marched in a parade honoring King George VI and Queen Elizabeth, and the event received extensive coverage in the St. Cloud newspaper.

If G. Oliver sent Hertz a telegram congratulating him for this honor, it wasn't mentioned in the *St. Cloud Times-Journal*, which proclaimed pride in the Tech band and in all the city's ensembles and said: "When honors come to any of these musicians, we are all happy as members of the great St. Cloud family."[32]

Ronald's high school band didn't travel out of the country that spring, but the school board commended Ronald for his work and offered him a raise. He turned it down to take a job directing the St. Cloud Teachers College band and supervising student band directors. It paid $1,730 a year—not as much as the $2,307 Percy made, but a bump up in pay and prestige from Thief River. G. Oliver, with four decades of experience, made $2,160 a year.[33]

Ronald's final responsibility was to lead the Lincoln High School band in its first-ever appearance at the Minnesota State Fair. But the excitement was tempered by sobering news: on September 1, the Germans invaded Poland. Two days later, Britain, France, Australia, and New Zealand declared war on Germany, which had previously signed pacts with Italy and the Soviet Union, and on September 10, Canada declared war on Germany, too.

Another world war had begun.

THROUGHOUT THE FALL, while the US government maintained its neutrality, war developments filled the radio airwaves and the newspaper pages. In September, the Soviets invaded Poland, and later divided it with the Nazis. In October, Germany attacked Britain, and in early November, Hitler survived an assassination attempt. Mindful of events overseas, organizers of the Armistice Day services in St. Cloud emphasized their desire for peace. Post Commander W. H. Mulligan noted that twenty-one years had passed since the signing of the treaty that ended the Great War.

The municipal band participated, as it always did, by marching to the Paramount Theatre and playing the "Star Spangled Banner." At 11 a.m., cornetists stationed at downtown intersections played "Taps," and all traffic halted for two minutes.[34]

G. Oliver and Hertz both helped organize the Minnesota Music Educators Association music clinic that winter, held in January at the University of Minnesota. Among the speakers was Percy, who discussed music's important role in keeping young people out of trouble. He had studied records at the St. Cloud Reformatory and, according to a *Times-Journal* article, found that "out of 6,000 inmates, only .0037 percent, or about 16 youths, had ever received previous training in instrumental music. No juvenile receiving such training had ever been convicted in St. Joseph (Indiana) county, Riggs said. He added that a study of Sing Sing prison records in New York revealed that no active professional musician ever had been committed to that institution."[35]

The municipal band members stayed out of trouble by preparing for the annual spring program at the Paramount. It featured a piano solo by Islea and a cornet trio by Bill Goblish, Lloyd McNeal, and William Sherin. G. Oliver listed the names of the city commissioners in the program and included a bandmaster's note: "It is again a pleasure to call attention to the cordial cooperation between the three Municipal Band Groups and the various school and college bands and orchestras. There are, at present, 165 boys and young men under the Municipal Band Director's teaching and supervision. Many of these members are at present numbered in the ranks of the various musical organizations of the Technical High School, Cathedral High School, St. John's University and the St. Cloud State Teachers' College."[36]

A *St. Cloud Times-Journal* editorial the next day reinforced the idea that cooperation among musical ensembles benefited the community. "The enthusiastic reception given to the well selected program was proof of the fact that the people of this community

G. Oliver directs the St. Cloud municipal band and granddaughter Mary Jane sings at a concert at the Colonial Gardens, August 22, 1940.

appreciate what has been accomplished under the municipal band director's teaching and supervision."[37]

G. Oliver and Islea planned to share the stage again in March for a joint concert of the St. Cloud Civic Chorus and the Municipal Band. But Islea became ill, and her friend Helen Griem accompanied the sixty-voice chorus instead. By April, Islea's health improved, while G. Oliver's worsened. He was admitted to the hospital for a week, for reasons not specified in the newspaper.

At the end of July, Ronald spoke to the Kiwanis Club about the history of band music. He explained that the greatest advance occurred after the Great War, when "music companies were faced with the problem of popularizing music to maintain their expanded factories and great advertising campaigns brought about the desired results." He concluded by noting that St. Cloud alone had ten bands, including the newly formed 101st Anti-Aircraft Regimental National Guard band.[38]

The following month, G. Oliver prepared a special program for the penultimate summer band concert. Granddaughter Mary Jane performed three vocal solos, including "God Bless America" by Irving Berlin. She wore a plaid skirt and a hooded jacket, and standing in front of the microphone she looked as poised as a professional. The newspaper ran a photo of the twelve-year-old soloist the next day, with G. Oliver in the background, his baton raised in the air.[39]

In the fall, as war raged on in Europe, Congress passed the Selective Training and Service Act establishing the first peacetime military draft in US history. All men between the ages of twenty-one and thirty-six had to register. This included several older municipal band members. That October G. Oliver took the band to Brainerd for a Republican rally attended by Governor Harold Stassen and a half a dozen other state and local candidates. Stassen handily won reelection, but the national Republican candidate didn't fare as well. Wendell Wilkie had tried to portray the President as being in favor of joining the war—in response, Roosevelt promised he wouldn't enter a foreign war if elected. The President was re-elected by a landslide, but he would not keep his promise.

Six days later, a fierce blizzard cancelled Armistice Day services in St. Cloud. Sixteen inches of snow fell, in some places forming drifts twelve feet high. All roads in central Minnesota were blocked, schools and businesses closed, and hundreds of people were marooned at work or inside their vehicles. The blizzard killed forty-nine people in Minnesota, although none in St. Cloud.

G. Oliver refused to let the snow win. He convinced a few cornetists to blow taps in front of the Paramount Theatre at 11 a.m., to commemorate the 22nd anniversary of the signing of the armistice. That was the extent of the memorial service for 1940.[40]

Three days before Thanksgiving, St. Cloud said goodbye to the first five men who signed up for training under the national defense act. The Chamber of Commerce hosted a lunch for them, and the Tech High School band serenaded the men before they boarded the train for Fort Snelling.[41] The scene would repeat many times in the years to come.

25

CONVERSATIONS WITH A BONEHEAD

One week after my phone conversation with Theodore Paper-master, I drove to his nursing home in St. Louis Park. It was the day before Thanksgiving in 2012. Big, fluffy flakes of snow landed on the windshield as I backed out of my driveway, but I was undeterred; it would take more than a blizzard to keep me from the interview. On the way, I stopped to get a latte and some items for the next day's feast. In the checkout line I caught sight of a package of three sugar cookies shaped like turkeys and added it to the conveyor belt on impulse, thinking Ted might appreciate a treat.

As I signed in at the nursing home desk, my stomach was unsettled. What if Ted didn't like me? What if it was hard to communicate with him? I found his room on the third floor, knocked, and entered.

As I walked into the L-shaped room, I saw a chair near the wall and the foot of a narrow, hospital-type bed. A bookcase filled with books stood along one wall. Above it was a framed portrait of a young, dark-haired man wearing a military cap and uniform. A much older man with white hair, the same facial structure, and clouded green eyes sat on the bed, dressed in comfortable trousers and a zipped-up sweatshirt.

He greeted me warmly. "Are you Joy? I've been waiting for you."

"It's so wonderful to meet you, Ted," I responded.

264

We both cried tears of happiness. I offered him the cookies, but he politely refused, saying he kept kosher. "Oh," I said, momentarily flummoxed, as I set them aside. Then I pulled the chair close to the bed and set up my recording equipment. Ted turned on his hearing-assistance device and handed me a microphone so he could hear my questions.

I switched into reporter mode. "OK, first of all, you lived in St. Cloud. You were born there."

Ted nodded affirmatively. "I was born March 30, 1914. That makes me 98 now. I went to medical school at the University of Minnesota, graduated in 1938, and then I went into pediatrics and became a pediatrician. However, World War II came as I was starting my third year of residency. I applied for a commission before we got into the war. And they said, 'you've got to go home and wait for the paperwork.' It takes a long time for the Army and the government to do things. So then I started my third year of a pediatric residency, and of course the war came along December 7 of 1941 ... I got a telegram finally from the adjutant general saying—"

He pointed at the wall. "There's my picture."

I glanced at the photo again. "Oh, wow."

"—One First Lieutenant Papermaster, report to Gowen Field, Boise, Idaho, for the Army. They put me in the Air Force; ultimately they sent me to flight surgeon school. I went to North Africa with a B-17 group, was with them a year, they transferred me to a P-38 group, a fighter group, and I was with them for two years."

I was no expert on the North Africa campaign—Sebastian could fill me in later—but I knew Ted easily could have been among the more than 416,000 US servicemen and women who died in the war. Instead, we were sitting together in the relative safety of a suburban nursing home.

"There's an old saying, there are three ways to do things: the right way, the wrong way and the Army's way," Ted said. "I say it about this institution, the Shalom Home."

I smiled at his punch line. Ted's style of storytelling resembled my dad's.

Ted said his parents moved to St. Cloud in 1912. His father,

Bert, encouraged Ted to join the boys' band, and Ted chose to play clarinet because that's what his father played in the adult municipal band.

"G. Oliver had the eight best clarinet players in the front row, and I was number 5," he said.

That seemed like my cue to take out the photo I'd brought; I had a printing shop create a five-foot-long, laminated copy of the 1925 boys' band photo, so Ted could more easily see the faces.

He peered at it. "Harry Atwood, Red Scofield, Streitz, Strobel." He pointed to his eleven-year-old self. "This is me, Ted Papermaster. This is a friend of mine, another Jewish boy, Sidney Kaufman. This boy—I know him, I can't remember the name. This guy, I'm not quite sure I remember—Opitz?"

Seeing Eddie Shuster, a cornetist who'd had a Saint Bernard, reminded him of a story about Islea.

"I never knew her first name. We always called her Mrs. Riggs," Ted said. "She was a very wonderful, sweet lady and a very fine performer and a very fine teacher. We got along fine. I took lessons until I was about a junior in high school."

He paused for a second, retrieving a memory.

"She was going to have a recital of all of her regular students. One of the numbers was a trio. Sidney Kaufman was the bass, I was in the middle, and on the upper register was Jay Redding, who played trombone in the band. We three played a trio on one piano, six hands. We went over to her house, we were practicing, and she had a beautiful dog. It was a collie, a gorgeous dog. He was sitting there on the floor—there was no rug ..."

"What kind of dog?" I interrupted.

Images of Riggs family photos flashed into my head: the children with a collie named Prince, and a collie pup named Laddie. Was Ted talking about Laddie? As if it wasn't remarkable enough that he knew my great-grandparents, my grandfather and my great-uncle, Ted also apparently knew one of their pets.

"A collie," Ted confirmed. "We were playing away on this trio—I can't tell you the name of it ... Da da *dat* da da *dat* da da da ..." he sang a few bars. "Anyway, the dog started to urinate on the floor. We three teenagers were listening to that, and we broke out into uncontrollable laughter. When it was over, Redding made a poem: 'There we sat in silent bliss, listening to the rippling piss.'"

He laughed heartily. I laughed, too. It was not the kind of story I expected him to tell.

"It was embarrassing for Mrs. Riggs, she had to get up and clean it up. It's strange how these things come back to you."

I searched through a folder of materials and handed him an article about a 1924 piano recital. It listed Ted, Sidney, and Jay, but not as a trio; that must have been a different recital. I also showed him a list of the 1923 boys' band members, which led to another story.

"One time the band was playing at the dedication of the St. Cloud hospital, and a big storm came up. One tree was falling over, and this fellow, Joe Tessari, who was a big fellow—he later became about six foot two or six foot three—he saw that this guy here, Vern Cotton," Ted said, pointing to the photo, "a little kid, who played drums, was running around, and Joe threw him on the ground and covered him with his own body so the tree would fall on Joe instead of the kid. It was an amazing act of personal bravery and danger, and I don't think anybody knows about that."

When I asked what G. Oliver was like, Ted described him as a strict disciplinarian and a good musician. I handed Ted a copy of a portrait of G. Oliver from 1910.

"That's him all right. He was proud of being a Scotch-Irishman. One of the things he said about himself was that a Scotch-Irishman has a wide thing here," Ted pointed to his philtrum, the vertical indentation between his upper lip and his nose. "That it was longer in that group, and I can see here he's probably right."

I had never noticed this before about G. Oliver, but I could see it now.

"So, he didn't play too often for you?"

Ted smiled and launched into yet another story I'd never heard from anyone else.

"When the adult band had a picnic, he used to play the violin while they'd sing. There was one song that was led by a man named Pete Dinndorf, who played sousaphone. He was a fun guy, he was in the paint business. Anyway, you know St. Cloud has a lot of Germans—German Catholics and German Lutherans. So they were singing these German songs. For one of the songs, they would point to various pictures on a chart, and Pete Dinndorf would lead them. G. Oliver would be playing his violin, and we'd sing to the accompaniment. The song was '*Ist das nicht eine Schnitzelbank? Ja, das ist eine Schnitzelbank.*'"

Ted sang the lyrics in what I assumed was German.

"You know what a schnitzelbank is?"

"No." I shook my head. I took French from my mom in high school, and I had one year of Russian in college, but my German was limited to what I'd learned watching *Hogan's Heroes* with my dad.

"It's a sawhorse!" He sang the line again. "It went on with other kinds of things. It's funny that I remember that."

When I asked about the 1925 Kiwanis Convention in St. Paul, Ted remembered sleeping on mattresses in a gymnasium, and riding on the train.

"They served ham sandwiches, and I don't eat ham because I'm a Jew. My father was there to help out. I said, 'Dad, what do I do?' He says, 'Well, give the ham to your non-Jewish neighbor and you can eat the bread.' That's how we handled that situation."

Ted had no memories of the banquet where G. Oliver announced his plans to resign. But he did recall G. Oliver's replacement, Albert Koehler, whom he described as a capable director and good man.

"He had cancer of the prostate, and he died, and then they got another man who was an old Army bandmaster. His name was Steinmetz. He was kind of a character, and I didn't think he had the background that G. Oliver did. He lasted a short time. While he was there we got a change of uniform, which I didn't like. They had these funny hats."

I pulled out a photo of the 1927 band. He was right about the white, floppy brimmed hats—they looked more suitable for a band of beach bums than a band of serious musicians.

Ted was still in the band when it went to Des Moines in 1931, but he had no memories of Junior the bear. The handler must have tried, wisely, to keep Junior away from the tempting, tender band boys.

Toward the end of our conversation, I brought up one more topic.

"The twins that you took care of, Ronald's grandchildren, my cousins? One of them has twin boys," I said.

"Is that so? Where are the twins now?" Ted asked.

"They live pretty close to here," I said.

I didn't have a map in front of me, but it occurred to me that they lived within fifteen miles of Ted's nursing home. They were practically neighbors.

"I think they wanted to get a doctor closer to them. I only saw them when they were a couple of months old. But I remember seeing the Riggs twins," Ted said.

"One of them has twins, and the other one has a little boy that they named Griffin Oliver Riggs," I said.

"They called him G. Oliver? That's very nice," Ted said. "I never knew what the G stood for—was it George?"

"George," I confirmed. "And he didn't like it."

"But you say there's another pair of twins, too—one of the twins had twins? Oh, that's great."

Ted chuckled, but his eyes drooped, and his shoulders slumped. So I gathered my things and told him I'd return soon.

A few days later, I blogged about finding Ted. Scott and Brent, their sister, Kristina, and their mom, Karen, were excited to hear the news. But I knew I had struck reaction gold when my understated uncle sent me a note containing multiple exclamation points.

"This is just an amazing story! I did not remember that he was Scott and Brent's pediatrician!!! Great work in following up and getting to meet him!" Bob wrote.

At Dad's suggestion, I emailed the post to Ted's daughter. Gail wrote back to say that Ted found two things he wanted to show me: a photo, and a letter.

"He is thinking of other stories that you can collect for your archives. This experience has been a mood lifter for him," she said.

The day after Christmas, I signed onto Facebook and was stunned to see a post from my second cousin Kae. Her brother Chris, who had sent me the old watch, had died in a fire at his house on Christmas Day. I took the watch down from the shelf above my desk. The local jeweler hadn't been able to fix it: its hands were still frozen in place.

When I returned to the Shalom Home on December 27, Ted eagerly launched into show-and-tell. First, he handed me a black-and-white photo taken outside his family's St. Cloud home. Ted held a clarinet, his brother, Ralph, held a saxophone, and both boys wore band uniforms. They were not Steinmetz-era uniforms: the military-style caps were non-floppy.

"What color were the uniforms?" I asked.

"Medium blue with a red stripe down the leg. They were beautiful uniforms, and they made a great impression. It was wonderful to see one hundred and fifty guys marching down the street; it was so impressive," Ted said. "I loved the band. I didn't realize it at that time, what effect it would have."

The second item was a typewritten letter from 1941, addressed to the Adjutant General of the US Army:

Dear Sir:

I have known Theodore Papermaster since April 1923. I have known his father since 1909 and his mother a great many years and can truthfully say that I know of no family that I would place on a higher level. I also knew his grandfather, who was a Rabbi, and certainly I never knew a finer man.

I am called on to give recommendations to young men very often on account, I presume, of the fact that I have worked among boys and young men for over fifty years. Some young men do not receive as good recommendations as Theodore Papermaster is entitled to.

I consider him one of the finest young men I have ever known, in every respect.

Yours truly,

G. Oliver Riggs

My first reaction was: *Wow. Sincere, glowing praise from G. Oliver.* Then, my brain fixated on the year 1909. According to this, G. Oliver and Bert met fourteen years before G. Oliver moved to

St. Cloud. Was that possible? And how did G. Oliver know Ted's grandfather?

"Ted, it says in this letter that G. Oliver met your dad in 1909. How did they meet?"

"I didn't realize that," Ted said. He glanced at the letter. "He must have met him in—probably Crookston. My father came from Grand Forks. My grandfather was born in Lithuania, and he came over to be the rabbi for North Dakota. He was a highly powerful, spiritually powerful man, a wonderful man, the greatest man I ever knew. He went to Grand Forks. He was the rabbi there from 1890 to 1934. He died in 1934 when I was a freshman in medical school. His name was Benjamin Papermaster."

"Was he musical, too?"

"He was musical in terms

Brothers Ralph and Ted Papermaster, outside their St. Cloud home.

of canting the prayers," Ted said. "Now, my father grew up in Grand Forks and left around 1908 or so, and he always liked the clarinet. Whenever a band played he liked to go and stand by the clarinet player, and he learned to play the clarinet."

Ted glanced at his notes to see what else he'd wanted to tell me, and remarked that he was "slowing down" at age ninety-eight.

I responded over-enthusiastically, "You look fantastic."

This made him laugh, for reasons that became clear.

"I might as well tell you the story. I hope it doesn't hurt your feelings," he began. "Three women were discussing what their husbands did for them during the past winter. One girl said her husband took her to Europe and bought her ten fur coats, none less than $10,000 a piece. So the other woman said, 'Fantastic.' The next woman says, 'We went to France, to a dressmaker, and he bought me ten dresses, none of which were less than $5,000.' The other two said, 'Fantastic.' They looked at the third woman and said, 'What did your husband do for you?' 'Oh, he sent me to charm school.' They said, 'What did you learn at charm school?' 'Well, they taught me to say fantastic instead of bullshit.'"

Ted chuckled. "If you're going to hang around with me, you're going to hear stories like that."

I would never think of the word fantastic in the same way again.

Although G. Oliver liked to lecture, he never cursed, Ted said. Instead, when he was angry, he used the word "bonehead." Years later, Ted and his friend Fritz Thielman began using that word in a new way. Fritz played baritone in the boys' band, and although they didn't attend the same high school—Fritz went to the Catholic school—they often swam or played tennis together.

"We'd meet each other and play tennis and say, 'Hey, bone-head!' We used to call each other that, and the term was one of affection and love and friendship. It meant, 'I love you. You're my best friend. You're a great guy. Hey, bonehead.' Isn't that something?" He smiled at the memory. "We learned that from G. Oliver. Bonehead."

Before I left, Ted thanked me for listening to his stories. His eyes brimmed with tears.

"I'm so glad you came up so I could get all these things off my chest. It's strange how you got in touch with me through my daughter. That's God, that's what I think. That's the way I think. How else should I think when I had a grandfather for a rabbi?"

He told me one more story, about his father.

"He was a little guy, five foot three and a half. In World War I there was a draft, and they couldn't take him because he was too short. On the third draft they lowered it to five foot three, so he was going to be drafted. And you know what? The Germans quit! They heard he was coming."

Ted's face widened into a smile. "It's a family joke. They heard Bert Papermaster's coming, 'we quit.' It's a wonderful story. There's nothing wrong with a good story. I love to tell stories. There's a word for that—you know what it is?"

A word popped into my head. "Raconteur?"

"Yes, raconteur."

He looked pleased that I knew the word. A burst of pride surged through my chest. I felt I had passed some kind of test.

TED'S STORIES FLOATED in and out of my brain over the next few days, as we prepared to host Steve's family for Christmas. The puzzle pieces finally fit together on January 1, as I reviewed my notes.

Herman "Bert" Papermaster, a St. Cloud businessman and band supporter.

Grand Forks. The year 1909. Oh my gosh, was it possible? My fingers shook as I sifted through a stack of photocopied articles until I found it: A *Grand Forks Herald* article dated June 24, 1909. That evening's band concert included a clarinet duet by Carl Lukkason and Burt Papermaister. Bert's first and last names were misspelled, but it didn't matter. I had uncovered something even Ted didn't know: his dad had belonged to G. Oliver's Grand Forks band.

I couldn't stop smiling. The friendship between the Riggs and Papermaster families went back one hundred and three years. The realization gave me goosebumps.

When I poked my head into Ted's room again the following week, he said, "Hi, bonehead!"

I laughed and sat next to him on the bed.

"I told you about bonehead, right? I wanted you to know that I recognized you."

"Yes, you told me," I assured him.

I handed him a copy of the 1909 article.

"Look at this, Ted. Your dad was in the Grand Forks band that G. Oliver directed in 1909."

Ted put on his glasses and examined the piece of paper.

"That makes him about twenty-three years old," he mused, as

he read. "Oh, my dad played a duet? Oh my gosh, isn't that something. Is this for me?"

"Yes," I said.

"Thank you. Thank you."

I handed him a second article about the same concert.

"Duet for clarinets. Bert Papermaster—they spell his name Papermaister," Ted noted. "G. Oliver must have thought highly of him—isn't that something. I never thought he was that great of a player!"

He shook his head in disbelief and chuckled.

Ted had new stories to tell me. One was about his brother, Ralph, who also fought in World War II and also became a doctor. Ralph, three years younger than Ted, had started in band on the soprano saxophone. When the band lost its oboe player, G. Oliver obtained an oboe and gave it to Ralph. But after a month, G. Oliver moved Ralph back to the soprano sax.

"I wondered, why did he do that? I figured out that the bandmaster figured that Ralph was going away to school in a year or so, and he was going to lose him, so he'd waste all that time training an oboe player," Ted said. "It's nobody's fault, it's just the way it is. I don't know who got the thing, but my brother liked the oboe and he wanted to play it, and he felt kind of bad about having to give it up. He told me that years later."

The next story concerned his friend Fritz's brother, Robert, who played trombone in the band. When G. Oliver had a bleeding ulcer, Robert donated blood for the transfusion. "I must have been out of college at the time," Ted said. "G. Oliver was in his late 60s or early 70s."

I wished Ted could provide more details about that incident. But it wouldn't change the point of his story: the bond between G. Oliver and some players had been so strong, one of them literally gave his blood for his bandmaster.

When I mentioned that G. Oliver and Islea had two children who died young, Ted said, "I wanted to ask you about that. I heard that Mrs. Riggs had a daughter, but I never saw her, so I didn't know what happened to the daughter."

I explained that Rosalie died from complications of an ear infection.

"Is that so? That was before the days of antibiotics, before the sulfa drugs, even. They would have easily saved her nowadays. That's too bad. I never knew that."

Ted claimed he was out of stories, but he said I was welcome to ask additional questions.

"It's nice to talk to a person like you. Parts of my life in the Army weren't so happy, and some parts in college weren't so happy, but I had a wonderful childhood in St. Cloud. You bring back the finest parts of my life."

I didn't see Ted again for six months. Before school ended, Louisa and I flew to Georgia to tour the Savannah College of Art and Design. It amused me to note that if she attended the college, she wouldn't be the first Yankee in the family to locate in Savannah: Jasper was stationed there in December 1864.

When I returned to the Shalom Home on July 3, despite what he'd said, Ted told me a new story about a time G. Oliver got upset with the boys for not playing a song correctly.

"'Make your dotted quarter longer and your eighth note shorter.' He kept repeating it," Ted said. "He took special issue with the trumpet section, and he gave them hell. He wanted it done right! But I got a little tired of that."

Toward the end of the visit, Ted talked about World War II, and his eyes lost their sparkle.

"All you have to do to make me cry is say two words: the war. I don't know how many veterans act that way, but I do, and I'm not ashamed of it. I hope that your kids never have to fight a war. It's awful. It's awful," he sobbed.

Tears streamed down his face. I patted his leg gently until he regained his composure and said, "It was a pleasure meeting you. Be well, be well. Have a good Fourth of July."

STEVE SPENT THE SUMMER rehearsing the role of one of the barbershop/school board characters for a Northfield production of *The Music Man*. Three of the performances coincided with the 2013 Vintage Band Festival. The cross-promotion was intentional. Steve wasn't the only family member involved in the musical: his sister Beth played the comedic role of the mayor's wife; Louisa and Sebastian were in the tech booth, running lights and sound; and at the director's invitation, I put together an exhibit in the theater lobby about G. Oliver, a real-life music man.

During the four-day band festival, I attended as many concerts as I could. My favorite moment came on Saturday evening, when Kenny Carr and the Tigers took the stage.

Dressed in a white T-shirt, white pants, and a white ball cap, Carr held a polished trombone in his left hand. The black bandleader looked out at the mostly white crowd from behind dark glasses and raised his right arm in the air.

"C'mon Northfield, c'mon Northfield, give us some love, Northfield. C'mon Northfield, c'mon Northfield, give us some love, Northfield."

The audience clapped tentatively. Braver souls swayed in lawn chairs. Undeterred, Carr repeated his entreaty. He had not traveled all the way from North Carolina to entertain a *seated* audience.

"C'mon Northfield!"

The drummer kept the beat, and the brass players launched into a jazz tune fused with gospel. The music washed over the downtown square like a tonic. People smiled. Toes tapped. As the circle sun dropped below the horizon, hundreds of stolid Midwesterners rose to their feet, raised their arms in the air, and danced with visitors from the East Coast and the South.

Once the blaze of gold and orange faded from the sky, you could no longer see individual faces, you could no longer see skin color or age or gender or other ways in which we judge each other. You could only make out inky silhouettes, like notes on a music staff, against the backdrop of the lighted stage. You could feel the beat of the music, the pulse of the crowd, and the movement of bodies around you. In this sliver of time, you could feel the pure, expansive love of being alive.

MY CONVERSATIONS WITH Ted remained in the back of my mind that fall, and when Louisa's high school choir performed with thirty-five other groups at the 111th annual St. Olaf College Choral Festival in November, I couldn't help but think of the band boys. Before the closing number, St. Olaf choral director Anton Armstrong spoke passionately about the role the arts play in educating young people.

"We will not have a society that can go forth if they don't know how to live and make beautiful things together. My colleagues and I have been saying that if we can get Congress to sing together in a choir, they might be able to govern the country. Because you have how many shades of varieties of thought and beliefs up here," Armstrong said, pointing toward the massed choir, "but they sing together as one. That's what the arts have to give: they transform the mind, they transform the heart, they transform the very spirit and essence of who we are."

I left the concert feeling inspired to return to my book project. Even though Ted claimed he had no new material for me, I didn't believe it. I needed to see him again.

26

The Night We Called It a Day

In his State of the Union speech on January 6, 1941, a week before his unprecedented third inauguration, President Franklin Delano Roosevelt tried to convince Americans of the need to intervene in the war and support Britain. He spoke about the threat Hitler's regime posed to democracies worldwide, and of the need to fight for four essential freedoms that he insisted all people were due: freedom of speech, freedom of religion, freedom from want, and freedom from fear.

It would be almost a year before the United States entered the war, but two weeks later, two hundred and fifty National Guard members from St. Cloud were called to active duty with the 217th Coast Artillery, including the thirty-two-piece regimental band. Led by Chester Heinzel, the band included eight other G. Oliver-trained men. The youngest, William Sherin, was a Cathedral High School student. The city threw a party for them, which Governor Harold Stassen attended,[1] and when they boarded a train for California on February 20, a crowd saw them off at the depot.

Islea did not attend the festivities. Heart problems slowed her down that winter, and she spent two weeks in the hospital. By mid-March, she had resumed her piano work.

Despite worries G. Oliver must have had about Islea's health, he proceeded with a joint concert that month with the St. Cloud Civic Chorus. One week later, Congress approved the Lend-Lease

278

The St. Cloud Municipal Band performs at Memorial Day services on the St. Germain Street Bridge in St. Cloud, May 30, 1941.

Act, which authorized the President to provide arms and supplies to Britain. This moved the United States closer to entering the war.

The fact that so many countries had become involved in another world war weighed heavily on G. Oliver's friend George Landers. The eighty-one-year-old bandleader believed music could be a tool to unite people and prevent future wars. While attending the American Bandmasters Association convention in Madison, Wisconsin, on March 2, Landers gave a speech, "Music as Peace Insurance," in which he advocated for organizing a band, orchestra, and chorus that would tour the war-torn countries after the war.[2]

G. Oliver did not attend the conference, but he surely knew about the speech; he and Landers regularly kept in touch through letters.

In mid-March, G. Oliver's new fifty-piece boys' band gave its first public concert, for parents gathered at the rehearsal hall. Budget cuts prevented outfitting all the boys with uniforms. Despite waning financial support, G. Oliver kept looking for ways to make the band relevant to community life. Later that spring, the older boys and young men performed at a boxing match, and for the opening of baseball season.

In June, G. Oliver attended the fourteenth annual Iowa Bandmasters convention in Cedar Rapids, as one of two out-of-state speakers. He demonstrated the proper method of teaching cornet, which he had learned from Alfred F. Weldon, founder of the "light pressure method of playing cup mouthpiece instruments."[3] It was the first time G. Oliver had been invited to speak to the group, although he had known its members for years, including Landers. It must have pleased G. Oliver to be thus honored.

Shortly after G. Oliver's return from Iowa, Islea visited Percy and his family for two weeks, and at the end of July, she and G. Oliver took a vacation in northern Minnesota. While his parents were gone, Ronald directed a municipal band concert for his father, and he led the municipal band in a citywide pageant at Tech High School.

Islea apparently felt bad about missing the activities in St. Cloud. She wrote to her daughter-in-law Eleanor from Grace Lake:

> *The time goes very slowly to me out here, and I won't be sorry to be going home. I felt so bad last Sat. that I almost did go home, but I got better again, and don't like to have Father go before his time is up. He is enjoying it so much, and I think it does him a lot of good. But I hope I never have to stay here another 4 weeks without some one to keep me company.*
>
> *Sat. I was really not well, besides being lonesome. My old "ticker" didn't seem to want to work at all—guess the Digitalis slowed it down too much. We are to leave here Sat., although Father said we could go sooner if I said so. I don't think I'll say so. . . .*
>
> *Tell Bill A-Ma will soon be seeing him. I'll be so glad, too. Guess Ronald is having a lot to do—almost too much I'd say...*"[4]

That fall, as German forces approached Moscow, President Roosevelt approved a lend-lease agreement with the Soviet Union, providing that country with $1 billion in aid. While many eyes focused on Moscow, the US Ambassador to Japan, Joseph Grew, warned the State Department that Japan planned to launch an attack at Pearl Harbor in Hawai'i. His warning was ignored.[5]

On December 8, a day after Japanese planes and submarines attacked Pearl Harbor, the United States entered the war. That evening, the *St. Cloud Times-Journal* declared that Japan's action would lead to Hitler's demise, and that it had united Americans behind the goal of fighting the axis powers and spreading liberty to nations enslaved by dictators.

"We lost the first World war at the peace table because we refused to carry on with the League of Nations. We will profit by our mistake and this time we will fight as hard for peace as we are going to fight for victory," the editorial said.[6]

G. Oliver believed his band played an important service by boosting morale in a time of war. He arranged for the February concert to be broadcast over the radio, to reach a wider audience.

Two days before the concert, the newspaper ran a lengthy article about G. Oliver's career.

Islea's health did not improve, and she suspended her music activities in March, and at 8:30 in the evening on April 4, the day before Easter, she died at home of heart failure.

The funeral was held on April 7 at St. John's Episcopal Church, where she had served as organist and music director. A former student of hers played the organ, and six members of the St. Cloud Municipal Band served as pallbearers. Her obituary in the *St. Cloud Daily Times* credited her with organizing some of the first musical societies in northern Minnesota,

Islea Graham Riggs, 1874-1942

and noted that she was active with music clubs and work since moving to St. Cloud.[7] Members of St. Cloud's Music and Drama Club sent a letter to the family expressing their distress at losing a valued member and friend.[8]

G. OLIVER MUST have found it difficult to adjust to her absence, and he may have found solace in his work. A week after Islea's death, he accompanied Ronald on a trip to Aitkin, Minnesota, where Ronald judged a high school band contest. At the end of the month, both men participated in a massed band concert that was part of the Stearns County Music Festival and was broadcast over KFAM radio. Ronald directed the "Star Spangled Banner," and G. Oliver directed a patriotic medley, "United We Stand." A news story said organizers believed that "music is important as a real force in keeping high the people's morale."[9]

Hertz was elected president of the Minnesota Music Educators Association that spring, and Ronald became secretary-treasurer. This must have made for interesting conversations between father and son. Ronald and Hertz attended the same church, and their jobs provided them with frequent opportunities for collaboration.

In the fall of 1942, G. Oliver created a new sign-up card for the 1942–43 Municipal band. It said: "Members of the Municipal Band have shown true American spirit by playing on all patriotic occasions as assigned to them, in addition to regular service. People of St. Cloud appreciate this splendid demonstration of citizenship. Many of our band members have been called by our government to serve in this war—more will be called. That means that those of us who are not called, must do our duty at home."[10]

In October, G. Oliver invited the mayor, the city commissioners, and Hertz to a municipal band banquet at the Teachers College. Ronald served as toastmaster, and the featured speaker was Andrew Vavricka, a professional musician and boys' band alumnus. The city leaders had cut the annual band budget from $4,065 to $3,800 that year, and G. Oliver may have felt it worthwhile to curry favor with them. A photo taken at the event showed G. Oliver and Ronald laughing and talking with the guests.[11]

The next month, Ronald and Eleanor's second son, Robert Graham, was born. His middle name honored the grandmother he didn't get to meet.

G. Oliver concluded the year with a trip to Chicago, where he purchased new pieces for the band. He visited his friend Hale VanderCook, director of the VanderCook School of Music, and he stayed with Percy and his family. Percy had quit his South Bend job and moved to Chicago to pursue an advanced degree at the Chicago Musical College. G. Oliver also visited his sister, Daisy, in Rock Island, Illinois. When he returned to St. Cloud, he reported that all the servicemen he met and talked to during his trip "were well satisfied with their treatment by the United States government and morale was good."[12]

In early 1943, St. Cloud residents learned that William Sherin had died in California. He had left the regimental band to join the Army Air Corps and was making one of his first solo flights when he crashed. The municipal band acted as honorary escort for Sherin's funeral, and five cornetists who played in the boys' band with Sherin played "Taps."[13]

The municipal and boys' bands merged that spring, and in late May, the fifty-five-piece band presented a concert of patriotic music at the Veterans Facility. It also marched in the Memorial Day and Flag Day parades. But the musicians voted not to participate in the city's Fourth of July festivities, breaking a longstanding tradition. By then, membership had dropped to forty-four, which, G. Oliver said, made it difficult to stage a "good showing."[14]

G. Oliver formed a band out of the remaining youth members and a dozen adult volunteers, including Ronald. Three concerts were scheduled for the fall and winter.

As band numbers declined, G. Oliver must have felt anxious about the future of his job. He told the newspaper, "So far as I know, people wish us to continue doing the best we can until the boys return. More members for the regular band are needed and beginners will also be given suitable separate instruction. More recruits and members must be had or your famous and helpful band may die an 'unnecessary death.' I would say 'everybody hold the band.'"[15]

In November, boys' band alumnus Pvt. Oliver Kerben wrote to G. Oliver from overseas. The letter said: "I think so often of the times we had in the band. All the heartaches and disappointments of some of those periods of preparation. Then came the time when we reached the peak and then a little tapering off. Then came the tournament, the great test; and we walked away with everything in our class."

He continued, "Mr. Riggs, I have to make this short and snappy but you may rest assured I will write soon again. I hope your present band is going well and continues successfully. St. Cloud certainly owes you an immense debt for the young fellows of the community. The influence of your good work has been felt all along the line. We need more men like you."[16]

IN DECEMBER OF 1923, G. Oliver traveled to Joy, Illinois, to attend his sister Daisy's funeral. Her death, on the day after Christmas, meant G. Oliver was more alone than ever.

The precariousness of G. Oliver's job grew as the war continued, and he announced on February 12, 1944, that he was scheduling a meeting for young women interested in permanently joining the band. He declared, "girls as well as boys are capable of good musical performances,"[17] and he said several young women had already contacted him; most preferred to play the saxophone. No further mention was made in the newspaper about the meeting.

In April, G. Oliver began planning the summer concert season. Granddaughter Mary Jane had won a regional vocal contest in Chicago, and he hoped she could perform again with his band.

G. Oliver's hopes did not materialize.

On April 17, incumbent Mayor Phil Collignon won a fourth term, defeating former mayor James Murphy by 295 votes. William Burkhard was re-elected finance commissioner, and incumbent streets commissioner Nat Fish lost to L.I. Stanley. The following week, the new city commission terminated G. Oliver's contract as band director effective May 1.[18]

It was the second time in his career that St. Cloud officials had forced G. Oliver out of a job.

Parents, musicians, and band committee members attended a farewell party for him on May 1 in the rehearsal hall. Murphy thanked G. Oliver for bringing honor to the city through his untiring efforts with the band.

G. Oliver told the crowd, "I appreciate the friendship which has been accorded me throughout the past years. Our municipal band has always made a good record wherever it has gone." He also said his "last wish was for the band to 'keep going.'"[19]

St. Cloud Times writer Harold Schoelkopf devoted his May 3 column to G. Oliver's retirement, and the training he provided to hundreds of boys.

When Mr. Riggs came here in 1923, the schools of the city did not have well-developed music programs. Youngsters received their individual training in the city band. In later years, the schools perfected excellent music courses, so that, in effect, the municipal band was duplicating the work of the schools. It was probably that realization that brought about the change.

Since both the school systems here now maintain their own bands and orchestras, what the city seems to need is an adult band into which these younger players can graduate when they finish their school work. That may be started in the near future. Whatever may be done, however, St. Cloud owes a vote of thanks to Mr. Riggs who pioneered in band work here, and whose musical organizations won fame and high praise in the northwest.[20]

Schoelkopf's column explained why the city felt a municipal boys' band was no longer necessary, but it didn't explain why G. Oliver wasn't asked to direct an adult municipal band.

G. Oliver stopped by the newspaper office to say goodbye before leaving for Bemidji. The staff printed an excerpt of the discussion in an editorial titled, "Not Tough—But Sincere."

"We popped this question at Mr. Riggs: 'We understand that you have always been pretty tough to the youngsters and insisted on perfect discipline at all times—yet the boys seemed to love to work under you. How did you do it?' Mr. Riggs' answer was 'I always tried to be fair to the boys, but of course, to get anywhere with a band, perfect discipline was most necessary. If I had to be tough to obtain it, the majority of the boys understood the necessity and always realized that I was trying sincerely to make each band member a good musician and a good citizen and realized that to obtain such results they would have to be disciplined just as they were taught discipline from their own parents—and they took mine the same way.'"[21]

Two days before Memorial Day, the ex-bandmaster took out an ad in the *St. Cloud Daily Times*, to send a message to his former band boys in service across the world. It said:

I had hoped to keep the Municipal Band intact until your return, but the Mayor and City Commission have decided against me. On May 1st, 1944 there were 38 young men and 14 older men playing in the organization. I will return to St. Cloud to greet you when the war is over, but so far as I know, I will not be your Bandmaster.

During our many happy years of association we learned much from each other. I know you are doing your duty, whatever that may be. I wish you Good Health and a safe return.

My address during the summer will be R.R. No. 3, Bemidji, Minn. [22]

Memorial Day services continued without him, and without a municipal band, for the first time since 1929. G. Oliver spent the summer at the cabin, with an air horn his sons gave him in case he had a medical problem and needed to alert the neighbors.

The Eagles Band and the Sauk Rapids municipal band put on concerts that summer, and the Tech and Cathedral bands made some appearances. But the absence of a band dedicated to civic service was noticed. Both the annual Flag Day parade and the Fourth of July parade were canceled because no band could lead them.

In September, the city hired Hertz to organize a new municipal orchestra and band program, open to men and women. Orchestra season would run from October through March, and the band season from April through September. [23]

In the course of 1945, news arrived that several of G. Oliver's former pupils had died. The *St. Cloud Daily Times* printed an editorial estimating that more than one hundred men from St. Cloud had lost their lives. [24] G. Oliver was undoubtedly relieved to receive a letter in March from a former band member who was very much alive. Warren Raymond wrote:

I hope this letter finds you in good health. I have a favor to ask of you and hope you will help me. There is a cornet player in the band that is interested in the no-pressure system and diaphragm breathing. I told him that my former bandmaster was an expert on the subject and offered to write a letter to you for him. He is a very good musician and is serious about study. Right now I am somewhere in Germany. I'm still repairing instruments and playing trombone. The other day, one of the fellows brought in a German French horn that he found. It's one of the best horns that we have in the band. The tone is as clear as a bell and it has fine workmanship.[25]

Keeping up with news events that spring was a challenge, even for a retired bandmaster. In mid-April, President Roosevelt died in his sleep. Less than two weeks later, St. Cloud Mayor Phil Collignon died of a heart attack, and the city commission appointed former mayor James Murphy to the vacancy. At the end of April, Hitler committed suicide, and on May 7, Americans welcomed the end to the war in Europe. The war against Japan continued until early August, when the United States dropped atomic bombs on Hiroshima and Nagasaki. Japan surrendered to the Allies on August 14, 1945.

The transition from war to peace was a slow process. More than three hundred thousand men and women from Minnesota had served in the war. They began returning home in November— around the time G. Oliver announced that he had accepted a part-time position directing a school band on the Red Lake Reservation, twenty-five miles northwest of Bemidji. The superintendent, Gordon Ose, wanted to add music and art to the curriculum. The

Family at the cabin on Grace Lake in 1945. From left to right: G. Oliver Riggs, Charles Johnson, Bill Riggs, Bob Riggs, Ronald Riggs, Alice Johnson.

school's principal, Nels Thorson, was a friend from G. Oliver's Crookston days, and the older brother of Ted Thorson, the Crookston band director.

"There has been no band in the reservation school before; in fact most of the youngsters there probably are not even familiar with band instruments, Mr. Riggs said. But the school, enthusiastic now over the program, is securing $1,500 worth of instruments as a starter. Mr. Riggs will give instruction three days a week and hopes to build up a 50-piece band," the *St. Cloud Daily Times* reported.[26]

G. Oliver spent December with Percy's family in Chicago, and Percy drove his father back to Minnesota in early January. During their last conversation, Percy wrote later, "I had tried to convince him of the great help that he had given to so many people, and the profound changes in the musical life of various communities that had been the direct result of his efforts. He admitted that I was probably right, but wondered what would have happened to his career as a soloist if he had never left Chicago for Minnesota."[27]

G. Oliver rented a room at the Hotel Markham in Bemidji and took a bus to the school. Seventy-five Ojibwe and white students attended the first meeting, and thirty-nine signed up. He held the first two rehearsals on Thursday and Friday of the next week.

The next Tuesday, G. Oliver sat in the hotel lobby and wrote to his elder son:

Dear Ronald,

You may consider this letter as a start of a weekly report. First, I have $20.00 coming to me from the Red Lake School. I have 47 boys and girls signed up for band. Now, here is a problem for you to figure out for me, 47 members and 26 instruments. I got a much larger band than Superintendent Ose thought possible.

At present we are having more than one taking their instruction on one instrument. He (Supt) appears to be afraid of his school board or someone else. He cooperates with me fine on most things.

I have made a request for enough instruments to supply each band member with an instrument. Mr. Thorson has been of great help to me and after my Thur (3 to 4) meeting made a written report to the Supt. And I think Mr. Ose sees the situation differently now.

I have 1 girl (Indian) on clarinet who is <u>very</u> musical and also equally intelligent. One Indian girl on trombone of Tom Peterson [sic]type.

As a rule the boys are <u>much more</u> intelligent than the girls.

I have 1 big, husky Indian boy on bass and he is a dandy.

There is a curling event in Bemidji and my letter has been interrupted by a bunch that have bought me my 4th cup of coffee but I got out of it O.K., so I guess I have a little of the old stuff left.

I came back from Red Lake Friday night and felt the best I have felt for several months. Didn't feel quite so good yesterday and am a little nervous this morning.

I think the work with the band at R.L. is going to do me some good.

I have a good room, good bed and fine place to eat so you may feel that you did the right thing for me when you advised me to take over the R.L. Band.

Mr. Ose was all set to have me put in more time but I showed him your card and he saw the point. I told him I depended on your <u>fine memory</u> and had asked you to write me the understanding and he said he "hoped Ronald would not think he was trying to over-work his father." He has another surprise coming to him when we have the parents meeting. How those old Indians will like me.

We have white children also but so far the Indian children are doing the best work.

Thursday I assigned 3 white girls to cornets and all I could get out of them was giggles. I finally got two to stop giggling and the other girl got mad, sullen. I told her she could either stop giggling or leave the room. I gave her a few minutes to make her choice and she finally said she would stop giggling.

Ose thought I did right. The principal at Redby, a small woman, licked a boy with a strap and Ose said O.K. The boy had ran off—got to Chinook Mont.

Well the curlers are busy again so I will close.
Write me again some.
Your father,
G. Oliver Riggs[28]

G. Oliver returned to Red Lake on January 24 to rehearse the band, and he stayed overnight at the school. During the night or early morning, he became ill. Ose drove G. Oliver to Bemidji, and before they reached the hospital, G. Oliver had a heart attack. He stopped breathing and couldn't be revived.

His sons arranged a service at a Bemidji funeral home. Vocal music was provided by Carl Thompson of the Bemidji Teachers College, and G. Oliver was buried in Crookston next to Islea.

Newspapers in Bemidji, Crookston, and St. Cloud ran obituaries, and Ronald received condolences from several people, including George Landers, who expressed shock. "While we all have to go—I never thought that your father was *near the end*," he wrote. "Sympathy at a time like this does not amount to much in a way. However your father was an *outstanding* man. He had done much to assist youngsters in making this old world a better place to live in with *music*."[29]

Ronald also received a letter from Ose and eight dollars from the school staff for a memorial.

"Your father's passing was a great shock to all of us and I assure you that he is sadly missed here. It was so destined that I happened to spend the last four hours of your father's life with him, and I want you to know that he was his old lovable self right up to the time he was stricken. He was truly a bandmaster to the very last and you and Percy have every reason to be proud of him," Ose wrote.[30]

Ronald and Percy sold the cabin on Grace Lake and the land their father owned north of Bemidji. Once G. Oliver's legal affairs were settled, they did what their parents would have hoped and expected. They turned their attention back to their careers and their growing families.

They had work to do. The music waited.

27

SHALOM

On one of my last visits to Ted—he had recently celebrated his 100th birthday—I had something to show him: a portrait of G. Oliver, Islea, and their family in 1910, around the time they left Grand Forks (and the year that Ted's dad played in G. Oliver's band). G. Oliver wore a suit, vest and tie; a pocket watch chain peeked out from his vest. Islea wore a high-necked dress, Percy and Ronald wore dark suits and ties, and two-year-old Rosalie wore a white dress; her hair was pulled back by a thick white bow.

"I see G. Oliver—is that his wife?" Ted asked, pointing at Islea. "Yes."

"She has an unusual name. I never knew her name until you came. I always wanted to. She's the opposite of him. He was a crusty old guy, and she was just a lovely lady. She was kind of fat. But—did I tell you …"

He launched into a new story about a St. Cloud municipal band picnic he attended as a kid. For fun, the band members' wives picked up the instruments and pretended to play.

"My mother was a little lady, five foot three, and she took—she took the fellow's soprano saxophone, she was blowing on this thing and she didn't know what she was doing, and *she*," Ted said, referring to Islea, "she was playing the sousaphone."

"She was?" I tried to picture Islea with a sousaphone.

Ted continued, as though reading my mind. "I have a picture

291

The Riggs family in 1910, left to right: Percy, age 6; G. Oliver; Rosalie, age 2; Islea, and Ronald, age 8.

someplace in my home of her and my mother."

"You have a picture of that? I would love to see it."

Ted's gaze returned to the 1910 picture.

"Percy ran a high school band for a while. He once asked me to play for his band. He needed a clarinet player to play at the county fair, so I did. I had fun, and he came up to me and gave me a dollar. A dollar!"

"Wow," I said, imagining that would seem like a fortune to a boy in the 1920s.

Ted, again as though reading my mind, said, "That's a million dollars! I remember that very well." He handed the photograph back to me. "That's a wonderful picture."

I hated to end the conversation that afternoon because I knew he would be sad. He also seemed hesitant to say goodbye.

"I'm talking longer than I had planned because I may not be here when you come next, and I—I may not be alive. Who knows?"

His voice trailed off.

"I like to talk about the things I know most about, put it that way—I'm not going to talk about *football.*"

We both laughed. We were kindred spirits as far as that topic was concerned.

"You drive carefully because I do want to see you again," he said. "But I don't have much more to tell you, so if I don't see you again, be well and do well. As they say, shalom. You know what shalom means?"

"It means peace?" I hoped this was the answer he was looking for.

He nodded. "It means peace. It also means goodbye. I'll tell you the story about that one day."

I worried about him on the drive home. Maybe he knew something I didn't. Maybe he would die tonight, alone. Maybe I should have said what was in my heart: that if we didn't see each other again, I was grateful we had become friends. That meeting him felt like a gift from God, whatever god was looking over us, the observant Jew and the doubting Catholic.

Months went by; I kept plugging away at the G. Oliver project, but I didn't make it a priority until that fall, when I cut back on freelance work and refocused on writing the book. I hadn't seen Ted for six months, so I emailed his daughter, Gail, to ask about her dad's health and to inquire about the picnic photo he'd mentioned on our last visit.

Gail responded, "My dad is doing as well as could be expected for someone who is 100 1/2. He loves your visits. I think Wednesdays or Thursdays in the afternoon are best. I don't ever remember seeing the picture you described, but I will try to locate it. Thank you so much for your visits and your interest in my Dad. I think you lift his spirits and help him continue to feel a part of a community."

The sun-filled days were warmer than usual in Minnesota that fall, and the red, orange, and brown tones of the leaves seemed more vibrant. By October 29, temperatures had dropped to the mid-40s. Weather forecasters predicted that the trick-or-treaters would need to bundle up.

Although many trees along the interstate had lost their leaves, it was still a lovely drive from Northfield to the Shalom Home. On my way in, I noticed, for the first time, the inscription on the wall of the building, set in a square of concrete. At the top were Hebrew words and below them an English translation: "Cast me not off in times of old age." –Psalms 71:9.

When I reached Ted's room, I noticed the door was slightly ajar. I listened for sounds of movement from inside. It was quiet. Was he sleeping? I knocked softly before I entered. As I peered around the corner I spotted Ted, sitting on the side of his bed. He looked alert and expectant.

"Hey, bonehead," I called out.

He looked gleeful.

"I have a *surprise* for you," he said. He nearly sang the words.

"You do?"

My heart beat a little faster. I guessed what that meant, but I didn't want to get my hopes up.

"There's a thick book over there on the shelf, right in the middle—do you see it? Can you get it for me?"

"*Full Harvest?*"

"Yes, that's it."

I maneuvered between the bed and his walker and reached for the nine-hundred-page historical novel. I needed both hands to lift it. I sat next to him on the bed and waited in suspense.

Ted opened the book to a bookmarked chapter about his grandfather. But that wasn't the object of his search. He then turned to the back of the book, where three loose, black and white photos had been placed. Two were the size of my iPhone; the third was almost half that size.

My eyes widened. I sensed that my guess had been right.

"Here's what I had in mind for you. Some pictures," Ted said.

The smallest one showed a dozen middle-aged women holding

Wives of the St. Cloud Municipal Band members at a picnic in about 1924.

band instruments. The women wore long dresses and kneeled or stood in the grass, with trees and a lake behind them.

"Oh my gosh!"

I peered through my "graduated lenses," wishing I had a magnifying glass or younger eyes. I pointed to a woman in the front right corner.

"Is that your mom?"

Ted put on his glasses and read the words scrawled in black ink on the back of the photo: "St. Cloud Municipal Band Picnic. Ladies pictured with instruments. Some front row ..."

I interrupted. "Does that say Sonia—your mom?"

"Yes. Sonia, front row, 1924 or '25—I wasn't sure which year that was," he said. "They took the men's instruments, which they can't play, and they did that for a joke."

He turned the photo over so we could see the women's faces again. Sonia wore a white dress, and her dark hair was pulled back from her face. She held an alto saxophone.

"Yes, that's my mother," Ted confirmed.

He moved on to a second picture, the one he *really* wanted to show me. Six women appeared to play band instruments. Ted's mom was second from the left. On the right was a woman with an ample figure holding a sousaphone. She had not been in the previous photo. But she looked familiar anyway.

"One of these ladies is Mrs. Riggs," Ted said, peering at the faces. He pointed to the figure with the sousaphone. "I think that's her. Is she kind of a fat lady?"

"Yes, that looks like it could be her," I agreed.

"That's your great-grandmother!" he pronounced triumphantly. The surprise was revealed.

He read the words on the back: "St. Cloud Municipal Band Picnic. Ladies with the instruments for a fun picture."

We both laughed.

The third photo showed young Ted, playing clarinet, and his brother, playing soprano saxophone, outside their house. It resembled the photo he gave me on a previous visit.

He handed all three photos to me.

"They're yours forever," he said. "Guard them with your life!"

He didn't appear to be joking.

Now it was my turn. From my purse I removed the pocket watch. I had slipped it into my purse before I'd left my house. Even though I believed Chris' hunch—that G. Oliver received it as a gift from his parents—it occurred to me that Ted might recognize it.

I pried open the gold-plated cover, revealing the creamy white clock face, the motionless hands, and the black spidery Roman numerals.

"We think that it belonged to G. Oliver, that it was his pocket watch. Do you remember him having a pocket watch?"

Ted examined it with the discerning gaze of an experienced pediatrician.

"I don't remember that. No, that escapes me," he said, after a pause. He shook his head.

I tried not to feel too disappointed. It was a long shot—and I would have kicked myself if I hadn't asked him about the watch. It would likely remain one of those unknowns in this epic tale of a music man, like when and where G. Oliver played with Sousa's band.

When I stood up to leave, Ted returned to the topic of the picnic photos.

"Don't lose any of those," he admonished. "I don't have any secondary ones. If I find some more, I'll get in touch with you. I

296

don't think there will be any more, but I was delighted to find what we did."

"Thank you so much—it means a lot."

He promised to tell me more stories about the war next time, even though he shouldn't because I was "a nice girl."

We both laughed.

"You are!" he insisted. "We can laugh about it, and that's good. I like to laugh."

His smile faded, and he changed topics abruptly.

"What kind of car do you have?"

Shoot. I probably would have answered honestly. But I had recently listened to the recording of the visit where he had emphatically explained his opposition to his family driving Japanese or German-made cars—even now, nearly seventy years after the war.

I could say "Mini Cooper," which was Steve's car, but wasn't that made by BMW? Afraid of disappointing him, I blurted out the first American car company that came to mind: "It's a Ford."

"A what?" Ted's hearing-assisted device was acting up. He fiddled with it and turned it off.

"A Ford." I repeated.

I decided to leave before he asked me what kind of Ford I had. I was a terrible liar.

"I'm going to go home and work on my book, and I'm going to tell my dad about the pictures," I said.

Ted watched me leave from the bed. "Goodbye. Drive carefully, and take care of the pictures."

"I will. I will see you soon."

He wasn't done. He had one more thing to say.

"If you ever publish it, I'd like to see your book," he said. "OK, bye-bye."

The last time I left Ted's room, I had felt sad. This time, I was mad at myself. Why did I lie to a one-hundred-year-old man about my car? I should have deflected the question, if I was so worried about upsetting him. I hadn't even known him when I bought my car.

It wasn't until I got to the parking lot and unlocked my Mazda5 that I remembered an article I'd recently read about Henry

Ford's awful, anti-Semitic views. Crap. I should have told the truth. And I couldn't count on Ted forgetting—he never forgot anything. I could only hope he hadn't heard me.

The next day, I wrote a blog post about the visit (minus the part about the car). I concluded:

"Every visit I have with you is a gift, Ted. Thank you.

With love and gratitude,

Your favorite bonehead"

A week and a half later, I received a message from Gail. I was sitting in the living room, checking email while Steve and the boys watched TV. I clicked on the message, thinking she was writing to tell me about Ted's reaction to my post. But that wasn't it. Ted had died.

He developed pneumonia three days ago, she wrote. He became progressively weaker, then unresponsive. He died at about one o'clock that afternoon.

I glanced at Steve. "Ted died earlier today." As soon as the words left my throat, my eyes filled up with tears. "I just got a message from his daughter."

Tears made it difficult for my eyes to focus as I read the message aloud in a shaky voice. Steve, Sebastian, and Elias came over and hugged me. "We're sorry, Mom," Seb said. Elias gave my leg a comforting squeeze.

I tried to prepare myself for this eventuality; one should not expect to form a long-lasting friendship with someone as old as the Panama Canal. And yet, it came as a shock. He looked so chipper during my last visit. I meant to ask an aide to take a picture of Ted and me, but I forgot in the excitement of Ted's surprise. Now it would never happen. There would be no photo to document the friendship of two boneheads.

ALTHOUGH SEEING OTHER people grieve usually made me cry, I found funerals fascinating. The type of service and the choices in music usually showed what the deceased person valued, or what their families valued. A funeral also served as a reality check. Was I living the life I wanted to live? If I died tomorrow, what would be said about me, and who would grieve?

I had attended many funerals, for personal reasons, and on assignment; once, in Mississippi, I attended the Baptist funeral of a young man who died in a shooting. It was a cultural experience, for sure, for a young white Catholic woman from Minnesota to watch black Southern women cry and grieve openly, to the point of fainting, and to hear people shout "Amen" throughout the service.

But I had never attended a Jewish funeral. So I asked Google for advice.

The how-to steps on "My Jewish Learning.com" seemed not so different from a Protestant or Catholic funeral:

No. 1: *Decide whether you are going.* OK, that was easy. Yes.

No. 2: *Dress appropriately.* For Minnesota in November, appropriate meant a down jacket, gloves, and a warm hat. But the writer of the article focused on indoor clothing: for women, a dress, and for men, a coat and tie. The article also noted that it was customary for men to wear a *yarmulke* on their heads. No worries—this did not apply to me. I decided to wear a skirt, tights, a sweater, and my brown leather boots.

No. 3: *Arrive early.* Always a good idea.

No. 4: *Follow directions.* The funeral director would let people know whether to sit or stand. Sign the guest book if there is one. Got it.

No. 5: *Do not greet the mourners.* "That's what the guest book is for, or let them know how you reacted to the eulogy when you see them during a shiva call. If you are very, very close family or friends, it may be appropriate to see the mourners before the service begins or approach them after the graveside service."

Well, I wasn't planning on making a shiva call, and I wasn't a close family member or friend, so I would hang back and play the role of observer/journalist.

The remaining steps that most interested me were 11, 12 and 13:

No. 11: *Surround the family at the graveside.* "When you reach the cemetery, you will be directed to the graveside. There you will find a row of chairs for the mourners. Stand behind and around the graveside. When the family arrives, do not greet them. Let them take their places for the graveside service."

No. 12: *Participate in the ritual at graveside.* "The casket may be lowered and friends invited to place dirt into the grave. Normally, the officiants begin this ritual, followed by the mourners and their family members. Then, you can take a place in line to do this most meaningful and important *mitzvah*. When your turn arrives, pick up a handful of dirt with your hands or with a shovel and place it into the grave. Some do this three times. Place the shovel back into the pile of dirt; do not hand it to the next person."

No. 13: *Offer your condolences.* "As the mourners leave the gravesite, form two rows in the crowd creating a path for their exit. As they pass, say the ancient words of consolation, '*Ha-Makom yenahem etkhem b'tokh sha ar aveilei Tzion vYerushalayim*—May the Omnipresent comfort you among all the mourners of Zion and Jerusalem.' Generally, you do not approach the mourners at this time. If you do, they must acknowledge your presence rather than cope with their own grief. Of course, if the mourner reaches out to you, respond with a hug and an additional word of condolence."

I did not think I could learn the ancient words of consolation in time, nor did I think anyone would expect that of me. I would do my best with the rest of it.

The cemetery was in a wooded, hilly area and had a little creek running through it. An inch of snow covered the ground. My car told me the outside temperature was 22 degrees above zero. I entered the one-story chapel and sat toward the back, next to the wall. The room held about one hundred and twenty padded chairs, arranged in rows. Two gray tablets that looked like the Ten Commandments adorned the front wall. Underneath the tablets was a menorah; the candles were lit, but their warmth did not compensate for the building's lack of heat. I kept my coat on.

Mourners streamed in, and most seemed to know each other. The men wore *yarmulkes*, and the rabbi wore a broad-brimmed black hat. He had a salt-and-pepper beard and could have been thirty or fifty; the beard made it hard to discern his age. When the service began, he first spoke in Hebrew, and then he spoke in English, about how Ted grew up in St. Cloud and was the grandson of a North Dakota rabbi; how he loved to speak his mind and study Judaism; how he was an amazing clinical diagnostician; how he loved to fish.

The oldest grandchild, Brian, spoke next. He, his wife, and his daughter surprised Ted with a visit about a week before he died. Ted told them about a blog post—"he didn't know what a blog was, so he called it an article," Brian explained—written by a woman whose great-grandfather had been Ted's band director, and Ted had given her some special photos.

My cheeks flushed, and my eyes welled with tears. Although I was not family, and had never met anyone in the room except Ted's wife, Dorothy, Ted felt like family to me. It made me happy to know that he was talking about that visit a few days later.

Grandsons Seth and Herschel and granddaughter Ilana also spoke, and last was David, the only grandchild to become a pediatrician like Ted. David said the job was much harder than he had expected, based on Ted's keen ability to speedily diagnose illnesses. He said he wished he could go back in time and ask his grandfather how he did it.

When the service ended, I followed the convoy of mourners to an area farther away from the cemetery entrance. It would be a beautiful spot in the summer. But today, with no protection from the wind, it was not a welcoming place for the living to linger.

Ted's wife, son, and two daughters sat in chairs underneath a green tent, and family and friends gathered behind them and to the side of the tent, facing the open grave. The rabbi spoke again, and the Hebrew words sounded mysteriously comforting, like Latin in an old-school Catholic Mass. I couldn't see much of what was going on from where I stood, toward the back. I wiggled my toes inside my boots and pulled my hat down tighter over my ears. When the rabbi invited people to come forward to place dirt on the casket, I was glad I had done my research—even though he said anyone was welcome to participate, I might have hesitated otherwise.

When my turn came, I grasped the shovel handle with a gloved hand, grasped the wooden shaft with my other hand, and pulled the blade out of the dirt. I turned the blade over, scooped up some dirt, and tossed it onto the casket below.

One.

It looked down cold in that hole. Ted's body was inside the casket, getting colder by the minute.

Two.

His soul was elsewhere, though. Perhaps he was reunited with his parents, whom he loved and missed so dearly.

Three.

I had never participated in a ritual like this, and it felt right. People help us into the world during birth—with different tools—and people help us leave it. We all return to the earth.

I tossed one final scoop of dirt onto the casket.

Shalom, my friend.

I turned away and plunged the shovel blade into the mound of dirt. I wiped a few loose tears from my cheeks as I joined the other mourners shivering in the cold.

I wanted to let Gail know I had been there, but I didn't want to seek her out. Also, I wasn't sure what she looked like, although logic told me she was one of the two women who had sat next to Dorothy. As I considered my next move, her son Brian walked past me. I caught his eye and said: "Hi, Brian. I'm Joy Riggs."

He looked at me blankly. I realized my mistake; the name Riggs was not as familiar to him as it had been to his grandfather. Duh. I was an idiot.

"I'm sorry," I stammered, trying to clarify. "I'm the woman who wrote the blog."

"Oh, yes," he nodded in recognition. "It's nice to meet you."

We spoke for a few minutes about the surprise of Ted dying so soon after our respective visits. Brian then excused himself.

"I've got to go—I need to join my family."

I felt like more of an idiot. I had forgotten the rules.

As I strode toward my car, someone called my name. I turned around. One of the two women I'd identified as Ted's daughters approached with her arms outstretched.

"I'm Gail. I recognized you from your photo on the blog. Thank you so much for coming."

She had bobbed hair and a warm smile, and she enveloped me in a hug. I fought back tears as she mentioned how much Ted enjoyed talking about our friendship. It felt like she was consoling me more than I was consoling her. I promised to keep in touch, and we hugged again.

I almost reached my car when a man asked, "Are you Joy?"

I turned to look at him. "Yes."

His face was not familiar.

"I just read your blog post this morning. I enjoyed it," he said. "Ted was quite a character."

The woman standing next to him added, "We're the neighbors."

"Yes, he was definitely a character." I agreed. "It was nice to meet you both."

I smiled as I got into my car. I wondered if Ted ever thought about the lives he influenced over the years, in ways large and small. Our lives all had a ripple effect. It reminded me of the movie *It's a Wonderful Life*. Take away one person, one action, and everything is changed.

I would never know how many people G. Oliver Riggs influenced. I did have a good idea, though, about how important he was to his family and his band boys. And I had some idea of how Ted created his own ripples, in the service, as a gifted doctor, and in those last years of life when he recounted memories to a kindred spirit eager to learn more about her ancestors.

One hundred and five years after the Riggs and Papermaster families met in Grand Forks, North Dakota, I had become the beneficiary of all those ripples; I was awash in the resulting waves of inspiration and aspiration, of loss and love, of music and family. It was my responsibility to take up the mantle of the raconteur. I would continue the story.

Acknowledgments

I started this project when my youngest child was in kindergarten; as I write this in late May of 2019, he is preparing to graduate from high school. Where does the time go? I'm sure it's a question my great-grandfather asked himself at different points in his life, and it's a question I returned to many times while researching and writing this book.

Because our time on earth is fleeting, sharing our stories with each other is important; it's a way to bridge differences, enhance understanding, and build community.

I extend my heartfelt thanks to Roman Schneider, Laverne Jung, Ray Galarneault, and Gary Heinzel for sharing their stories with me. Gail Papermaster Bender Satz, I can never thank you enough for your warm embrace of my out-of-the-blue inquiry; you are a true bonehead in the best sense of the word.

I'm grateful to Leonard "Lennie" Jung (1919–2016), Howard Pramann (1918–2016), and Francis Schellinger (1922–2014) for talking to me about their band experiences. The men live on in the memories of those who loved them, and in the pages of this book. Polly Streitz (1926–2013), I hope you and Herb are tooling around together on that heavenly golf cart. And to my favorite bonehead, Ted Papermaster (1914–2014), I can't wait to visit the cemetery and show you my book.

To Norton Stillman, my publisher, thank you for saying "Yes" one day before my 51st birthday, thus raising the bar impossibly high for future birthday presents; and to John Toren, my editor and book designer, thank you for your insight and sage suggestions.

Kate Hopper, my writing teacher, mentor, and friend (and one heck of a bass player—G. Oliver would be impressed!), you have provided a seemingly infinite supply of guidance and encouragement, and I can't imagine where I'd be without you. Possibly stuck on Chapter 6.

Members of my writing community buoyed me throughout the lengthy writing and revising process. To Myrna CG Mibus and Christine Bernier Lienke, thank you for believing in me from the beginning. To Heidi Fettig Parton, thanks for being the ideas person behind our literary endeavors and for your unwavering support. To all the Fisher Cats, whose words never fail to inspire and move me—you rock. I'm especially grateful to those of you who provided feedback on early scenes and chapters (Lucinda Cummins, Erin Erickson, Cindy Lehew-Nehrbass, Sara Martin, Amber D. Stoner, Tamara Robinson, Kara Douglass Thom) offered publishing advice (Kathleen English Cadmus, Janine Kovac) and gave me pep talks/ confidence boosts (Ann Kempke, Ann V. Klotz, Debra Palmquist, Heidi Schneider, Krista Westendorp, and Lisa Witz).

Thank you to the Beltrami County Historical Society, the Minnesota Historical Society, the Polk County Historical Society, and the Stearns History Museum for the use of photos; to John Decker and Steve Penick at Stearns for their steadfast support; and to Lynn Ellsworth, former archivist at Iowa Wesleyan, for unearthing articles about G. Oliver and for the warm hospitality during our visit in 2012.

I'm grateful to the Southeastern Minnesota Arts Council for the emerging artist grant, and to Paul Niemisto, Dan Bergeson, Jan Stevens, and the Vintage Band Festival board for promoting my book project.

Thanks to *Topology Magazine* for publishing an excerpt from the book; and to Northfield Poet Laureate Rob Hardy, the City of Northfield, and the Northfield Arts and Culture Commission for publishing two excerpts as part of Writers Night events in 2017 and 2018.

This book wouldn't exist without stellar journalism mentors Robert Woodward (the real Bob Woodward), my adviser at Drake University; and Joan Gandy, my editor at the *Natchez Democrat*. I continue to be grateful for all the lessons they taught me. Thanks to former *Minnesota Parent* editors Tricia Cornell and Kathleen Stoehr for the opportunity to bolster my journalism skills as a teen/

tween columnist; and to Loft Literary Center teachers Ashley Shelby, Mary Jean Port, and Rachael Hanel for helping me grow as a creative nonfiction writer.

I'm grateful to DeWayne Wee, one of the kindest, most patient souls I've ever met, for teaching piano to all three of my kids; and to other educators who fostered my children's love of music, including Liz Shepley, Anton Armstrong, the late Roger Jenni, Heather Olivier, Paul Beck, Ethan Freier, Kyle Eastman, and Mary Williams.

Thank you to Laurie Cuccia Oliver and Grace Healy for your valuable feedback on early drafts of the book; to Carolyn Porter for your expert suggestions on a late draft of the book; to Melissa Berthelsen and Wendy Cloak for going to Chicago with me; to Randy Brown, for brainstorming sessions that lead to great ideas; and to Lee and Laurel Engquist, who kindly listened to book updates on all those Wednesdays at the Ole Store.

Thanks to other friends who assisted me or cheered me on, especially Amy Boxrud, Doug Bratland, Cheryl Buck, Mary Crippen, Carrie Duba, Kathy Granger, Mary Hahn, Steve Hahn, Ellen Iverson, Patrick J. Kearney, Mike Legvold, Tania Legvold, Maria Leuthard, Tim Mahr, Jay Moad, Diana Powell, Amy Shonka (and my REVAMP pals), and Colleen Wood.

I am grateful to extended family members for providing photos and other assistance, especially the late Chris Duncan, Kae Kessler, Lorenda Stoner, Patricia Tester, and my dad's siblings, Dana Lowell and Bob Riggs.

To my brother, Pete, and my parents, Anne Falvey Riggs and William Riggs: I am grateful for everything you've done for me, and for your unconditional love.

Finally, I want to thank my children, Louisa, Sebastian, and Elias, and my leading man, Steve Lawler, for allowing me to include my great-grandfather in our family vacations, for entertaining me with your songs and stories, and for making me feel like I live in the best musical ever written. I love you.

Let's keep the music going.

NOTES

The historical account of my great-grandparents' lives is drawn extensively from newspaper accounts, magazine and journal articles, city directories, census records, death certificates, concert programs, yearbooks, photos, family letters and scrapbooks, and other documents. I recorded most interviews with former boys' band members, and I took extensive notes during other conversations and research trips. No names have been changed.

Chapter 1
1. *St. Cloud Times*, May 18, 2003, p. 1C.
2. *St. Cloud Daily Times*, Aug. 31, 1977, p. 11.
3. *Escape to the Minnesota Good Times*, undated, p. 13.

Chapter 2
1. Undated, Riggs family scrapbook.
2. *St. Cloud Daily Times*, undated, 1944, Riggs family files.
3. Essay by Percy Riggs, Riggs family files.
4. Stephen Rhodes, "A History of the Wind Band," http://www.lipscomb.edu/windbandhistory/rhodeswindband_06_19thcenturyamerican.htm
5. Clayton H. Tiede, *The Development of Minnesota Community Bands during the Nineteenth Century* (PhD thesis, University of Minnesota, 1970).
6. Margaret Hindle Hazen and Robert M. Hazen, *The Music Men: An Illustrated History of Brass Bands in America, 1800–1920* (Smithsonian Institution Press, 1987), p. 8.
7. Letter from G. Oliver Riggs to Ted Thorson, Feb. 5, 1939, Riggs family files.
8. *Crookston People's Press*, Nov. 18, 1898.
9. *Polk County Journal*, Jan. 12, 1899, p. 1.
10. Islea Graham's commencement speech, Riggs family files.
11. *Aledo Democrat*, June 14–July 5, 1894.
12. *Polk County Journal*, Jan. 19, 1899, p. 1
13. *Crookston People's Press*, Jan. 21, 1899, p. 1.
14. *Crookston People's Press*, April 1, 1899, p. 1.
15. Ibid.
16. *Crookston Daily Times*, Oct. 14, 1899, p. 4.
17. *The Dominant*, 1900, Riggs family files.

Chapter 4
1. *Bemidji Pioneer*, Nov. 7, 1901, p. 1.
2. *Crookston Daily Journal*, 1901, undated, Riggs family files

3. *Crookston Daily Journal*, March 6, 1903, Riggs family files.
4. *The Metronome*, February 1905.
5. *Crookston Daily Times,* Nov. 28, 1906, p. 7.
6. https://www.nps.gov/vick/learn/historyculture/copy-of-troops-in-the-campaign-siege-and-defense-of-vicksburg.htm.
7. https://www.nps.gov/vick/learn/historyculture/illinois-memorial.htm.
8. *Vicksburg Daily Herald*, Nov. 15, 1906
9. Ernest Sherman, *Dedicating in Dixie* (Press of the Record Printing Company, 1907), p. 27.
10. *Des Moines Register*, Nov. 16, 1906, p. 2.
11. *Chicago Tribune*, Oct. 27, 1906, p. 5.
12. William C. Lowe, "A Grand and Patriotic Pilgrimage: The Iowa Civil War Monuments Dedication Tour of 1906." *The Annals of Iowa* 69 (2010), p. 23.
13. *Crookston Daily Times*, Nov. 28, 1906, p. 7.
14. *Dedicating in Dixie*, p. 49.
15. *Crookston Daily Times*, Nov. 28, 1906, p. 7.
16. *Dedication of Monuments Erected by the State of Iowa* (E. H. English, state printer, 1908), p. 101.
17. *Dedicating in Dixie*, p. 57.
18. *Dedication of Monuments*, p. 213.

Chapter 5
1. *St. Cloud Daily Times*, Aug. 31, 1977, p. 11.

Chapter 6
1. Essay by Percy Riggs, Riggs family files.
2. *Polk County Journal*, Oct. 17, 1907, p. 3.
3. Ibid.
4. *Bismarck Tribune*, Jan. 6, 2013, p. 4C.
5. *Fargo Morning Call/Fargo Daily Argus*, July 1908, Riggs family files.
6. *Crookston Daily Times*, March 16, 1909.
7. *Polk County Journal*, March 18, 1909, p. 1.
8. *Grand Forks Herald*, April 1, 1909, p. 10.
9. *Grand Forks Herald*, March 30, 1909, p. 4 (reprint of a *Crookston Daily Times* article).
10. *Crookston Chronicle*, April 9, 1909.
11. *Crookston Evening Times*, April 29, 1909.
12. *Minneapolis Morning Tribune*, April 25, 1909, p. 6.
13. *Grand Forks Evening Times*, May 13, 1909, p. 6.
14. *Grand Forks Evening Times*, July 22, 1909, p. 8.
15. *The Metronome*, June 1909.
16. Albert Bigelow Paine, *Mark Twain: A Biography*, chapter 282.
17. *Tacoma Daily News*, Jan. 21, 1910.
18. *Tacoma Daily News*, Feb. 10, 1910.
19. *Grand Forks Herald*, March 1, 1910, p. 10.
20. *Grand Forks Herald*, March 8, 1910, p. 5.
21. *Grand Forks Evening Times*, March 19, 1910, p. 10.
22. *Tacoma Daily News*, undated article, 1910.
23. *Tacoma Daily News*, April 18, 1910.
24. *Tacoma Tribune*, April 18, 1910.
25. *Tacoma Daily News*, April 18, 1910.

26. *Tacoma Ledger*, April 22, 1910.
27. *Tacoma News and Tacoma Ledger*, April 1910.
28. Postcard from G. Oliver Riggs to Ronald Riggs, Riggs family files.
29. *Tacoma Times*, May 30, 1910, p. 4.
30. *Grand Forks Herald*, June 14, 1910, p. 2 (reprint of a *Tacoma Daily News* article).
31. Ibid.
32. Aledo newspaper clipping from Riggs family files, August 11, 1910.
33. Letter from Alfred F. Weldon to G. Oliver Riggs, dated Oct. 11, 1910, Riggs family files.
34. *Ottumwa Courier*, undated, 1911, Riggs family files.
35. *Burlington Hawkeye*, undated, April 1911, Riggs family files.

Chapter 8
1. Gary A. Wilson, *Honky-Tonk Town: Havre, Montana's Lawless Era* (Globe Pequot/ TwoDot, 2006), p. 24.
2. Ibid., p. 10.
3. US Department of Interior report, National Register of Historic Places, section E, pp. 12, 15.
4. Ibid., p. 12.
5. *Havre Plaindealer*, June 17, 1911, p. 1.
6. *Hunnewell* (Missouri) *Graphic*, undated, Riggs family files.
7. *Havre Promoter*, April 19, 1912, p. 4.
8. *Havre Plaindealer*, April 20, 1912, p. 4.
9. *Hill County Democrat*, July 13, 1912, p. 1.
10. *Portland Oregonian*, July 10, 1912, p. 1.
11. *Oregon Daily Journal*, July 12, 1912, p. 18.
12. *Who's Who in Minnesota, 1941* (Minnesota Editorial Association, 1942), p. 505.
13. *Anaconda Standard*, Sept. 19, 1912, p. 12.
14. Biloine W. Young with Eileen R. McCormack, "He Had a Flair for the Colorful: Louis W. Hill and Glacier National Park," *Ramsey County History*, Summer 2010, p. 8.
15. *Grand Forks Herald*, Nov. 9, 1912, p. 10.
16. *Grand Forks Herald*, Nov. 15, 1912, p. 8.
17. *Minneapolis Morning Tribune*, Nov. 19, 1912, p. 1.
18. *Minneapolis Journal*, Nov. 21, 1912, p. 1.
19. *Chicago Evening Post*, Nov. 23, 1912, p. 1.
20. Ibid.
21. *Chicago Daily Tribune*, Nov. 23, 1912, p. 1.
22. *Chicago Evening Post*, Nov. 23, 1912, p. 1.
23. *Chicago Sunday Tribune*, Nov. 24, 1912, sporting section, part 3, p. 1.
24. *Chicago Evening Post*, Nov. 27, 1912, p. 13.
25. *Chicago Sunday Tribune*, Nov. 24, 1912, land show section, p. 1.
26. Letter from Fred Big Top to Louis Hill, Louis W. Hill collection, Minnesota Historical Society.
27. *Havre Promoter*, Dec. 6, 1912, p. 5.
28. *Havre Plaindealer*, Dec. 14, 1912, p. 1.
29. *Hill County Democrat*, Dec. 7, 1912, p. 5.
30. *Grand Forks Evening Times*, Jan. 25, 1913, p. 6.
31. *American Musician and Art Journal*, Dec. 13, 1913, p. 3.
32. Ibid.
33. Undated clipping from unnamed newspaper, Riggs family files.

Chapter 10

1. *Crookston Daily Times*, April 1, 1914, p. 5.
2. *Crookston Daily Times*, July 11, 1914, p. 4.
3. *Crookston Daily Times*, Aug. 24, 1914, p. 1.
4. Letter from G. Oliver Riggs to Rebecca Riggs, dated Aug. 1, 1915, Riggs family files.
5. *Crookston Daily Times*, July 10, 1916, p. 8.
6. *Crookston Daily Times*, July 11, 1916, p. 1.
7. *Crookston Daily Times*, July 12, 1916, p. 8.
8. *Crookston Daily Times*, Aug. 4, 1916, p. 8.
9. *St. Paul Dispatch*, Jan. 30, 1917, p. 1.
10. Ibid.
11. *St. Paul Daily News*, Jan. 30, 1917, p. 11.
12. Ibid.
13. *St. Paul Pioneer Press*, Jan. 31, 1917, p. 1.
14. *Polk County, Minnesota, in the World War* (C. E. Wentzel, 1922), p. 163.
15. *Crookston Daily Times*, Nov. 5, 1917, p. 6.
16. *Crookston Daily Times*, Dec. 13, 1917, p. 8.
17. *Crookston Daily Times*, Dec. 26, 1917, p. 6.
18. Ibid.
19. *Crookston Daily Times*, Jan. 5, 1918.
20. *Bemidji Daily Pioneer*, Jan. 18, 1919, p. 4.
21. *Bemidji Daily Pioneer*, Jan. 2, 1919, p. 1.

Chapter 12

1. http://www.ojibwe.org/home/about_anish.html
2. *Bemidji Pioneer*, June 5, 2015.
3. Cecelia Wattles McKeig, *Images of America: Bemidji* (Arcadia Publishing 2013), p. 7.
4. *Bemidji Sentinel*, Nov. 21, 1919, p. 12.
5. *Bemidji Daily Pioneer*, Nov. 26, 1919, p. 1.
6. *Bemidji Daily Pioneer*, Jan. 13, 1920, p. 1.
7. *Bemidji Daily Pioneer*, Jan. 14, 1920, p. 1.
8. *Bemidji Sentinel*, Jan. 23, 1920, p. 1.
9. *Bemidji Sentinel*, Jan. 9, 1920, p. 1.
10. http://www.flu.gov/pandemic/history/1918/the_pandemic
11. *Bemidji Daily Pioneer*, Feb. 26, 1920, p. 5.
12. *Bemidji Daily Pioneer*, Feb. 25, 1920, p. 1.
13. http://www.cdc.gov/mmwr/preview/mmwrhtml/00056803.htm
14. Biennial report of the Minnesota State Board of Health and Vital Statistics, 1920–21, pp. 120, 123
15. http://www.mnopedia.org/person/sanford-maria-1836-1920
16. *Bemidji Daily Pioneer*, April 9, 1920, p. 1.
17. *Bemidji Daily Pioneer*, Sept. 17, 1920, p. 1.
18. *Bemidji Daily Pioneer*, Nov. 2, 1920, p. 3.
19. *Bemidji Daily Pioneer*, Nov. 3, 1920, p. 1.
20. *Bemidji Daily Pioneer*, Jan. 13, 1921, p. 4.
21. *Bemidji Daily Pioneer*, June 14, 1921, p. 1.
22. *Bemidji Daily Pioneer*, June 16, 1921, p. 1.
23. *Bemidji Daily Pioneer*, Sept. 7, 1922, p. 1.
24. *Bemidji Daily Pioneer*, March 7, 1922, p. 1.

25. *Bemidji Daily Pioneer*, April 3, 1922 p. 1.
26. *Bemidji Daily Pioneer*, May 23, 1922, p. 1.
27. *Bemidji Daily Pioneer*, June 16, 1922, p. 1.
28. *Minneapolis Journal*, Sept. 2, 1922.
29. *Minnesota Daily Star*, Sept. 7, 1922, p. 2.
30. G. Oliver cited this quote in his publicity report to the city. It differs from a page 1 account in the Sept. 11, 1922, *Bemidji Daily Pioneer*, which says Snyder introduced them as the "world's most famous boys' band." That article was based on the reporter's conversation with G. Oliver a few days after the event. I've been unable to resolve the discrepancy.
31. *Bemidji Daily Pioneer*, Sept. 16, 1922 p. 1.
32. *Bemidji Sentinel*, Sept. 22, 1922, p. 4.
33. *Bemidji Daily Pioneer*, Nov. 3, 1922, p. 1.
34. *Grand Forks Herald*, Dec. 7, 1922, p. 12.
35. *Bemidji Daily Pioneer*, Dec. 28, 1922, p. 1.
36. Bemidji Boys' Band report to the city, Riggs family files.

Chapter 13
1. Michelle Poland Devlin, *The Contributions of Tommy Pederson (1920-1998) to Trombone Performance and Literature in the Twentieth Century: A Lecture Recital and Document* (DMA thesis, University of North Carolina–Greensboro, 2007), p. 8.
2. *Mount Pleasant Journal*, Oct. 17, 1895
3. *Mount Pleasant Journal*, Nov. 7, 1895

Chapter 14
1. *St. Cloud Daily Journal-Press*, Feb. 28, 1923, p. 5.
2. *Bemidji Daily Pioneer*, March 16, 1923, p. 3.
3. *St. Cloud Daily Times*, June 23, 1923.
4. Ibid.
5. *St. Cloud Daily Times*, July 10, 1923, p. 4.
6. *St. Cloud Daily Times*, July 11, 1924.
7. *St. Cloud Daily Times*, Aug. 5, 1924, p. 1.
8. *St. Cloud Daily Times*, Aug. 6, 1924, p. 5.
9. *St. Cloud Daily Times*, Aug. 7, 1924, p. 4.
10. *St. Cloud Daily Journal-Press*, Nov. 6, 1924, p. 8.
11. *St. Cloud Daily Journal-Press*, Nov. 17, 1924, p. 5.
12. *St. Cloud Daily Times*, April 22, 1925, p. 5.
13. *St. Cloud Daily Journal-Press*, May 4, 1925, p. 1.
14. *St. Cloud Daily Times*, May 22, 1925, p. 1.
15. Ibid.
16. *St. Cloud Daily Times*, May 21, 1925, p. 4.
17. *St. Cloud Daily Times*, May 29, 1925, p. 5.
18. *St. Cloud Daily Times*, June 3, 1925, p. 4A.
19. *St. Cloud Daily Times*, June 11, 1925, p. 4.
20. *St. Cloud Daily Journal-Press*, June 19, 1925, p. 6.
21. *St. Cloud Daily Journal-Press*, June 23, 1925, p. 5.
22. Tim Mahoney, *Secret Partners: Big Tom Brown and the Barker Gang* (Minnesota Historical Society Press, 2013), p. 17.
23. http://www.mnopedia.org/gangster-era-st-paul-1900-1936
24. *St. Paul Daily News*, June 22, 1925.

25. *St. Paul Dispatch*, June 22, 1925, p. 1.
26. Ibid.
27. http://collections.mnhs.org/governors/index.php/10004492
28. *St. Cloud Daily Journal-Press*, June 23, 1925, p. 5.
29. *St. Cloud Daily Times*, June 23, 1925, p. 1.
30. *St. Cloud Daily Times*, July 6, 1925, p. 5.
31. *St. Cloud Daily Times*, July 7, 1925.
32. http://historyapolis.com/community-sing-1925/
33. *St. Cloud Daily Times*, Aug. 21, 1925, p. 4.
34. *St. Cloud Daily Times*, Oct. 6, 1925, p. 1.
35. *St. Cloud Daily Journal-Press*, Oct. 6, 1925.
36. *St. Cloud Daily Journal-Press*, Nov. 6, 1925, p. 12.

Chapter 16
1. *St. Cloud Daily Journal-Press*, October 6, 1925.
2. Ibid.
3. *St. Cloud Daily Journal-Press*, Oct. 31, 1925.
4. Ibid.
5. *St. Cloud Daily Times*, Oct. 31, 1925, p. 3.
6. *St. Cloud Daily Times*, Nov. 3, 1925, p. 5.
7. *St. Cloud Daily Journal-Press*, Nov. 3, 1925, p. 7.
8. *St. Cloud Daily Times*, Nov. 3, 1925, p. 5.
9. *St. Cloud Daily Journal-Press*, Nov. 4, 1925.
10. *St. Cloud Daily Times*, Nov. 4, 1925, p. 5.
11. *St. Cloud Daily Journal-Press*, Nov. 6, 1925, p. 12.
12. *Minneapolis Daily Star*, Nov. 18, 1925, pp. 3, 7.
13. *St. Cloud Daily Journal-Press*, Nov. 25, 1925, p. 5.
14. Ibid, p. 3.
15. *St. Cloud Daily Journal-Press*, Dec. 9, 1925, p. 1.
16. *Bemidji Daily Pioneer*, March 1, 1926, p. 2.
17. *St. Cloud Daily Times*, Jan. 28, 1926, p. 5.
18. A Trip to Yellowstone scrapbook by Ronald Riggs, Riggs family files.
19. *St. Cloud Daily Times*, Dec. 7, 1926, p. 1.
20. *St. Cloud Daily Times*, Dec. 13, 1926, p. 1.
21. *St. Cloud Daily Times*, Dec. 27, 1926, p. 1.
22. Speech by George Landers, Landers' files, State Historical Society of Iowa in Iowa City.
23. *St. Cloud Daily Times*, Feb. 17, 1927, p. 5.
24. *Sauk Centre Herald*, March 31, 1927, p. 1.
25. Murrae N. Freng, "A History of the Minnesota Music Educators Association," *Gopher Music Notes*, October 1963.
26. *St. Cloud Daily Times*, May 12, 1927, p. 1.
27. *St. Cloud Daily Times*, Nov. 30, 1927, p. 1.
28. *St. Cloud Daily Times*, Dec. 1, 1927, p. 1.
29. *St. Cloud Daily Times*, Jan. 23, 1928, p. 5.
30. *St. Cloud Daily Times*, April 3, 1928, p. 1.
31. *St. Cloud Daily Times*, June 23, 1928, p. 1.

Chapter 17
1. *St. Cloud Daily Times*, June 3, 1925.
2. Tony Horwitz, *Confederates in the Attic: Dispatches from the Unfinished Civil War*

(Vintage Books, 1999) p. 175.

Chapter 18
1. https://www.history.com/topics/roaring-twenties/roaring-twenties-history
2. http://www.digitalhistory.uh.edu/topic_display.cfm?tcid=124
3. *The Bandmaster*, January 1929, p. 7.
4. Margaret Hindle Hazen and Robert M. Hazen, *The Music Men: An Illustrated History of Brass Bands in America, 1800–1920* (Smithsonian Institution Press, 1987), pp. 193-194.
5. *St. Cloud Daily Times*, Jan. 25, 1929, p. 4.
6. *St. Paul Pioneer Press*, June 22, 1929, p. 1.
7. Ibid.
8. Ibid.
9. Ibid., p. 7.
10. *The Bandmaster*, July 1929, p. 11.
11. *St. Cloud Daily Times*, June 24, 1929, p. 1.
12. Ibid., p. 2.
13. *St. Cloud Daily Journal-Press*, July 1, 1929 p. 12.
14. *St. Cloud Daily Times*, Sept. 4, 1929, p. 3.
15. Ibid, p. 10.
16. *Windom Cottonwood County Citizen*, Oct. 9, 1929, p. 1.
17. *The Bandmaster*, November 1929, p. 19.
18. *St. Cloud Daily Times*, Feb. 21, 1930, p. 3.
19. *St. Paul Pioneer Press*, June 21, 1930, p. 1.
20. Ibid., p. 6.
21. *St. Paul Pioneer Press*, June 20, 1930, p. 3.
22. *St. Cloud Daily Times*, June 23, 1930, p. 1.
23. *The Bandmaster*, July 1930, p. 8.
24. Ibid.
25. *Northwest Musical Herald*, January 1931, p. 1.
26. Ibid., p. 4.
27. Ibid.
28. Ibid., p. 6.
29. *St. Paul Dispatch*, June 10, 1931, p. 1.
30. *St. Cloud Daily Times*, June 15, 1931, p. 2.
31. *Des Moines Tribune-Capital*, June 13, 1931. p. 8.
32. *St. Paul Dispatch*, June 12, 1931, p. 12.
33. *St. Cloud Daily Times*, June 15, 1931, p. 2.
34. *Des Moines Tribune-Capital*, June 13, 1931, p. 8.
35. *Mason City Globe*, June 15, 1931, p. 5.
36. *St. Cloud Daily Times*, June 19, 1931, p. 3.

Chapter 20
1. https://www.history.com/topics/great-depression/hoovervilles
2. *St. Cloud Daily Times/Journal-Press*, Oct. 7, 1931, p. 10.
3. *St. Cloud Daily Times/Journal-Press*, Sept. 5, 1931, p. 4.
4. *St. Cloud Daily Times/Journal-Press*, Sept. 8, 1931.
5. *St. Cloud Daily Times/Journal-Press*, Sept. 22, 1931, p. 7.
6. Ibid.
7. *St. Cloud Daily Times/Journal Press*, Oct. 31, 1931, p. 1.
8. *St. Cloud Daily Times/Journal-Press*, Dec. 1, 1931, p. 1.

9. *St. Cloud Daily Times/Journal-Press*, Dec. 3, 1931, p. 4.
10. *St. Cloud Daily Times/Journal-Press*, March 31, 1932, p. 1.
11. *St. Cloud Daily Times/Journal-Press*, April 25, 1932, p. 1.
12. *St. Cloud Daily Times/Journal-Press*, May 28, 1932, p. 4.
13. *St. Cloud Daily Times/Journal-Press*, Sept. 9, 1932, p. 1.
14. *St. Cloud Daily Times/Journal-Press*, Nov. 5, 1932, p. 3.
15. *St. Cloud Daily Times/Journal-Press*, Jan. 2, 1933, p. 4.
16. *St. Cloud Daily Times/Journal-Press*, Jan. 3, 1933, p. 3.
17. *St. Cloud Daily Times/Journal-Press*, March 31, 1933, p. 1.
18. *St. Cloud Daily Times/Journal-Press*, April 24, 1933, p. 1.
19. *St. Cloud Daily Times/Journal-Press*, May 22, 1933, p. 2.
20. *St. Cloud Daily Times/Journal-Press*, May 31, 1933, p. 2.
21. *St. Cloud Daily Times/Journal Press*, June 22, 1933, p. 3.
22. *St. Cloud Daily Times/Journal Press*, Aug. 11, p. 3.
23. *St. Cloud Daily Times/Journal Press*, Aug. 19, 1933, p. 3.
24. *St. Cloud Daily Times/Journal Press*, Aug. 15, p. 3.
25. *St. Cloud Daily Times/Journal Press*, Sept. 11, 1933, p.3.
26. *St. Cloud Daily Times/Journal Press*, Jan. 23, 1934, p. 2.
27. *St. Cloud Daily Times/Journal Press*, Jan. 26, 1934, p. 4.
28. *St. Cloud Daily Times/Journal Press*, June 5, 1934, p. 1.
29. *St. Cloud Daily Times/Journal Press*, Aug. 6, 1934, p. 3.
30. *Duluth News-Tribune*, Aug. 7, 1934, p. 1.
31. *Duluth News-Tribune*, Aug. 6, 1934.
32. *Duluth News-Tribune*, Aug. 8, 1934, p. 7.

Chapter 22
1. http://www.english.illinois.edu/MAPS/DEPRESSION/dustbowl.htm
2. http://www.mnopedia.org/person/olson-floyd-b-1891-1936
3. *St. Cloud Daily Times/Journal-Press*, Oct. 17, 1934, p. 1.
4. *St. Cloud Daily Times/Journal-Press*, Nov. 8, 1934, p. 1.
5. Letter from G. Oliver Riggs to Ronald Riggs, dated Dec. 13, 1934, Riggs family files.
6. *St. Cloud Daily Times/Journal-Press*, March 11, 1935, p. 8.
7. *St. Cloud Daily Times/Journal-Press*, March 20, 1935, p. 4.
8. Ibid.
9. *St. Cloud Daily Times/Journal-Press*, April 26, 1935, p. 4.
10. *St. Cloud Daily Times/Journal-Press*, June 11, 1935, p. 3.
11. *St. Cloud Daily Times/Journal-Press*, June 14, 1935, p. 4.
12. *The Notre Dame Scholastic*, Dec. 6, 1935, p. 5.
13. *St. Cloud Daily Times/Journal-Press*, Dec. 19, 1935, p. 4.
14. Letter from Bert Keck to Percy Riggs, dated Sept. 24, 1958, Riggs family files. Keck wrote that the last letter he'd received from G. Oliver Riggs was dated Dec. 28, 1935, and he wondered whether G. Oliver and Islea were still alive.
15. *St. Cloud Daily Times/Journal-Press*, Jan. 10, 1936, p. 4.
16. Ibid.
17. *St. Cloud Daily Times/Journal-Press*, Feb. 17, 1936, p. 4.
18. *St. Cloud Daily Times/Journal-Press*, Feb. 18, 1936, p. 5.
19. *St. Cloud Daily Times/Journal-Press*, Feb. 19, 1936, p. 5.
20. *St. Cloud Daily Times/Journal-Press*, March 16, 1936, p. 3.
21. *St. Cloud Daily Times/Journal-Press*, March 27, 1936, p. 6.
22. Newspaper clipping from Riggs family files, dated April 1936.
23. *St. Cloud Daily Times/Journal-Press*, April 29, 1936, p. 1.

24. Undated newspaper article, Riggs family files.
25. *St. Cloud Daily Times/Journal-Press*, July 24, 1936, p. 3.
26. Letter from G. Oliver Riggs to Ronald Riggs, Riggs family files.
27. *St. Cloud Daily Times/Journal-Press*, Aug. 19, 1936, p. 7.
28. *St. Cloud Daily Times/Journal-Press*, Aug. 24, 1936, p. 4.
29. Letter from Islea G. Riggs to Eleanor Johnson, Oct. 18, 1936, Riggs family files.
30. Letter from Islea to Eleanor, Nov. 29, 1936, Riggs family files.
31. *St. Cloud Daily Times/Journal-Press*, Dec. 29, 1936, p. 3.

Chapter 23
1. Undated newspaper clipping, Riggs family files.
2. *Manitoba Free Press*, July 15, 1899, p. 1.

Chapter 24
1. http://historymatters.gmu.edu/d/5105/
2. *St. Cloud Daily Times/Press-Journal*, March 8, 1937, p. 4.
3. Murrae N. Freng, "A History of the Minnesota Music Educators Association," *Gopher Music Notes*, October 1963.
4. *St. Cloud Daily Times/Journal-Press*, April 12, 1937, p. 3.
5. *St. Cloud Daily Times/Journal-Press*, May 18, 1937, p. 5.
6. Undated 1937 clipping, Riggs family files.
7. *St. Cloud Daily Times/Journal-Press*, May 24, 1937, p. 5.
8. *St. Cloud Daily Times/Journal-Press*, July 17, 1937, p. 6.
9. *St. Cloud Daily Times/Journal-Press*, July 29, 1937, p. 9.
10. Essay by Percy Riggs, Riggs family files
11. *St. Cloud Daily Times/Journal-Press*, Aug. 5, 1937, p. 4.
12. *St. Cloud Daily Times/Journal-Press*, Aug. 6, 1937, p. 3.
13. *St. Cloud Daily Times/Journal-Press*, Sept. 8, 1937, p. 4.
14. *Thief River Falls Times*, Oct. 7, 1937, p. 10.
15. *St. Cloud Daily Times/Journal-Press*, Nov. 12, 1937, p. 5.
16. *St. Cloud Daily Times/Journal-*Press, Nov. 17, 1937, p. 11.
17. *St. Cloud Daily Times/Journal-Press*, Dec. 13, 1937, p. 6.
18. "A History of the Minnesota Music Educators Association," *Gopher Music Notes*, October 1963.
19. Letter from George Landers to Ronald Riggs, dated Feb. 12, 1946, Riggs family files.
20. *St. Cloud Daily Times/Journal-Press*, March 3, 1938, p. 3.
21. *St. Cloud Daily Times/Journal-Press*, July 13, 1938, p. 4.
22. *St. Cloud Daily Times/Journal-Press*, July 27, 1938, p. 4.
23. *St. Cloud Daily Times/Journal-Press*, Sept. 8, 1938, p. 9.
24. *St. Cloud Daily Times/Journal-Press*, Sept. 22, 1938, p. 14.
25. *Crookston Daily Times*, Sept. 23, 1938.
26. *St. Cloud Daily Times/Journal-Press*, Oct. 31, 1938, p. 1.
27. *St. Cloud Daily Times/Journal-Press*, Nov. 15, 1938, p. 1.
28. *St. Cloud Daily Times/Journal-Press*, Dec. 2, 1938, p. 10.
29. https://encyclopedia.ushmm.org/content/en/article/franklin-delano-roosevelt
30. *St. Cloud Daily Times/Journal-Press*, Jan. 13, 1939, p. 1.
31. Letter from G. Oliver Riggs to Ted Thorson, dated Feb. 5, 1939, Riggs family files.
32. *St. Cloud Daily Times/Journal-Press*, May 24, 1939, p. 10.
33. 1940 US Census data

34. *St. Cloud Daily Times/Journal-Press*, Nov. 11, 1939, p. 3.
35. *St. Cloud Daily Times/Journal-Press*, Jan. 4, 1940, p. 3.
36. Concert program, Riggs family files
37. *St. Cloud Daily Times/Journal-Press*, Feb. 12, 1940, p. 4.
38. *St. Cloud Daily Times/Journal-Press*, July 30, 1940, p. 3.
39. *St. Cloud Daily Times/Journal-Press*, Aug. 23, 1940, p. 9.
40. *St. Cloud DailyTimes/Journal-Press*, Nov. 11, 1940, p. 3.
41. *St. Cloud Daily Times/Journal-Press*, Nov. 26, 1940, p. 3.

Chapter 26
1. *St. Cloud Daily Times*, Feb. 12, 1941, p. 3.
2. Speech by George Landers, March 1941, Landers files, State Historical Society of Iowa in Iowa City
3. *St. Cloud Daily Times*, May 17, 1941, p. 3.
4. Letter from Islea Riggs to Eleanor Johnson Riggs, dated Aug. 11, 1941, Riggs family files
5. https://www.freep.com/pages/interactives/pearl-harbor-anniversary-timeline/
6. *St. Cloud Daily Times*, Dec. 8, 1941, p. 8.
7. *St. Cloud Daily Times*, April 6, 1942, p. 5.
8. Letter from club secretary to family, dated April 13, 1942, Riggs family files.
9. *St. Cloud Daily Times*, April 27, 1942, p. 3.
10. Card, Riggs family files.
11. *St. Cloud Daily Times*, Oct. 13, 1942, p. 5.
12. *St. Cloud Daily Times*, Jan. 28, 1943, p. 9.
13. *St. Cloud Daily Times*, April 3, 1943, p. 3.
14. *St. Cloud Daily Times*, June 28, 1943, p. 5.
15. *St. Cloud Daily Times*, Sept. 13, 1943, p. 3.
16. *St. Cloud Daily Times*, Nov. 10, 1943, p. 5.
17. *St. Cloud Daily Times*, Feb. 12, 1944, p. 5.
18. *St. Cloud Daily Times*, April 26, 1944, p. 7.
19. *St. Cloud Daily Times*, May 2, 1944, p. 3.
20. *St. Cloud Daily Times*, May 3, 1944, p. 8.
21. Undated newspaper clipping, Riggs family files
22. *St. Cloud Daily Times*, May 27, 1944, p. 3.
23. *St. Cloud Daily Times*, Sept. 18, 1944, p. 5.
24. *St. Cloud Daily Times*, Jan. 31, 1945, p. 8.
25. *St. Cloud Daily Times*, March 12, 1945.
26. *St. Cloud Daily Times*, Nov. 16, 1945, p. 3.
27. Essay by Percy Riggs, Riggs family files.
28. Letter from G. Oliver to Ronald, Riggs family files.
29. Letter from George Landers to Ronald Riggs, dated Feb. 12, 1946, Riggs family files.
30. Letter from Gordon Ose to Ronald Riggs, dated Feb. 1, 1946, Riggs family files

photo: Tania Legvold

J oy Riggs grew up in Alexandria, Minnesota, and graduated from Drake University in Des Moines, Iowa, in 1990 with a bachelor's degree in news-editorial journalism. She specializes in writing about history, travel, and parenting. Her award-winning columns, essays, and articles have appeared in numerous publications, including the *Star Tribune*, *Minnesota Parent*, *Minnesota Monthly*, and the *Des Moines Register*. She lives in Northfield, Minnesota, where she serves on the boards of the Vintage Band Festival and the Northfield Historical Society. For more of her writing, visit www.joyriggs.com.